Criminal Justice and Neoliberalism

Criminal Justice and Neoliberalism

Emma Bell
University of Savoie, France

First published 2011 by
PALGRAVE MACMILLAN

Palgrave Macmillan in the UK is an imprint of Macmillan Publishers Limited, registered in England, company number 785998, of Houndmills, Basingstoke, Hampshire RG21 6XS.

Palgrave Macmillan in the US is a division of St Martin's Press LLC, 175 Fifth Avenue, New York, NY 10010.

Palgrave Macmillan is the global academic imprint of the above companies and has companies and representatives throughout the world.

Palgrave® and Macmillan® are registered trademarks in the United States, the United Kingdom, Europe and other countries

ISBN 978-0-230-25197-7   hardback

This book is printed on paper suitable for recycling and made from fully managed and sustained forest sources. Logging, pulping and manufacturing processes are expected to conform to the environmental regulations of the country of origin.

A catalogue record for this book is available from the British Library.

A catalogue record for this book is available from the Library of Congress.

10   9   8   7   6   5   4   3   2   1
20   19   18   17   16   15   14   13   12   11

Printed and bound in Great Britain by
CPI Antony Rowe, Chippenham and Eastbourne

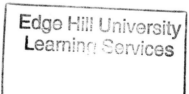

Contents

Foreword

During the last four decades profound social and cultural changes have set into reverse key features of a trajectory of emancipation that can be traced back over the five centuries since the Renaissance. I have in mind here what David Garland has referred to as the 'solidarity project', the long march of increasing social inclusiveness and equal citizenship (Garland, 2001, p. 199). This is not to postulate a Whig grand narrative of inevitable or unbroken progress. The project faced constant opposition across a broad front of interests and ideologies. And throughout there were massive setbacks, not least the industrialised mass slaughter and destruction of the twentieth century's world wars.

Nonetheless, after each bloodbath, and despite continuing critique, the ideals and social imaginary encapsulated in the French Revolutionary slogan – liberty, equality, fraternity – seemed to become more deeply and widely realised and embedded, most evidently in the post-World War II decades of social democratic predominance. This process was celebrated in democratic socialist and liberal histories, quintessentially T. H. Marshall's classic lectures on citizenship (Marshall, 1950). But its seeming irreversibility was also perceived by those who railed against it, as indicated by Evelyn Waugh's famous lament that 'the trouble with the Conservative Party is it has not turned back the clock one second'.

In the more specific spheres of crime and criminal justice the project was associated with a civilising process *à la* Norbert Elias, whereby violence by citizens unevenly but steadily declined (Eisner, 2001; Spierenberg, 2008). The use of force by criminal justice agencies also became less prominent, signified by the rise of penal welfarism and policing by consent (Garland, 1985; Reiner, 2010a, pp. 250–2, 2010b: Chap. 3). The highpoint of the march towards greater social incorporation, and more welfarist approaches to criminal justice, was the post-World War II dominance of Keynesian and social democratic economic management and social policy (including its US version, the New Deal). The rapid rupturing of these political-economic and penal strategies since the 1970s by the rise of their nemesis, what has come to be called 'neoliberalism', is the focus of the complex, sophisticated and scholarly analysis in this book.

Speaking for myself, I feel there has been something of a *trahison de clercs* (although in the reverse political direction from Benda's original formulation accusing intellectuals of surrendering to socialism) in the relative absence of critical attention given to this monumental development, at any rate until relatively recently. In the early stages of neoliberalism's rise, during the later 1970s and 80s, conservative criminologists cheered the neoliberal turn (heralded by Wilson, 1975). But *soi-disant* radical criminology also attenuated its critique of criminal justice in a variety of ways, ranging from the espousal of left realism and a proliferation of administrative, policy-oriented research. I have always been persuaded of the validity of left realism's central claim that criminal victimisation (and not just the injustices of criminal justice) must be taken seriously as a left issue. And much of what the left realists somewhat caustically dubbed administrative criminology provides invaluable material for the understanding and analysis of crime and justice, and is often very critical of official policies in its implications. Nonetheless the various strands of the realist turn after the 1970s did until recently imply a change in the subject, diverting attention from the large-scale social and cultural forces that were restructuring crime and criminal justice (Chap. 7 of this book discusses how changes in funding and career opportunities for academic criminologists encouraged this). Altogether there was a temporary bracketing-out of the significance of political economy (Reiner, 2007a).

One aspect of the increasing hegemony of neoliberalism was a revival of interest in the *economics* of crime and criminal justice on the part of some criminologists and neo-classical economists. This was paralleled by administrative criminologists' rediscovery of classical conceptions of crime as a rational choice and a focus on crime control through manipulation of the immediate situations and contexts of offending (explored in Chap. 7 of this book).

It has only been since the late 1990s that some criminologists have begun to probe the broad spectrum of changes in crime and criminal justice, and their deeper socio-cultural sources. The widest-ranging and most influential interpretation is without doubt David Garland's seminal *The Culture of Control* (Garland, 2001), which attributes the transformation to a multi-stranded conception of late modernity. Other analyses of the overall trends in crime and control include Currie, 1998; Taylor, 1999, Young, 1999, 2007; Tonry, 2004; Pratt *et al.*, 2005; Cavadino and Dignan, 2006; Reiner, 2007b; Simon, 2007; Hall *et al.*, 2008; Lacey, 2008; Wacquant, 2009 (as well as a growing body of papers including many by these same authors).

These earlier interpretations are influential in this book, but also subject to shrewd critical assessment. Emma Bell's analysis offers the most rigorous and complete account to-date of neoliberalism and the British criminal justice experience (including useful comparisons throughout of the variations between England and Wales, and Scotland and Northern Ireland). She documents convincingly that there has indeed been a 'punitive turn', whilst also paying due attention to the continuities and indeed reversals in penal policy. She traces in detail the politicisation in law and order since the 1970s, in particular following the electoral exploitation of the issue by the Conservatives under Margaret Thatcher (as indicated by the study of election manifestos in Downes and Morgan, 2007).

The intensification of penality has not, however, been a continuous development, as the present book shows. For all Margaret Thatcher's tough rhetoric her governments largely mounted what I have called a 'phoney war' against crime (Reiner, 2007b, p. 129), and indeed they presided over an unprecedented crime explosion. This is not to say that all the Iron Lady's fiery speeches were mere sound and fury signifying nothing. In some ways, notably the militarisation of public order policing, they were every bit as hard as promised. But in criminal justice policy more broadly the real shift to toughness came in the early 1990s when Michael Howard as Home Secretary and Tony Blair as his Shadow began a bidding-war on boosting penal severity and police powers (whilst watering down the countervailing due process safeguards in the 1984 *Police and Criminal Evidence Act* which in its time had attracted opprobrium as heralding an Orwellian expansion of police power).

The causes and consequences of the embedding of tough law and order policies are analysed insightfully and comprehensively in the chapters below. There is particular attention given to the growth of 'out-of-court justice' (ASBOS, Penalty Notices for Disorder, cautioning), and New Labour's proclivity to expand what Garland called the 'welfare sanction', the combination of welfare measures backed by potential criminal sanctioning, as its way of delivering on its pledge to be tough on the causes of crime. The increasing commercialisation of punishment and security, through privatisation and the importation of New Public Management models to state agencies, is assessed critically. These criminal justice trends are dialectically related to growing social inequality and exclusion. They are responses to the crime and disorder generated by the inequality, long-term unemployment and social dislocation produced by neoliberalism. But in turn they exacerbate crime through segregation and labeling. As Polanyi, Gamble and others have shown, the 'free economy' requires a 'strong state' to handle the tensions and conflicts it spawns (Polanyi, 1944; Gamble, 1994).

The book is not only a comprehensive account of penal transformation but a rigorous analysis of its roots in the political economy of neoliberalism. This is no straightforward economic determinism. Neoliberalism is not a one-dimensional economic category. It refers to a political economy in which a particular form of economic theory holds sway, which can be referred to as market fundamentalism: the view that unfettered markets promote maximal efficiency and prosperity. But this has complex cultural, social and political conditions of existence and consequences.

The links between neoliberalism as contrasted with other forms of political economy and patterns of crime and control is complex, dialectical and multi-dimensional. The relationship is mediated by particular processes and institutions, for example the affinity between unregulated, risky and highly competitive markets, a moral culture of egoistic individualism and utilitarian, risk-based managerial and governmental mentalities. But whilst *laissez-faire* economics may be conducive to *laissez-faire* ethics, as noted earlier the fallout of this mix in terms of crime and disorder encourages strong state security strategies. Moreover, Emma Bell adopts the useful notion of 'actually existing neoliberalism' to analyse the incomplete and varying realisation of neoliberal economic theory in specific social and political formations, introducing a further degree of complexity.

Altogether this book offers the most comprehensive and rigorous account to-date of the complex inter-relations of neoliberalism, crime and criminal justice. But there is of course much work still to be done. Despite the burgeoning literature on the subject indicated above, there are still mysteries in explaining the sudden rise of neoliberalism to dominance in the 1970s, sweeping away so rapidly the post-World War II social democratic consensus that had delivered so much in terms of widely shared growth in material prosperity and security, as well as relatively low crime and benign control strategies by historical standards. Even more important practically, and at least as mysterious: where are we going now? It is remarkable that so soon after the economic and financial crunch in late 2007 seemed to discredit the neoliberal model, its savagely deflationary prescriptions for dealing with the sovereign debt crisis (resulting from governmental support for banking) are the new orthodoxy. How can this zombie neoliberalism be accounted for? And what will it mean for criminal justice in Britain, in the hands of the new Conservative-Liberal Democrat coalition?

Many liberals have been impressed and surprised by early signs of willingness to reverse some of the trends to harsher punitiveness and the erosion of civil liberties under New Labour (and of course the Michael Howard regime at the Home Office before that). For example, a landmark speech by Justice Secretary Kenneth Clarke on 30 June 2010 at the Centre for Crime and Justice Studies harked back to the philosophy articulated by the White Paper preceding the 1991 *Criminal Justice Act*, that prison was an expensive way of making bad people worse. For the first time in nearly 20 years there was government questioning of Howard's mantra that prison works. This apparent conversion is very welcome, even if it is largely prompted by economic considerations. But the arguments and evidence in this book suggest that these liberal ambitions will be frustrated in practice by the crime and disorder rise flowing from the financial cuts and downturn. As before, the 'freeing' of the economy will engender a strong state penal and policing response to the social dislocation it produces. Neoliberalism entails social injustice and thus undermines liberal approaches to criminal justice.

Robert Reiner

Professor of Criminology in the Law Department,
London School of Economics, UK

References

Cavadino, M. and Dignan, J. (2006) *Penal Systems: A Comparative Approach* (London: Sage).

Currie, E. (1998) *Crime and Punishment in America* (New York: Holt).

Downes, D. and Morgan, R. (2007) 'No Turning Back: The Politics of Law and Order into the Millennium' in Maguire, M., Morgan, R. and Reiner, R. (eds.), *The Oxford Handbook of Criminology*, 4th edn (Oxford: Oxford University Press).

Eisner, M. (2001) 'Modernisation, Self-control and Lethal Violence: The Long-term Dynamics of European Homicide Rates in Theoretical Perspective', *British Journal of Criminology*, 41, 618–38.

Gamble, A. (1994) *The Free Economy and the Strong State* (London: Macmillan).

Garland, D. (1985) *Punishment and Welfare* (Aldershot: Gower).

Garland, D. (2001) *The Culture of Control* (Oxford: Oxford University Press).

Hall, S., Winlow, S. and Ancrum, C. (2008) *Criminal Identities and Consumer Culture: Crime, Exclusion and the New Culture of Narcissism* (Cullompton: Willan).

Lacey, N. (2008) *The Prisoners' Dilemma: Political Economy and Punishment in Contemporary Democracies* (Cambridge: Cambridge University Press).

Marshall, T. M. [1950] (1963) *Citizenship and Social Class* (Cambridge: Cambridge University Press). Reprinted in Marshall, T. H. (1963) *Sociology at the Crossroads* Chap. IV (London: Heinemann).

Polanyi, K. [1944] (2001) *The Great Transformation* (Boston: Beacon).

Pratt, J., Brown, D., Brown, M., Hallsworth, S. and Morrison, W. (2005) (eds.) *The New Punitiveness* (Cullompton: Willan).

Reiner, R. (2007a) 'Political Economy, Crime and Criminal Justice', in Maguire, M., Morgan, R. and Reiner, R. (eds.), *The Oxford Handbook of Criminology*, 4th edn (Oxford: Oxford University Press).

Reiner, R. (2007b) *Law and Order: An Honest Citizen's Guide to Crime and Control* (Cambridge: Polity Press).

Reiner, R. (2010a) 'Citizenship, Crime, Criminalisation: Marshalling a Social Democratic Perspective', *New Criminal Law Review*, 13/2, 241–61.

Reiner, R. (2010b) *The Politics of the Police*, 4th edn (Oxford: Oxford University Press).

Simon, J. (2007) *Governing Through Crime* (New York: Oxford University Press).

Spierenburg, P. (2008) *A History of Murder* (Cambridge: Polity Press).

Taylor, I. (1999) *Crime in Context* (Cambridge: Polity).

Tonry, M. (2004) *Thinking About Crime* (New York: Oxford University Press).

Wacquant, L. (2009) *Punishing the Poor: The Neoliberal Government of Social Security* (Durham: Duke University Press).

Wilson, J. Q. (1975) *Thinking About Crime* (New York: Vintage).

Young, J. (1999) *The Exclusive Society* (London: Sage).

Young, J. (2007) *The Vertigo of Late Modernity* (London: Sage).

Acknowledgements

I am indebted to the many people without whose help and encouragement this book would surely never have been written. Thanks to Keith Dixon and Neil Davie at Lyon II University for their guidance and unstinting support. I am grateful to Gilles Christoph who happily shared his expertise on neoliberalism with me and who has proved to be an invaluable friend throughout the course of my research.

I would like to thank those who pushed me to publish my work (notably Agnès Alexandre-Collier and Emmanuelle Avril), to David Scott who helped me to prepare my proposal and who kindly agreed to reread the manuscript (any remaining errors are, of course, my own), and to Philippa Grand and Olivia Middleton at Palgrave Macmillan for being prepared to publish the work of a little-known and (relatively) young researcher like myself. I am extremely grateful to Robert Reiner for having accepted to write the foreword to this book. I also owe him a considerable intellectual debt.

It would be simply impossible to provide the names of all the scholars who have influenced my work. However, it can be said that the ideas which I have formed since beginning research on this book have been greatly shaped by my participation in research groups with colleagues at Lyon II University. The significant body of work published by the Centre for Crime and Justice Studies at King's College, London has proved an invaluable source of information. I'd like to thank Peter Moodie and John Baldwin for stimulating my initial interest in criminology back when I was a law student at the University of Birmingham.

Thanks are also due to those who agreed to talk to me about their own experiences with the criminal justice system, whether as staff in penal institutions, as prisoners or, in the case of David Blunkett, as policymakers. Rod Morgan kindly agreed to discuss his time spent as head of the Youth Justice Board with me.

I'd also like to thank TRIANGLE, the research laboratory at the École Normale Supérieure in Lyon, which supported me throughout my research for this book. Thanks also to my colleagues and my research laboratory at the Université de Savoie (LLS) for providing me with the teaching relief necessary to write.

I am forever grateful to the friends who helped me to keep my sanity whilst writing this book, to my parents for their indefatigable support and encouragement, and to John who remained kind and good-humoured throughout, patiently putting up with my moods and jeremiads.

List of Relevant UK Legislation

Penitentiary Act 1779
Vagrancy Act 1824
Reformatory Schools Act 1854
Habitual Criminals Act 1869
Licensing Act 1872
Prisons Act 1898
Probation of Offenders Act 1907
Children's Act 1908
Old Age Pensions Act 1908
Prevention of Crime Act 1908
National Insurance Act 1911
Criminal Justice Administration Act 1914
Probation of Offenders (Scotland) Act 1931
Criminal Justice Act 1948
Murder (Abolition of the Death Penalty) Act 1965
Criminal Justice Act 1967
Social Work (Scotland) Act 1968
Children and Young Persons' Act 1969
Criminal Justice Act 1972
Local Government Act 1972
Highways Act 1980
Criminal Justice Act 1982
Police and Criminal Evidence Act 1984
Public Order Act 1986
Local Government Act 1988
Criminal Justice Act 1991
Criminal Justice Act 1993
Criminal Justice and Public Order Act 1994
Children (Scotland) Act 1995
Housing Act 1996
Crime Sentences Act 1997
Police Act 1997
Prevention of Harassment Act 1997
Crime and Disorder Act 1998
Human Rights Act 1998
National Minimum Wage Act 1998

Northern Ireland (Sentences) Act 1998
Youth Justice and Criminal Evidence Act 1999
Criminal Justice and Court Services Act 2000
Freedom of Information Act 2000
Powers of Criminal Courts (Sentencing) Act 2000
Regulation of Investigatory Powers Act 2000
Sexual Offences (Amendment) Act 2000
Terrorism Act 2000
Anti-Terrorism Crime and Security Act 2001
Criminal Justice and Police Act 2001
Justice (Northern Ireland) Act 2002
Police Reform Act 2002
Antisocial Behaviour Act 2003
Criminal Justice Act 2003
Local Government Act 2003
Sexual Offences Act 2003
Antisocial Behaviour (Northern Ireland) Order 2004
Antisocial Behaviour (Scotland) Act 2004
Civil Partnerships Act 2004
Crime and Victims Act 2004
Constitutional Reform Act 2005
Prevention of Terrorism Act 2005
Serious Organised Crime and Police Act 2005
Equality Act 2006
Police and Justice Act 2006
Road Safety Act 2006
Terrorism Act 2006
Violent Crime Reduction Act 2006
Corporate Manslaughter and Corporate Homicide Act 2007
Offender Management Act 2007
Serious Crime Act 2007
Criminal Justice and Immigration Act 2008
Criminal Justice (Northern Ireland) Order 2008
Coroners and Justice Act 2009
Children's Hearings (Scotland) Bill 2010
Crime and Security Act 2010

Introduction

In most contemporary societies, criminal justice has become what might be termed a 'hot topic', widely discussed in the media and ignored by ambitious politicians at their peril. Although crime itself has long been the object of popular fear and fascination (Pearson, 1983), it is only in relatively recent years that the criminal justice system itself has become the subject of such widespread public scrutiny and political debate. This trend has been accompanied by a proliferation of legislation in the field of criminal justice which has resulted in a wide extension of police powers and increased criminalisation, particularly of the most visible forms of 'deviant' behaviour. Consequently, the number of people placed under the watchful eye of criminal justice agencies and their partners from the private and voluntary sectors, whether in prison or in the community, has increased exponentially. A number of commentators have summed up this hardening of the criminal law as the 'new punitiveness' (Pratt *et al.*, 2005; Goldson, 2002) or the 'punitive turn' (Garland, 2001a, p. 142). Pratt *et al.*, in their critical exposé of the phenomenon, cite amongst its principal indicators a rapid expansion of the prison population, the displacement of proportionality as a guide to sentencing (as exemplified by the much-discussed 'three strikes' legislation), the restriction to the civil liberties of ex-offenders (notably via the creation of sexual offenders' registers), the return of the public shaming of offenders, increased police numbers, and a halt to prison reform efforts (Pratt *et al.*, 2005). Garland also highlights harsher sentencing and increased reliance on imprisonment, paedophile registers and penal austerity, as well as the imprisonment of children, zero tolerance policing and Antisocial Behaviour Orders (Garland, 2001a, p. 142). In America, he notes the revival of chain gangs and corporal punishment, 'boot camps' and

1

'supermax' prisons, as well as the multiplication of capital offences and executions (Garland, 2001, p. 142).

It is clear that some, although not all, of these indicators are present in most modern industrialised societies, suggesting that the trend towards increased punitiveness in criminal justice is to at least some extent global. Indeed, even countries previously noted for their tolerance in their approach to the crime problem, such as the Netherlands (Downes, 1993) and Scandinavia (Pratt, 2008b), have become increasingly tough in this field (Van Swaaningen, 2005; Tham, 2001).This has led many commentators to attempt to explain the punitive trend by pinpointing factors common to most Western nations rather than specifically national characteristics. David Garland, for instance, has highlighted the role played by late modernity which he regards as being principally characterised by widespread insecurity (Garland, 2001a). It is this feeling of insecurity, prompted by the social and economic transformations which have affected nearly all Western nations to differing degrees since the 1970s, but particularly Britain and the United States, which he claims has fuelled demands for increased protection against all forms of risk, notably that posed by crime.

Garland is certainly correct to point out that feelings of insecurity run high, this despite the fact that the overall crime rate has actually declined in most developed countries over the past decade and more (van Dijk *et al.*, 2008). Indeed, increasing punitiveness in penal policy can be regarded as being as much a response to fear of crime as to the crime problem itself (Garland, 2001a). It is also the case that the options available to the modern State to respond to the crime problem have been severely limited by the peculiar context in which it has had to operate. Many commentators, however, have preferred to view that context as one of neoliberalism rather than of late modernity. It is arguably this specific political conjecture which is responsible for many of the problems of late modernity. With its focus on individual rather than state responsibility for the social and economic dislocations of which crime is but one manifestation, it has been argued that neoliberalism has severely limited the extent to which national governments might attempt to tackle the root causes of crime (Reiner, 2007). In such a context, it is argued that reintegrative welfare-oriented approaches to criminal justice have been displaced in favour of those advanced by conservative criminologists who regard offenders as rational actors primarily responsive to state interventions which aim to render the costs of crime higher than its benefits. Such an approach favours deterrent and punitive sentencing. It is, however, advanced in the present text that it is the extension rather than the total displacement of welfarist approaches, combined with an emphasis on individual responsibility for the crime problem which has been the prime driver of punitive policies in recent years in Britain.

The link between neoliberalism and punitive penal practice – the primary focus of this book – has been much discussed in recent years (Cavadino and Dignan, 2006; Reiner, 2007; Wacquant, 2009). Cavadino and Dignan, in their ambitious comparative study of different developed nations, conclude that countries which have adopted harsh neoliberal policies, such as the USA, England and Wales, Australia, New Zealand and South Africa, also tend to have harsh penal policies, largely on account of the exclusionary attitude that prevails there. This exclusionary attitude may be aptly summed up in Garland's phrase, 'the criminology of the other', according to which crime policy is directed at excluding rather than reintegrating those who pose a threat to mainstream social norms. Such policies form part of what Garland describes as a growing 'culture of control' which has gradually replaced the postwar philosophy of penal welfarism (Garland, 2001a). Reiner, concentrating on the case of the UK, has also pointed to the link between neoliberalism and exclusionary attitudes, noting that neoliberal culture favours 'egotistic individualism' over the 'reciprocal individualism' which was promoted during the post-war period when social-democratic beliefs were prevalent (Reiner, 2007, p. 18). He argues that egotistic individualism implies a lack of concern for others, namely the socially excluded, whose ranks have swelled in recent years and whose exclusion neoliberal government remains relatively powerless to act upon (*ibid.*). In line with these commentators, Wacquant sees harsh penal and social policies as going hand in hand in the Neoliberal State. However, rather than placing them in the context of the development of a particularly punitive culture, he considers them as being intrinsic to the very practice of neoliberal statecraft. For him, harsh penal policy is not a response to criminal insecurity but rather to social insecurity. It is a way for the State to manage the social fallout generated by neoliberalism by containing and controlling problem populations.

The argument presented in this book is largely in agreement with elements of all of these theses and is indeed indebted to them. However, the present analysis diverges from them in several important ways. Firstly, unlike that of Wacquant, it does not regard punitiveness as being intrinsic to neoliberalism. Neoliberalism should not inevitably result in penal severity, even if this has most frequently been the practical outcome. The huge state expenditure required to sustain such a policy actually runs counter to neoliberal theory, as does the extra-ordinary level of state intervention into the lives of individuals that has occurred in many neoliberal countries in recent years, or the rise in disproportional punishment. Secondly, although accepting that neo-liberalism can generate a punitive climate conducive to punitive penal policy, the present argument suggests that the most important link between neoliberalism and punitiveness lies in the transformation of the Capitalist State. Wacquant also notes that neoliberalism has caused such a transformation, which he sums up as 'the amputation of its econ-omic arm, the retraction of its social bosom, and the massive expan-sion of its penal fist' (Wacquant, 2009, p. 4). But it is suggested here that this transformation is not as profound as Wacquant suggests: although globalisation has severely restricted the role which govern-ments play in managing their national economies, it is surely going too far to speak of the 'amputation of [their] economic arm'. States continued to intervene to a considerable extent in national economic policy right through the heyday of the neoliberal era of the 1980s and 1990s – for example, by continuing to control interest rates to keep inflation down – and, in the context of the current crisis, there has been a considerable rolling *forward* of the State in the economic field with national governments stepping in to save the banks and key industries from financial ruin. Furthermore, although nations which have adopted neoliberalism have seen a simultaneous retrenchment of welfare state programmes and an expansion of penal surveillance and control, it would be incorrect to suggest that there has necessarily been a direct inverse relationship between the two. In fact, if we take the UK as an example, social spending has actually continued to grow along-side spending on criminal justice (HM Treasury, 2009). In many ways the welfare state in Britain has actually been extended with the develop-ment of an ever-wider range of social programmes, although this does not necessarily mean that it has not become more punitive in this sphere.

In reality, the most significant transformation which the State has undergone as a result of neoliberalism is the move from its role as provider of public services to that of facilitator of market solutions. Garland has suggested that the modern State has become weak, yet it might be more convincingly argued that 'it is not that the state has become impotent, but that it is constrained to use its power to advance the process of commodification' (Leys, 2003, p. 2). Consequently, the efforts of the Neoliberal State have been focused on the need to liberate the market from restrictive forces of regulation (although it is argued here that regulation has paradoxically actually increased in other areas) and to carry out a fundamental reorganisation of public services in order to create new markets for expanding capital. The changes made to the criminal justice system must be seen in the wider context of neoliberal public service reform which has led to the privatisation and contracting out of core state functions and the importation of the logic of the free market into areas formerly thought to be immune from such influences. The penetration of the market logic of neoliberalism into the criminal justice system has led to punitiveness in a number of different ways. The spread of management ideology has gradually altered the culture of criminal justice services which have become increasingly concerned with meeting narrowly-defined targets. In the British Police Service, this has translated as an obsession with meeting government-set targets concerning the number of Offences Brought to Justice (OBTJ), contributing to a proliferation in the use of summary justice. The UK Prison Service has become increasingly concerned with meeting Key Performance Indicators (KPIs) with regard to issues such as prison escapes and rehabilitation, whilst the Probation Service has been reorganised in such a way as to transform the role of probation officers from that of 'befriending' ex-offenders to that of surveillance. Although the New Labour government remained committed to rehabilitation, this function had to compete alongside the aims of punishment, crime reduction, public protection and reparation (*Criminal Justice Act 2003*, s. 142). Offender 'management' is now the declared aim of the criminal justice system in England and Wales, as clearly demonstrated by the reorganisation of the Prison and Probation Services into the National Offender Management Service. As in the market, emphasis is now placed on the management of risk. This concern with risk management has legitimated ever-earlier intervention into the lives of potential offenders, whether they are adults or children. Indeed, the very definition of criminal behaviour has become extremely loose to include simply risky behaviour: 'nuisance' behaviour and 'incivilities'. Paradoxically, therefore, the contracting out of many functions of the criminal justice system to external agencies, and the offloading of state responsibilities for crime control onto individual communities, have resulted in more, not less, state intervention. If anything, state surveillance has simply been dispersed throughout an ever-expanding network of agencies in civil society. The potential for increased punitiveness is self-evident. Another problem is that the increase in the central power of the State has resulted in decreased accountability, as accountability pathways become increasingly complex. Accountability has also become a significant problem where, for example, the policing of large areas of public space are effectively transferred over to private security agencies who are at liberty to define problem behaviour according to the specific interests of their employers. Finally, as business becomes a key partner in the criminal justice policy-making process, the old barriers to punitiveness, namely small groups of professional élites, are pushed aside.

Another way in which the present analysis diverges from other work on penal severity and neoliberalism is that it attempts to address some issues which have to date been left unexplained. Firstly, if neoliberalism is the key source of punitiveness, why did the 'punitive turn' not occur until *circa* 1993 in the UK, whereas neoliberal policies had been applied there since the arrival of Margaret Thatcher to power in 1979, if not earlier? Secondly, as Wacquant has noted, neoliberal penality has been warmly embraced by centre-left parties in America, Britain and France. Yet, it is often unexplained precisely how the Left managed to reconcile such policies with their particular intellectual inheritance. For the British Left, for example, socially-interventionist yet punitive crime control policies must be situated in the context of the tradition of Christian socialism and more recent communitarian theory. It is thus important to show exactly how neoliberalism interacts with specific cultural and institutional factors in different contexts, producing variable results across and even within different nations at different times. Indeed, although the focus of this book is on the interaction between neoliberal political economy and punitive penal policy, the notion of 'political economy' is understood in its widest possible sense, including not just economic but also political, social and cultural factors. It is important to acknowledge Nicola Lacey's argument that 'political-economic forces at the macro level are mediated not only by cultural filters, but also by economic, political and social institutions' (Lacey, 2008, p. 57).

A final question concerns Wacquant's assertion, which is largely supported here, that penal policy represents an attempt by the Neoliberal State to manage and control certain 'undesirable' populations. It is argued here that this attempt has largely been a failure, at least in the British context. Indeed, the problem of poverty and social inequality remains highly visible. Moreover, the strategy may actually call the legitimacy of the government into question as fear of crime remains high and confidence in the criminal justice system is low (Thorpe and Hall, 2009). Why then is such a policy pursued? It is argued that it may nonetheless be understood in the specific context of the need for governments to find new means of legitimation in an age when legitimation is no longer derived from their ability to protect the public against the 'worst excesses' of capitalism by providing full employment or universally free public services, as they attempted to do during the period of 'embedded liberalism'. Despite the apparent failure of tough crime policy to restore confidence in the government, the question of law and order is one which tends to appeal to voters across traditional class lines. There are few other issues which enable the government to do so and it is almost certain that ignoring the question of law and order, once it has become so highly mediatised and politicised, is no longer a realistic option for modern government. Adopting tough penal policies may thus be regarded as just one way in which states may still *attempt* to seek legitimacy in a neoliberal world which has stripped them of their former role as service providers and fundamentally transformed how they function. Consequently, the link between neoliberalism and punitiveness is an indirect one.

A few points ought to be made about the terminology used in the book. All too often, the term neoliberalism is used in the absence of an adequate definition. Yet, the concept is in many ways as nebulous as that of late modernity. It is essential to avoid the trap of thinking of neoliberalism as a uniform, universally applicable concept. Neoliberalism is in reality a complex *system* which does not simply have an economic dimension but also social, political, legal, cultural and intellectual dimensions (Dardot and Laval, 2009; Christoph, 2010). Taking the example of Britain, it was an economic project in the sense that it aimed to 'free' the market from political and social constraints by retrenching the welfare state, creating a flexible labour market and promoting privatisation and deregulation. However, such an economic project also converged with the political project of Thatcherism to regain the centre-ground of British politics. Such a dramatic change of policy necessitated the legal framework to render it possible, a change in cultural sensibilities and intellectual support, largely provided by think tanks such as the Institute of Economic Affairs and the Centre for Policy Studies (Dixon, 1998).

Furthermore, there are often wide divergences between the theory and the practice of neoliberalism. Indeed, the frontiers of the Neoliberal State are often simultaneously rolled forward and backwards, leading to what Andrew Gamble has described as the paradox of the 'free economy' and the 'strong state' (Gamble, 1994). Indeed, the withdrawal of the State in the economic arena has led to increased state intervention in the social and legal spheres. For example, Margaret

Thatcher attempted to free the economy from regulation by using the law to severely curtail the power of the trade unions and to deregulate the labour market. In addition, neoliberalism can be both destructive and creative. This paradox has been appropriately described by Jamie Peck and Adam Tickell (2002) as 'roll back' and 'roll out' liberalism. The former may be used to describe the Thatcher and Reagan administrations which attempted to apply neoliberal philosophy by dismantling the key institutions of the Keynesian welfare state, whereas the latter more appropriately describes the attempts by the New Democrats in the USA and New Labour in Britain to consolidate the reforms of their predecessors by creating new policies and agencies to respond to the economic problems and social dislocations engendered by the first phase of neoliberalism. It is in this phase that neoliberalism became more of a social project, promoting increased state intervention in order to regulate problems of immigration, welfare reform, crime and the degeneration of the inner cities (*ibid.*, p. 389).

Given the contradictory nature of neoliberalism, it must be borne in mind that neoliberalism is applied in different ways in different contexts. We should therefore focus on what Neil Brenner and Nik Theodore describe as 'actually existing neoliberalism' (2002). Even within the same nation, neoliberalism may be applied in different ways – for example, it may be argued that weaker forms of neoliberalism have emerged within the UK, in Wales and in Scotland. Consequently, rather than attempting to provide a universal, catch-all definition of neoliberalism, the present argument attempts to theorise neoliberalism in the specific context of the UK and examine precisely how it is applied and how it interacts with other cultural and institutional factors. This enables us to adopt a much-needed empirical approach to the concept. Comparisons with other nations, where relevant, are not, however, excluded.

Two final points ought to be borne in mind about neoliberalism. Firstly, even if some experts such as Wacquant regard the spread of neoliberalism as inexorable, evidence is to be found to the contrary, as formidable resistance is mounted by certain interest groups and in certain countries such as France, Germany, Italy and Sweden (Cavadino and Dignan, 2006). Secondly, there is a danger that focus on the 'neo' of neoliberalism may result in an ahistorical approach being taken to the question of the link between punitiveness and neoliberalism. Yet, both these concepts need to be viewed in their historical context. There is considerable disagreement about the extent to which neoliberalism is really new. It has been suggested that it is actually nothing more than a simple return to the classical liberalism of the nineteenth century. Indeed, Serge Halimi's discussion of neoliberal politics carries the title, *The Great Leap Backwards* (*Le grand bond en arrière*, 2004), and experts have highlighted parallels with classical liberalism such as the attempt to restore power to the economic élites who were marginalised with the coming of twentieth century democracy (Harvey, 2007; Duménil and Lévy, 2004). Yet it might be argued, following Foucault, that the one great novelty of neoliberalism is the fact that it intervenes as never before in society as part of a strategy of governmentality which attempts to subject individuals to self-regulation (Foucault, 2004 [1978–9]).

Similarly, we should be wary of allowing a focus on the novelty of neoliberalism to lead us to view punitiveness itself as being entirely novel. Just as Halimi writes of a leap backwards in the economic and social arenas, Wacquant writes of a 'great penal leap backwards' (Wacquant, 2005), suggesting that modern penality is something of a reincarnation of earlier forms of punishment. Pratt *et al.* also suggest that contemporary penality marks a break with modern penality which focused on the reform of the offender and harks back to pre-modern arbitrary and disproportionate forms of punishment which seek merely to contain and control (Pratt *et al.*, pp. xii–xiii). It is argued here that contemporary penality tends to combine elements from across all historical periods. For example, although the 'spectacle of punishment', a distinctive feature of pre-modern penality (the prime example of which was, of course, the scaffold), is being re-emphasised – for example, via policies which encourage the 'naming and shaming' of offenders – it would be a mistake to suggest that the modern nineteenth and twentieth century emphasis on rehabilitation is dead. In reality, rehabilitation has been redefined: the modern Capitalist State still aims to create 'docile bodies' (Foucault, 1975) but, rather than reintegrating them, the State intervenes in an intrusive way to neutralise the risk they represent by forcing them to modify their personalities and to become 'self-regulating' (such is the focus of the cognitive behaviour programmes to which increasing numbers of offenders are subjected). As Joe Sim suggests, it is perhaps more appropriate to speak of the 'intensification' of punishment rather than of an entirely 'new punitiveness' (Sim, 2009, p. 15). Just as nineteenth century attempts to reform and rehabilitate the offender can best be understood in the context of classical liberalism which sought to 'discipline' workers and potential workers to conform to a new capitalist order, today's penal strategies may rather be understood in the context of neoliberal governmentality which aims to neutralise the risk that is presented to the new neoliberal order by the criminal or the simply unruly. It is in this sense that a historical approach may enable us to better understand the links between neoliberalism and penality.

The book is divided into two main parts. The first examines whether or not British penal policy has really become considerably more punitive. The case of Britain is of particular interest to the study of neoliberal penality since it is arguably the only democratic nation outside the United States to have experimented with both neoliberal policy *and* punitive penality to such a significant extent. It is also notable that the UK finds itself in the unusual position of being strongly subject to influences from both the United States and Europe. Whilst the former pulls her in a more punitive, neoliberal direction, it is possible to argue that the latter has been pulling her in the opposite direction. The focus is on England and Wales although the case of Scotland, Wales and Northern Ireland are also briefly studied in order to determine the extent to which they do or do not conform to the rest of the British model.

On account of the fact that the aim is to deal with contemporary penality, the book mainly deals with the past 13 years of New Labour government. It is obviously timely to provide a comprehensive review of New Labour policy in the field just as the party has exited power. It is hoped that this work will complement that already carried out by experts such as Michael Tonry and others (Tonry, 2003; Tonry, 2004a). It is nonetheless necessary to trace the 'punitive turn' back even further than New Labour, briefly examining the Thatcher and Major years and placing it in the context of the initial rise of neoliberalism in Britain. The less recent past is also studied in order to situate policies in a broader historical trajectory and thus examine their novelty.

A number of different indicators of punitiveness are examined. Firstly, the phenomenon of penal expansionism is elucidated. It is suggested that the current extraordinarily high prison population has largely resulted from the lengthening of prison sentences, the limitation of parole and the harsh enforcement of alternative sentences. Secondly, the focus is placed on the widening of the penal net to include not just criminal behaviour but also simple nuisance behaviour. The rise of summary justice is revealed as the main driver of this particular trend. It is shown that the widening of the penal net has meant that increasing numbers of people who would previously have been subject to welfarist interventions, notably children and young people, are becoming the target of the criminal law. Chapter 3 focuses on how a tougher approach has not just been adopted towards criminal and nuisance behaviour but also towards offenders themselves. This is exemplified by the development of a new rehabilitative philosophy which emphasises the control and surveillance of the offender and the management of risk to the detriment of welfare and reintegration. The fourth chapter deals with the erection of real and metaphorical boundaries between the 'law-abiding majority' and 'undesirable' groups and the extension of state control outside the prison walls, placing both offenders and potential offenders under surveillance. It is demonstrated how the forces of law and order play an ever-greater role in policing these boundaries. Historical references throughout these initial chapters allow us to address the question of the novelty of punitive penality. The final chapter in this section briefly draws some international comparisons in an attempt to situate the UK in a global context and to determine whether or not it is possible to speak of one single global punitive trend.

The second part of the book represents an attempt to explore the possible links between neoliberalism and penal punitiveness. Firstly, an overview is provided of the principal explanations which have been given of punitive trends before turning to those which focus specifically on neoliberalism. Neoliberalism cannot be considered as the sole cause of punitiveness nor, as noted above, can punitiveness be seen as inherent to neoliberalism. Yet, as the most significant political mutation of our times, it is surely essential to seek to understand how exactly it interacts with penality and other areas of government policy. A more comprehensive attempt to define the notion of neoliberalism is attempted here, before looking at how neoliberalism has been applied in the British context. The link between punitive penality and the neoliberal transformation of the Capitalist State is then studied in detail. Finally, an attempt is made to understand precisely why successive New Labour governments turned to 'populist punitiveness' (Bottoms, 1995) in this particular context.

The conclusion seeks to outline some possible futures for penal policy in the UK. It may have been thought that the ongoing economic crisis might have forced the State to depart in significant ways from the central tenets of neoliberalism but, despite short-lived state intervention into the economy to steer the country through the worst part of the crisis, it would appear that the neoliberal order has survived intact. It might also have been thought that the crisis might have distracted attention from the crime problem but, so far, this has not proved to be the case. Finally, it is asked if the incoming Conservative-Liberal Democrat coalition government is likely to break from the policy of its predecessors in any significant way that might check the current slide towards punitiveness.

Part I

The Intensification of Punishment

1
Lock 'em Up!

There is a widespread public perception in Britain that prison is under-used and sentencing too lenient. The most recent British Crime Survey found that 41 per cent of people interviewed in England and Wales believed that 'too lenient sentencing' was 'a major cause of crime' (Thorpe and Hall, 2009, p. 96). This view is shared by respondents to surveys in Scotland and Northern Ireland (Northern Ireland Office, 2005; Scottish Executive, 2007). Despite the fact that such views are more likely to be informed by ignorance than reality (Hough and Roberts, 1998), they are widely echoed by the media and even expressed by some senior ministers. For example, in 2006 *The Sun* seized on the case of Craig Sweeney, a convicted sex offender who, in the opinion of the tabloid, had received an unduly lenient penalty for sexually abusing a three-year-old child. It launched a campaign demanding that judges who handed down lenient penalties to murderers, rapists, paedophiles and other violent criminals be sacked. Under the headline, 'We Demand Real Justice', *The Sun* published the photos of ten judges accompanied by details of their 'lenient' sentencing history (*The Sun*, 2006). John Reid, then Home Secretary, soon joined the debate, declaring publicly that Sweeney's sentence was indeed 'unduly lenient' and requesting that the Attorney General send the case to the Court of Appeal for review. Such highly-publicised cases obviously help to fuel perceptions of leniency but it should be borne in mind that in England and Wales the cases of only 80 offenders whose sentences were considered to be unduly lenient were referred to the Court of Appeal in 2008 (Attorney General, 2009), representing a mere 0.01 per cent of all offenders sentenced that year (Ministry of Justice, 2010a).

The prison population explosion

The reality is that sentencing has been getting tougher over recent years as people have been spending ever-longer periods of time in prison. According to official Ministry of Justice reports, this has been a major cause of the exponential rise in the prison population, together with tougher enforcement rules and an increase in the seriousness of offences coming before the courts (Ministry of Justice, 2009a). Indeed, the prison population of England and Wales has risen by almost 88 per cent since 1992 (ICPS, 2010). In April 2010, just before New Labour left power, it stood at the historically high rate of 154 people incarcerated per 100,000 people (ICPS, 2010) or 85,086 people in total (HM Prison Service, 2010a). It is expected to hit a maximum high of 93,900 by 2015 (Ministry of Justice, 2009b). Scotland has also seen a considerable rise in its prison population – approximately 42 per cent since 1992 (ICPS, 2010). In early 2010, there were 7630 people incarcerated, representing a rate of 146 prisoners per 100,000 people. Although this annual rate of imprisonment is less than that of England and Wales, Scotland's *daily* rate is actually considerably higher – 753.9 new entrants to prison per 100,000 inhabitants per day – , placing it top of a Council of Europe league table measuring flow of entry to prisons (*The Herald*, 2008). Northern Ireland is the only apparent exception to these trends towards carceral inflation, having experienced a significant decrease in its total prison population. Since 1992, the population fell by almost 24 per cent and the region currently incarcerates 1377 people, corresponding to a rate of 77 inmates per 100,000 people (ICPS, 2010). However, this drop can largely be explained by the release of political prisoners – who represented a quarter of the total prison population – following the *Northern Ireland (Sentences) Act 1998*. These figures mask the fact that the population has actually been rising considerably since a low of 877 prisoners in 2001 (*ibid.*): this marks an increase of over 57 per cent in just nine years!

There are also more women, young people and foreign nationals in prison in the UK than in the past, although Northern Ireland represents an exception in the first two instances. The number of women in prison in England and Wales has almost doubled since 1996 – they now represent 5.1 per cent of the prison population (Berman, 2009, pp. 5–6). In Scotland, the average daily female population, which represents about 5 per cent of the total prison population, increased by 87 per cent between 1998/99 and 2007/08. Conversely, in Northern Ireland, the number of women in prison has remained relatively stable over the past ten years (O'Loan and McKibbin, 2008, p. 3).

Young people aged under 18 represent 2.2 per cent of the prison population in England and Wales, 12.2 per cent in Scotland and 0.7 per cent in Northern Ireland (ICPS, 2010). The number of under-18s held in custody in England and Wales is currently declining, after having risen considerably in the early part of the decade (YJB, 2010a). In addition, the number of juveniles sentenced by courts in England and Wales has also fallen: by nine per cent from 2007–2008 (Ministry of Justice, 2010a, p. 15). Yet, it should be noted that these figures may mask the increasing numbers of young people who are currently placed under the surveillance of the criminal justice system (see Chapter 3). For instance, the number of juveniles given a community sentence has more than doubled since 1998, rising from 34 to 68 per cent (Ministry of Justice, 2010a, p. 33). The extremely high rate of custody for young people in Scotland can partly be explained by the tough approach taken with regard to those aged over 16 who are effectively treated as if they are adults – those aged under 16 actually tend to receive more lenient treatment than in England and Wales, largely thanks to the unique system of Children's Hearings (Cavadino and Dignan, 2006, p. 22; see Chapter 3). In 2008 (the latest figures available) only three juveniles under the age of 16 were held in Scottish prisons and just 12 were held in young offender institutions (Scottish Parliament, 2009). The rate of incarceration for juveniles under 18 in Northern Ireland is considerably lower than that in either England or Scotland and it fell considerably between 1996 and 2006 (Jacobson and Gibbs, 2009, p. 22).

The number of foreign nationals held in custodial institutions has increased across the UK in recent years. In England and Wales, it increased from about 8 per cent of the total prison population in the mid-1990s to approximately 14 per cent in 2009 (Berman, 2009, p. 8). Approximately 71 per cent of foreign national prisoners were from a minority ethnic group (*ibid.*, p. 9). According to a recent report, foreign nationals account for disproportionately high numbers of prisoners in Scotland, yet on account of their small numbers they cannot account for the overall growth in the prison population (Audit Scotland, 2008, pp. 8–9). Although the percentage of foreign nationals held in Northern Irish prisons remains lower than in the rest of the UK, their number has been increasing in recent years and now stands at about 5 per cent of the total prison population (Northern Ireland Prison Service, 2008).

Despite the massive increase in the UK prison population in recent years, it remains low compared to that of the United States where the population exceeds two million people and the rate of incarceration is almost five times higher (753 prisoners/100,000 people: ICPS, 2010).

David Garland has described the situation in the United States as one of 'mass imprisonment' which he defines as follows: '[...] a rate of imprisonment and a size of prison population that is markedly above the historical and comparative norm for societies of this type. [...] Imprisonment becomes *mass imprisonment* when it ceases to be the incarceration of individual offenders and becomes the systematic incarceration of whole groups of the population' (Garland, 2001b, pp. 5–6). Although the UK cannot yet be described as experiencing imprisonment on anything like the scale of that in the USA, the two trends identified by Garland are nonetheless present. The current prison population of England and Wales is much higher than the historical norm – the rate of imprisonment for men is now twice what it was throughout the whole period extending from 1900–1990, whilst that for women is almost three times greater (Office for National Statistics, 2003a). The prison population rate for England and Wales is also higher than that of countries of a similar type. As we have just noted, it is higher than that of either Scotland or Northern Ireland. It is also considerably higher than that of its European neighbours such as France (96 prisoners per 100,000 people: ICPS, 2010), Germany (88 prisoners per 100,000 people: *ibid.*) or Italy (107 prisoners per 100,000 people: *ibid.*). It currently has the highest prison population rate in Western Europe with the exceptions of Luxembourg and Spain. Finally, although imprisonment does not yet have anything like the racial dimension that it has in the USA where 58 per cent of all sentenced prisoners under state and federal jurisdiction in 2008 were either Black or Hispanic (Sabol *et al.*, 2009), the percentage of prisoners from ethnic minorities in England and Wales has been growing considerably in recent years (Councell, 2003, p. 3). In 2008, over one quarter of the prison population in England and Wales were from a minority ethnic group (Berman, 2009, p. 9), even though non-White ethnic minorities only represent approximately 8 per cent of the total population (Office for National Statistics, 2004). In the UK it might be argued that there has indeed been 'systematic incarceration of whole groups of the population', yet this trend does not just have a racial dimension. Although there are no statistics specifically relating to the social background of prisoners, it is clear that they are largely drawn from the ranks of the poorest and most disadvantaged people in society. It is estimated that 80 per cent of all prisoners suffer from mental health problems (Scott, 2008, p. 116), that 80 per cent have writing skills at or below the level of an 11-year-old child and that prisoners are 13 times as likely to have been unemployed as people in the general population (Social Exclusion Unit, 2002, pp. 2–3). These figures are even higher than those revealed by the Prison Reform Trust almost 20 years ago (Prison Reform Trust, 1991), suggesting that the increase in the use of imprisonment has impacted most heavily upon whole swathes of the disadvantaged. It might be argued that the UK, or England and Wales at least, are now heading down the road towards mass imprisonment.

The crime-prison nexus

Before analysing the trend towards mass imprisonment in detail, it should first be noted that it is not a direct response to increased criminality, contrary to Jack Straw's affirmation, 'If crime is rising, the prison population is bound to rise' (Straw, cited by Richards, 1998, p. 27). Indeed, the exact reverse would appear to have been the case over the past two decades – crime has been falling whilst the prison population has been rising. According to both police statistics and the British Crime Survey, crime has been falling since 1995 (Walker *et al.*, 2009, pp. 2–3). The British Crime Survey registered an overall 45 per cent drop between 1995 and 2008/9 (*ibid.*). Meanwhile, as we have seen, the prison population has continued to climb. Far from regarding this trend as proof of the absence of any causal relationship between crime and imprisonment, certain conservative criminologists have seen it as confirmation of such a trend. Inversing the causal relationship postulated by Jack Straw, the right-wing think tank, CIVITAS, argues that the rise in the rate of incarceration since 1993 led directly to a corresponding drop in the crime rate. In an article published in *The Observer* in 2003, David Green, the director of CIVITAS, argued that what he calls the 'incapacitative effect' of imprisonment has meant that the incarceration of 12,000 extra people between 1997 and 2003 resulted 1.7 million fewer crime victims (Green, 2003). In another publication, CIVITAS argues that imprisonment also has a deterrent effect (CIVITAS, 2003). It bases its argument on a comparative study of crime rates in the United States and England and Wales, carried out by Patrick Langan and David Farrington, which showed that whilst the probability of being imprisoned increased in the United States between 1981 and 1995, it decreased in England and Wales over the same time period. Simultaneously, the crime rate fell in the States whilst it increased in England and Wales. CIVITAS draws the conclusion that when there is a relatively high risk of being imprisoned, potential offenders are dissuaded from committing crime and the crime rate consequently drops.

This argument is flawed in three main ways. Firstly, it is extremely difficult to compare crime rates across different countries since the counting rules may vary from place to place. Even within the same country, different crime statistics may reveal contradictory trends. For instance, the most recent British Crime Survey (BCS) registers an increase of 25 per cent in theft from the person whereas the official police statistics register a fall of 12 per cent (Walker *et al.*, 2009, p. 1). Indeed, crime statistics are notoriously unreliable (Morris, 1989; Maguire, 2007; Reiner, 2007). Changes in crime rates may actually be as much a reflection of changes to how these are collated than of crime trends themselves. For example, between 2000 and 2003 the official crime rate in England and Wales increased, not due to a change in criminal behaviour, but rather due to changes made to the counting rules which have meant that a whole range of summary offences are now to be included in the statistics. It is estimated that the change added 250,000 new crimes to the violent crime statistics (Maguire, 2007, p. 259). The BCS statistics have also been criticised. They are very subjective, only registering what the people questioned consider to be crimes. They are also far from exhaustive, excluding white collar crime, crime committed against homeless people, businesses and those aged under 16 (although, as of January 2009, the BCS covers crimes perpetrated against ten to 15 year olds), the crimes of assault, grievous bodily harm, sexual offences and homicide. The survey certainly goes some way to filling in the gap left by the police statistics – it is estimated that less than half of the crime it records is actually reported to the police (Walker *et al.*, 2009, p. 5). Nonetheless, there remains a substantial 'dark figure' of crime. Many offences remain 'hidden', such as violence within the home committed against women and children (Garside, 2006). A confidential report published under the *Freedom of Information Act* has estimated that there are 130 million serious crimes a year in England and Wales alone – 110 million more crimes that the maximum figures estimated by the British Crime Survey (Birt, 2000).

This leads us to the second problem with the CIVITAS argument – that of the incapacitative effect of imprisonment. If the dark figure of crime is as large as is suggested here, prison could only succeed in incarcerating a wholly insignificant proportion of those people likely to commit crime. Even if all these crimes were recorded, the chances of those responsible being incarcerated is slim: only 28 per cent of recorded crimes are cleared up and even then they do not necessarily result in imprisonment (a crime is said to be 'cleared up' when the offender is given a formal sanction: Walker *et al.*, 2009, p. 9).

Thirdly, the deterrent effect of imprisonment must also be questioned. During interviews conducted with over 80 male and female prisoners in February 2007, the author found that 68 per cent claimed to have committed their offence on the spur of the moment without any thought for the possible consequences (Bell, 2007). This would suggest that the relative severity of penalties has little effect on criminal behaviour. Furthermore, it would appear that prison has little future deterrent effect on those already incarcerated on account of the high rate of recidivism. It is estimated that in the two years following their release from prison 57.6 per cent of ex-offenders recommit a crime (Shepherd and Whiting, 2006). Some estimates even put this figure at as high as 67 per cent (Coalition on Social and Criminal Justice, 2006).

Although recognising that sentencing toughness and more stringent enforcement of penalties have contributed to the rise in the prison population, the Ministry of Justice also cites the increased seriousness of offences coming before the courts, noting the impact of violence against the person and drug offences (Ministry of Justice, 2009a, p. 9). However, other statistics suggest that the volume of these offences has not substantially increased in recent years, nor have they increased in seriousness. On the contrary, there has been a 15 per cent drop in offences of violence against the person between 2005/06 and 2008/09 (Walker *et al.*, 2009, p. 23). Even if these offences increased between 2002/03 and 2005/06, this increase may be accounted for by the impact of new counting rules (*ibid.*). Nor would these offences appear to have become more serious: weapons are used in one in five violent crimes, a figure which has remained stable over the past decade, and incidents of homicide are now at their lowest level in 20 years (Roe *et al.*, 2009, p. 43). Similarly, closer analysis of the statistics suggests that drug offences have not increased in seriousness. Although recorded drug offences have increased in recent years, it is suggested that these increases are mainly due to the increased recording of possession of cannabis offences which account for 69 per cent of all recorded drug offences (Moley, 2009, p. 87). In addition, the British Crime Survey found that overall illicit drug use amongst 16 to 59 year olds is now at its lowest level since the BCS began in 1981 (*ibid.*).

1993: The 'punitive turn'

All of this would suggest that the increase in the prison population is best explained by factors other than the crime rate. The start of the prison population increase can be dated to 1993, a date which many experts have pinpointed as the beginning of the 'punitive turn' in British penal policy, corresponding as it did with the arrival of Michael Howard as Home Secretary and the murder of the toddler James Bulger by two ten-year-old boys (Ashworth and Hough, 1996; Downes and Morgan, 2002a). The murder of James Bulger became symbolic not just of the rise in crime (in 1992–1993 the crime rate reached a peak, *cf.* Office for National Statistics, 2003a; Nicholas *et al.*, 2007) but rather of a more general moral breakdown in society, leading then Prime Minister John Major to launch a 'crusade against crime' and Tony Blair, then shadow Home Secretary, to deplore the descent into 'moral chaos' (Haydon and Scraton, 2000).

From the moment he was appointed as Home Secretary in 1993, Michael Howard was determined to adopt a tough stance on law and order. At the Conservative Party Conference of that year, he declared that 'prison works' and, in similar terms to those that would soon be adopted by his New Labour successors, he declared, 'In the last thirty years the balance in our criminal justice system has been tilted too far in favour of the criminal and against the protection of the public. The time has come to put that right' (Howard, 1993). Whilst at the Home Office, he ushered in a new culture of decision-making which was dominated by 'the politics of law and order' (Downes and Morgan, 2002a, p. 118) and which tended to exclude alternative viewpoints such as those presented by the prison reform lobby (Wilson, 2001, p. 141). During the course of his infamous 'prison works' speech, Howard announced 27 new crime-fighting measures, the majority of which were subsequently adopted by the *Criminal Justice Act 1993* and the *Criminal Justice and Public Order Act 1994*. Both these laws considerably toughened up the law. The first eroded the principle of proportionality in sentencing, whilst the second targeted whole categories of people engaged in 'undesirable' behaviour: ravers, squatters and travellers. This legislation undoubtedly had some impact on the rise of the prison population but, given the inevitable delay between the passage of legislation and its practical impact, it cannot be held directly responsible for provoking the initial rise. Perhaps more relevant was the politicisation of the issue of law and order. Indeed, Ashworth has suggested that the prison population from 1993 to 1997 rose independently of legislative changes and can be best explained by the fact that the judiciary was influenced by the punitive climate of public opinion (Ashworth, 1997). However, as the years have worn on and the prison population has continued to increase exponentially, it is plausible that legislative changes may also have played a significant role. This chapter is dedicated to analysing those changes which have impacted directly on the prison population. The question of the politicisation of the issue is dealt with in detail in Part II when an attempt is made to provide a detailed analysis of the forces driving legislative change. For now, focus is on examining the factors which have directly driven the prison population explosion, namely the extended periods of times that offenders now spend in prison and the tougher enforcement of sentences.

Keeping them locked up

Although the overall number of people sentenced actually decreased by 7 per cent between 1998 and 2008 (Ministry of Justice, 2010a, p. 15), sentencing severity increased. The average length of immediate determinate custodial sentences rose quite steadily, averaging 13.3 months in 2008. This is the longest average sentence length since 1997 (*ibid.*, p. 26), although there are considerable regional variations (*ibid.*, p. 44). In Scotland and Northern Ireland, average sentence lengths have also been increasing. In Scotland, average adult sentence lengths increased by over 20 per cent between 1998/99 and 2003/04 (Scottish Government, 2008a), although they had fallen again by 10 per cent by 2007/08. In Northern Ireland between 2001 and 2007 there was a significant increase in the number of prisoners serving determinate sentences of five years or more (O'Loan and McKibbin, 2008, pp. 4–5). In addition, there are increasing numbers of people in prison in England and Wales serving indeterminate sentences following the introduction of Indeterminate Sentences for Public Protection (IPPs) in April 2005. By July 2007, the number of people serving indeterminate life sentences and IPPs had already exceeded the number of people serving short sentences of a year or less (Prison Reform Trust, 2007, p. 2).

Although this trend towards increased sentence lengths has been exacerbated in recent years, it is not entirely new. In 1960, an official report attributed the rise in the prison population since the Second World War to the tendency of the courts to inflict more severe sentences than previously (Home Office, 1960, pp. 4–8). The trend continued in the 1960s and 1970s, with average sentence lengths increasing by at least 50 per cent (Morris, 1989, p. 136). Longer sentences increasingly became the norm: whereas in 1948 a ten-year sentence would have been considered long, in the 1960s a sentence of 25 years was handed down to the Kray brothers and 30 years to the Great Train Robbers (Morris, 1989, p. 136). Nevertheless, whilst the trend towards longer sentencing is not new, the proliferation of laws resulting in the lengthening of sentences certainly is. Since 1997, legislation has seriously eroded the principle of sentencing proportionality and limited the use of parole.

The erosion of proportionality

The recent erosion of the principle of sentencing proportionality might be regarded as a reversal of the philosophy which had dominated sentencing since the end of the eighteenth century when capital punishment was slowly replaced with sentences of imprisonment characterised by their uniformity (the same penalties were imposed for the same offences) and certainty (the length of penalties was fixed in advance). The new system was strongly inspired by Enlightenment ideas which questioned the arbitrariness of capital punishment, on account of the gap between theory and practice, and rejected a chaotic system of imprisonment which appeared to function in the absence of any coherent penal philosophy. The key influence of the period was the Italian legal philosopher Cesare Beccaria who, in his *opus magnum* of 1764, *Dei Delitti et delle Pene* (*On Crimes and Punishments*), denounced the excessive cruelty of the death penalty which only served to corrupt the public at large rather than deter crime. In its place, he recommended the development of a veritable science of punishment according to which laws would be clearly laid out and uniformly applied, and penalties calculated relative to the harm suffered by the offence and limited to what was strictly necessary to deter people from crime:

> In order for punishment not to be, in every instance, an act of public violence of one or many against a private citizen, it must be essentially public, prompt, necessary, the least possible in the given circumstance, proportionate to the crimes, dictated by laws (Beccaria, 1996, p. 13).

His ideas were in large part taken up in England by what is referred to today as the classical school of criminology which reacted against a system of vengeful, irrational and excessive punishment. One of its main proponents was Jeremy Bentham who considered that punishment should never be more severe than what is strictly necessary to deter the future offender from crime and thus to protect the happiness of the greatest number (McConville, 1981, p. 80). Yet the rise of proportionality did not necessarily lead to penal parsimony.

On the contrary, the prison population increased considerably over the course of the first three quarters of the nineteenth century (*ibid.*,

p. 198) – it was only after 1895 that the prison population began to fall considerably (Bailey, 1997) before rising again from the 1940s onwards (Office for National Statistics, 2003b, pp. 4–5). This initial surge in the population might be explained by the fact that the principle of proportionality may be defined in both a negative and a positive sense, often simultaneously. David Garland notes that the revival of the principle at the beginning of the 1990s under the label of 'just deserts' translated as both a preference for fixed penalties on the one hand and a discourse of vengeance on the other (Garland, 2001a, p. 9). Similarly, during what might be described as the Golden Age of classicism in the nineteenth century, there was considered to be no contradiction between proportionality and what would today be considered as extremely harsh punishment: indeed, up until 1965 in Britain the death penalty was considered to be perfectly commensurate with the seriousness of the offence of murder (even if it had been abolished for almost all other crimes in 1837). Although the *Criminal Justice Act 1991* might have been considered by some as the contemporary highpoint of the principle of proportionality (Koffman, 2006, p. 281), it was in reality both moderate and severe. It sought to limit imprisonment for minor offenders whilst demanding longer sentences for those found guilty of serious crimes. Consequently, section 2(2) stipulated that the court could impose an indeterminate penalty on any offender found guilty of having committed a violent or sexual offence when such a sentence would be 'necessary to protect the public from serious harm from the offender'. Yet this dualist approach, known as bifurcation, also clung to the notion of proportionality: section 2(2)(a) stipulated that the penalty imposed must be 'for such term (not exceeding the permitted maximum) as in the opinion of the court is commensurate with the seriousness of the offence'. In the same vein, section 1(2) dictated that custodial offences should only be handed down for an offence or combination of offences which are 'so serious that only such a sentence can be justified'.

Yet, the 1991 Act did not succeed in reducing the prison population. On the contrary, after having fallen from 50,000 people in 1987–88 to 42,500 people in 1991 (Downes and Morgan, 1997, p. 87), the population quickly started to climb again, only falling momentarily between the end of 1992 and the middle of 1993 (Office for National Statistics, 2003b). Although the Act aimed to limit judicial discretion in sentencing (Home Office, 1990), section 1(2) was interpreted broadly by the judges. On account of the fact that the concept of seriousness was not defined by law, the judges were left to interpret it as they saw fit. In the case of Keogh ([1994] 15 Cr. App. R. (S) 279), the Court of Appeal sentenced a defendant found guilty of having stolen goods worth £35 from a DIY store to one month's imprisonment because he had committed a 'serious' offence. In determining the meaning of seriousness, the Court applied the test developed by Lord Taylor in the case of Cox ([1993] 14 Cr. App. R. (S) 479 who declared that the court ought to ask itself if it is dealing with the type of crime that 'would make right-thinking members of the public, knowing all the facts, feel that justice had not been done by the passing of any sentence other than a custodial one' (cited in Ashworth and Hough, 1996, p. 783). In the punitive sentencing climate of recent years, it is easy to see how such a subjective test could easily result in an increase in the use of custodial sentences as well as a lengthening of the average penalty imposed. Indeed, it would appear that judges have tended to adopt a negative definition of the principle of proportionality. Consequently, the 1991 Act resulted in what Cavadino and Dignan have referred to as 'punitive bifurcation' whereby sentencing was punitive towards both more and less serious offenders (Cavadino and Dignan, 2006, p. 66).

Judges are not the only ones to have favoured a negative interpretation of the principle of proportionality. The British government soon departed from its support for penal parsimony as outlined in its 1990 White Paper (Home Office, 1990). The *Criminal Justice Act 1993* marked a turning point which has since seen the principle of proportionality gradually eroded by a focus on the past record of the offender and by the creation of automatic minimum sentences and indeterminate sentences. Whilst the *Criminal Justice Act 1991* allowed the court to take into account two previous offences linked to the current offence when determining offence seriousness, section 66(1) of the *Criminal Justice Act 1993* abolished this rule, allowing the court to examine any number of previous offences committed by the defendant provided that they are linked to the offence being judged. There is consequently nothing to stop a judge from grouping together a whole series of minor offences which may lead him to decide that, taken as a whole, they are sufficiently serious to merit imprisonment (Ashworth and Gibson, 1994, pp. 102–3). Such an approach would appear to have also been adopted by the Halliday Report of 2001 which led to the *Criminal Justice Act 2003*. Although the Report emphasised the importance of 'just deserts' and proportionality, it also proposed that there should be 'a clear presumption that sentencing severity should increase as a consequence of sufficiently recent and relevant previous convictions' (Halliday, 2001, p. 13). This recommendation was adopted by section 143(2) of the 2003 Act: when determining the seriousness of an offence committed by an offender who has at least one previous conviction, the court is now obliged to consider each conviction as an aggravating factor, provided that it was recent and relevant. For Geoff Dobson from the Prison Reform Trust, this represents a sort of double penalty and reverses the principle according to which one is considered innocent until proven guilty (Dobson, 2003, p. 16).

The idea that an offender can be sentenced not only for the crime for which he or she has been brought to court but also for all previous offences was pushed to its limit with the introduction of so-called 'three strikes' penalties in 1997. Up until 1997, there was only one automatic minimum sentence in English law – the life sentence for murder which was created by the *Murder (Abolition of the Death Penalty) Act 1965*. Then, in 1997, the *Crime Sentences Act* created mandatory minimum sentences for those found guilty of other serious offences. Section 3 created a minimum seven-year sentence for those convicted for their third offence for the trafficking of class A drugs, whilst section 4 created an automatic minimum penalty of three years for the third offence of domestic burglary. These penalties are mandatory unless the court considers them to be 'unjust in all the circumstances'. Section 2 created a mandatory minimum penalty of life imprisonment for those convicted for their second violent or sexual offence unless there are 'exceptional circumstances'. It was estimated at the time that the mandatory sentences for domestic burglars would alone cause an immediate increase in the prison population in the order of 4000 people (Rutherford, 1999, p. 82). There were also concerns that these penalties would have an indirect impact on other sentences, inciting judges to increase penalties across the board in the interest of uniformity (*ibid.*). However, in the event, these sentences appear to have had little impact on the prison population (Jones and Newburn, 2006, pp. 788–9). The mandatory sentence for domestic burglary was not actually implemented until December 1999 and even a year after its implementation, not a single three strikes sentence had been passed on a convicted burglar (*ibid.*, p. 788). Analysing the impact of these new sentences on the prison population by 2005, Jones and Newburn conclude that the minimum sentences for drug trafficking and burglary had had 'very small effects' and that even if there was more use made of mandatory minimums for sexual and violent offenders, there is no way of knowing whether these offenders would have received severe discretionary sentences in any case (*ibid.*, p. 789). In addition, the sentences soon ran up into trouble with the *Human Rights Act 1998* when it entered into force in 2000: the 'exceptional circumstances' which might prevent the court from imposing an automatic life sentence for violent and sexual offences were given a wide interpretation by the Court of Appeal which ruled that such an sentence should only be applied where an offender represented a risk to the public (*ibid.*, p. 788). However, more use has been made of the three strikes sentence for domestic burglary (now included in the *Powers of the Criminal Courts [Sentencing Act] 2000*) in recent years, with 500 such sentences being handed down in 2008 alone (Ministry of Justice, 2010a, p. 31). In addition, a mandatory minimum sentence of five years custody was created by the *Criminal Justice Act 2003* for offenders convicted of certain firearms offences unless exceptional circumstances apply, although the total number of people aged over 16 sentenced to minimum sentences for such offences has fallen in recent years (*ibid.*).

More significant than mandatory minimum sentences in terms of their effect on increasing the length of sentences served by offenders has been the new Indeterminate Sentence for Public Protection (IPP), introduced in 2005 by the *Criminal Justice Act 2003*, which now applies to adult offenders having committed violent or sexual offences after 4 April 2005 (offenders under 18 are subject to sentences of Detention for Public Protection – DPPs). Judges may impose a minimum period of imprisonment (tariff) on offenders, after the end of which they must remain in prison until the Parole Board considers that they no longer pose a threat to the public, at which point they may be released on licence. The new penalty is more severe than the 1997 mandatory minimum sentence: whilst the old penalty could only be applied once an offender had committed his second of one of 11 classified offences, the new penalty may be triggered by any one of 153 offences carrying a maximum penalty of ten years or more, even if it is a first offence, provided that the defendant is considered to pose a threat to the public (N.B. For offenders convicted of violent or sexual offences carrying maximum penalties of at least two years but less than ten years, the *Criminal Justice Act 2003* created Extended Sentences for Public Protection – EPPs). Not all of the offences which attract IPPs are necessarily particularly serious. Indeed, the majority of offences which have been sanctioned by such a penalty have in practice been minor ones. Twenty-eight of the first 707 IPPs were handed down to sanction crimes against children whilst 40 such sentences were given for rape, but the vast majority of them – 40 per cent of the total – were imposed for robbery, mostly street crimes or mugging (Rose, 2007).

The Ministry of Justice itself has recognised that IPPs have contributed to a considerable rise in the prison population since they were introduced in 2005 (Ministry of Justice, 2008, p. 5). IPPs seem to have been particularly problematic in terms of the increase in the prison population since they can effectively operate as a kind of life sentence. As of April 2009, just four years after the introduction of IPPs, there were a total of 5246 offenders serving such a sentence in England and Wales (Hansard, 2009a). Overall, there were over 12,000 prisoners serving indeterminate sentences – an increase of 12 per cent from the previous year (Ministry of Justice, 2009c). Although there was a slight reduction in the number of offenders sentenced by the courts to IPPs following changes introduced by the *Criminal Justice and Immigration Act 2008* which attempted to limit their use to the most dangerous offenders (Ministry of Justice, 2010a, p. 30), those who are already sentenced will continue to have an impact on the prison population for years to come (HM Inspectorate of Prisons, 2008). Indeed, even if indeterminate sentences cease to have a significant impact on receptions into prisons, they are likely to continue to affect the length of time that offenders spend there: up until the end of April 2009, only 60 offenders serving IPPs had been released from custody (Hansard, 2009a). This is not because they are necessarily serving particularly long tariffs but rather because the Parole Board is already over-stretched and is consequently having significant difficulty processing offenders on IPPs (Prison Reform Trust, 2007, p. 5). As prisons are increasingly subject to the pressures of overcrowding, places on rehabilitation programmes are limited, yet prisoners may not be considered for release before they have completed certain courses. Consequently, they may be obliged to remain in prison until a place becomes free (Nichol, 2006). In May 2009, the House of Lords overturned a High Court ruling of 2007 which had declared that the practice of detaining prisoners beyond their tariff in order to enable them to complete the courses necessary to demonstrate their safety for release to the Parole Board was 'arbitrary, unreasonable and unlawful' (Wells v Parole Board; Walker v Secretary of State for the Home Department [2007] EWHC 1835 (QB)); James v Secretary of State for Justice QBD (Admin) 20 August 2007). The House of Lords held that the failure of the Secretary of State for Justice to provide such courses did not render their post-tariff detention unlawful (R [James] v Secretary of State for Justice [Parole Board intervening]; R [Lee] v Same [Same intervening]; R [Wells] v Same [Same intervening] [on appeal from R [Walker] v Same (Same intervening)] [2009] UKHL 22; [2009] WLR (D) 145).

IPPs were introduced in Northern Ireland in May 2008 following the *Criminal Justice (Northern Ireland) Order 2008*. There, they are known as Indeterminate Custodial Sentences (ICSs). No statistics have yet been released on their use and their recent introduction means that the considerable rise in the prison population since 2001 has been fuelled by other factors. Scotland does not have an equivalent of IPPs but rather an Order for Lifelong Restriction, introduced in 2006 to deal with violent and sexual offenders who pose a continuing danger to the public. The new sentence certainly has the capacity to be highly puni-tive on account of the fact that high risk offenders are not just to be sentenced to life imprisonment but also to surveillance and risk assess-ment throughout their lifetime. However, unlike the IPP in England and Wales, it has, to date, been used sparingly: by February 2010, only 46 such sentences had been imposed since they were introduced in June 2006 (MacAskill, 2010).

Although there has been a considerable increase in the number of prisoners serving indeterminate sentences in England and Wales in recent years, the practice of indeterminate sentencing is not entirely new. Already in the 1860s the problem of recidivism attracted the attention of policy-makers who enacted the *Habitual Criminals Act* in 1869, placing certain kinds of recidivists under police surveillance during seven years following their release from prison. They could be returned to prison if a magistrate considered that they were behaving in a 'suspicious' manner or if they could not prove that they were earning an honest living (Davie, 2005, pp. 90–1). Then in 1908, the *Prevention of Crime Act* created indeterminate sentences for those who had already served a sentence of penal servitude of three years (Radzino-wicz and Hood, 1990, p. 275). However, at that time, on account of the visceral reaction on the part of the English against the idea of indeterm-inacy in sentencing, the penalty was rarely used. It was criticised by Winston Churchill when he was a member of the Asquith Cabinet – he worried about the arbitrary results such a system could have on account of its lack of regard for the principle of proportionality between crime and punishment (*ibid.*, p. 283). The judges themselves tended to impose the shortest period of incarceration possible (Bailey, 1997, p. 302) so that by 1921 the penalty had only been handed down to 577 prisoners (Radzino-wicz and Hood, 1990, p. 287). A second attempt to impose indeterminate sentences by the *Criminal Justice Act 1948* was equally unsuccessful and was later repealed by the *Criminal Justice Act 1967* on account of its ten-dency to imprison 'passive inadequate deviants' rather than dangerous criminals (Rose, 2007).

Today, however, indeterminacy in sentencing appears to cause no such qualms, at least in government circles, provided that it can be jus-tified by the need for public protection. Perhaps this change of policy may be explained by the increased confidence that government has in the capacity of criminal justice professionals to provide accurate risk assessments. However, in reality, it would seem that such assessments are no more reliable today than they ever were. Since April 2003, the Prison and Probation Services have been attempting to calculate offender risk using the Offender Assessment System (OASys) which provides an assessment of the probability that a given offender will reoffend based on an analysis of specific criminogenic factors. An inquiry by the Inspectorate of Probation into the case of Anthony Rice, a convicted offender who killed a woman in October 2005 while he was still on parole, found that while OASys is 'probably the most advanced tool for this purpose [risk assessment] in the world, ... like all such tools its value depends largely on the skill of the people using it as well as the efficiency of the IT system it runs on' (HM Inspectorate of Probation, 2006, p. 69). In this particular case the system failed to fulfil its role of public protection, but it might equally lead to the unnecessary incarceration of those who pose no public risk. Indeed, Diana Fitzgibbon has suggested that inexperienced practitioners working under tight budget constraints might easily exaggerate the risk presented by those placed under their surveillance (Fitzgibbon, 2007).

Given the risk of imposing wholly disproportionate sentences, the punitive potential of contemporary sentencing is evident. The move towards indeterminacy in sentencing, as well as the proliferation of mandatory minimum sentences, may be seen to represent a 'new' punitive direction in sentencing. Offenders are not just punished for the current offence for which they are brought before the court but also for past and potential future offences. Furthermore, it is not just the most serious offenders who are concerned by such trends but relatively minor offenders too – the UK has moved a long way from the principle of bifurcation which was so popular in the 1980s and early 1990s. In light of this discussion, it would be hard to disagree with the following assessment by the Prison Reform Trust in its discussion of IPPs: 'The "just desert" model of sentencing where a period of punishment is carefully measured out against the offence has been replaced by a belief that people can be held indefinitely, for a huge range of offences, until rehabilitation has been administered and somehow proven' (Prison Reform Trust, 2007).

Limitation of parole

Not only are the sentences handed down by the courts longer, but many prisoners are now less likely to be released before the end of their terms and those who are can expect to be placed under surveillance for longer periods of time. In recent years, there has been considerable reform of the system of parole which had long meant that most prisoners could expect to be released into the community before the end of their sentence. An early form of parole was first introduced in England around the middle of the nineteenth century. It was intended for convicts who would previously have been transported to the colonies but who were by that time sent to public works prisons such as those at Portland, Dartmoor, Portsmouth and Chatham (McGowen, 1995, p. 103; McConville, 1981, pp. 385–6). In 1856 a Royal Commission appointed to examine the convict system recommended that all convict prisoners be freed on 'tickets of leave' towards the end of their sentences. The system soon caused public uproar following a series of 'garottings' (theft by strangulation) in 1856 and in 1862 (Davis, 1980). The press and the public held ex-convicts released on tickets of leave responsible for these offences and called for the new system of early release to be abandoned (*ibid.*). Nonetheless, the system survived in a limited form, with the decision to free a convict before the end of his sentence being left to the discretion of the Home Secretary. It generally only applied to youths and those sentenced to life imprisonment.

However, in 1964, a Labour Party research group headed by Lord Longford recommended the creation of a specialist committee responsible for examining the dossiers of those eligible to apply for early release (Labour Party, 1964). The proposal was adopted by the *Criminal Justice Act 1967*: all prisoners having served one third of their sentence or 12 months, whichever was shortest, were granted the right to submit a request to the new Parole Board asking for parole (Morris, 1989, p. 116). Following their release, they would remain on parole until they had served two thirds of their original sentence. Following the introduction of the law, the prison population fell temporarily before starting to climb again (Thomas, 1995, p. 127), despite the fact that one of the principal aims of the law had specifically been a reduction in the prison population (Samuels, 1968, p. 16). The system was also introduced simultaneously in Scotland and Northern Ireland but it was not until the 1980s that parole led to the desired reduction in the prison population. In 1984, then Home Secretary Leon Brittan reformed the system in an attempt to allow more short-term prisoners to benefit from early release. Although the reform made it more difficult for those serving long sentences for sexual offences, violent crimes or drug offences to get parole, Bottoms notes that the change immediately led to a reduction in the prison population of 2000 people (Bottoms, 1995, p. 41). Indeed, Neil Morgan considers that by 1983 the parole system was acting as a 'vacuum cleaner' for the prison population (Morgan, 1983).

The *Criminal Justice Act 1991* replaced the old system of parole, granting automatic early release to prisoners serving sentences of less than four years and reserving discretionary release for those serving sentences of four years or longer. The former would normally be released on the recommendation of the Parole Board after having served half of their sentence (instead of just one third), whilst the latter could be obliged to serve up to between half and two thirds of their sentence before being considered for early release. The aim was to introduce more 'truth in sentencing' by narrowing the gap between the length of the sentence originally imposed and the length of time actually served (Home Office, 1990). However, the practical effect of the law was to reduce the number of prisoners released on parole, thus contributing to an increase in the prison population (Hoyle and Rose, 2001).

In 1997 the system was reformed once again. Under the *Crime Sentences Act*, prisoners serving sentences of between two months and three years could have their sentence reduced by six days per month whilst those serving sentences of three years or more could find they could only apply for early release after having served five sixths of their sentence. This meant that offenders were likely to spend even more time in prison than previously (Ashworth, 1997, p. 1117). This was not, however, the express intention of the law. On the contrary, in order to avoid such a situation, section 26 stipulated that judges impose sentences equivalent to only two thirds of the sentence they would have received before the law was enacted. However, Ashworth has argued that judges who followed the law to the letter and imposed lighter penalties than the norm risked opening themselves up to public ridicule in the popular press (*ibid.*). Consequently, they tended to impose the same penalties as they had previously.

The *Criminal Justice Act 2003* further modified the system of parole in an attempt to gain public confidence by ensuring that offenders would serve the entirety of their sentences, although not necessarily in prison (Halliday, 2001, p. 28). Some experts even suggested that the law heralded the end of parole (Broadhead, 2004, p. 1117). Section 244, in force since spring 2005, stipulates that those sentenced to determinate sentences of more than 12 months will be automatically released on parole after having served half of their sentence. Since June 2007, they may also apply to be released up to 18 days before this half-way point under an 'End of Custody Licence', although this scheme was only intended to be a temporary measure to relieve overcrowding and was to be phased out by April 2010 (Travis, 2010). In practice, the new early release scheme means that release on parole is no longer contingent on the behaviour of the prisoner. However, this does not mean that the new system is in any way less punitive. The offender is now placed under surveillance until the very end of his or her sentence, whereas originally surveillance ended once he or she had reached the two thirds point of their sentence. Indeed, the punitive potential of the new system was recognised by Halliday in his report which led to the White Paper preceding the *Criminal Justice Act 2003* (Halliday, 2001, p. 28). The Act is particularly strict with regard to dangerous offenders, i.e., those who are sentenced to life imprisonment, to an indeterminate sentence or an extended sentence. For them, parole remains discretionary – some may never get it (Woolf, cited by Zander, 2003, p. 1266). As noted above, the excessive use of IPPs introduced under the Act and the problems involved in processing offenders through the system has meant that release under licence has been considerably delayed for many. In addition, a considerable number of those who are released on licence find themselves returned to prison within a short space of time. In 2005, HM Inspectorate of Prisons estimated that in the previous five years there had been an increase in the number of offenders recalled to prison for breaching a licence condition – as a consequence, recalled prisoners constituted nearly 11 per cent of the population in local prisons (HM Inspectorate of Prisons, 2005, p. 5). The Ministry of Justice estimates that the increases in the number of offenders recalled to prison accounted for a 16 per cent increase in the prison population of England and Wales between 1995 and 2009 (Ministry of Justice, 2009a, p. 7). A higher recall rate has been partly caused by the extension of the period of supervision on licence introduced by the *Criminal Justice Act 2003* (*ibid.*). The automatic recall to prison of offenders who breach the conditions of their licence has been severely criticised by Lord Phillips who described the system as a 'trapdoor to prison' (Phillips, quoted by Travis, 2007). In Scotland too, the number of prisoners who have been recalled from supervision or licence has increased by almost 500 per cent. Indeed, offenders recalled to prison represent the fastest-growing prisoner group in Scotland (Scottish Prisons Commission, 2008, p. 13).

Furthermore, the *Criminal Justice Act 2003* limited the application of Home Detention Curfew (HDC), a system of home surveillance by electronic tag introduced in 1999 by the *Crime and Disorder Act 1998* for prisoners who present a low risk of reoffending and may thus be sent home before the end of their release date. The system was originally meant to apply to all offenders sentenced to more than three months' but less than four years' imprisonment who had successfully passed a risk evaluation assessment. However, since the passage of the *Criminal*

Justice Act 2003, which increased the number of offences which may attract a sentence of over four years, more offenders are now excluded from the system. According to the Prison Reform Trust, HDC 'has begun to wither on the vine' (Prison Reform Trust, 2007, p. 2). Fewer offenders are now being placed on HDC: between 2003 and 2007 there was a 46 per cent fall in the number of offenders released under the system (Prison Reform Trust, 2009, p. 15). The Prison Reform Trust suggests that this trend is indicative of 'a growing reluctance of governors and others to take any risk, however carefully calculated, on releasing people on tag' (Prison Reform Trust, 2007, p. 2). Indeed, although the 2003 Act specifically stated that prison should not be used unless 'the seriousness of the offence requires it', the emphasis placed on the need to guarantee public protection has meant that prison will continue to be considered as the best way of avoiding risk. Consequently, HDC would not appear to have contributed to a significant reduction in the prison population, despite a former Home Secretary's promise that it would reduce it by 3000 people (Straw, 1998, p. 14). In Scotland, there has conversely been an overall increase in the use of HDC between 2006 and 2008/09 but it must be borne in mind that it was only introduced there in 2006 so it is a little early to come to any definitive conclusions (Scottish Government, 2009a, p. 7).

The new emphasis on risk has led to a profound change in the philosophy guiding the system of parole and early release. Whilst in the past, from the beginnings of the system in the 1860s until the early 1990s, the decision to release an offender on parole was informed by his or her good behaviour, today it is based rather on a risk assessment. As was stated in the Halliday Report:

> 'Earned early release' may be helpful in prison management, but if not accompanied by strict risk assessment, can increase crime. To combine the two approaches would be confusing and potentially frustrating, for example to a prisoner who behaved well but was still assessed as high risk so could not be released (Halliday, 2001, p. 30).

The Report thus recommended the latter approach which was subsequently adopted by the Parole Board. The new preoccupation with risk is used to justify the surveillance of offenders right up until the very end of their sentences and even beyond (for example, in the case of the Scottish Order for Lifelong Restriction). Recently, the Scottish

Government invoked the argument of risk avoidance to propose the abolition of the system of early release for prisoners:

> We are committed to replacing the current arbitrary system of early release with one which is driven by the individual offender's risk to the community and not the length of the sentence... Under our plans, every single prisoner, regardless of the length of their sentence, will be subjected to restriction for the entire length of the sentence. Risk can never be eliminated but it can be reduced (spokesman for the Scottish Government, STV, 2010).

It is this same preoccupation with risk which might explain the increasing numbers of offenders being sent to prison in the first place and being sanctioned with custodial penalties for breach of community sentences.

Tightening the carceral net

According to the Ministry of Justice, offenders sentenced to immediate custody accounted for 78 per cent of the total rise in the prison population between 1995 and 2009 (Ministry of Justice, 2009a, p. 5). As explained above, the lengthening of sentences goes a long way towards explaining this increase. However, the creation of an increasing number of custodial offences over the past decade and more has also had some impact. In addition, offenders whom the courts originally intended to keep out of prison are increasingly finding themselves behind bars when they breach their community penalties. Overall, this latter category of offenders may only account for a relatively small rise in the prison population but the fact that prison is increasingly considered to be an appropriate means of dealing with it is certainly an indication of a move towards increased punitiveness in criminal justice.

Manufacturing criminals

In ten years, between 1997 and 2007, there were a total of 446 new imprisonable offences created in England and Wales alone (Hansard, 2009b). This trend towards such widespread criminalisation is not entirely novel. There were certainly periods of increased criminalisation in the past. In the eighteenth century, for instance, many previously tolerated customary practices such as gleaning (whereby peasants would be allowed to collect the stalks that remained after the corn had been harvested) were effectively criminalised (Briggs *et al.*, 1996, p. 93).

Similarly, in the nineteenth century a wide range of 'undesirable' behaviours, such as vagrancy (the *Vagrancy Act 1824*) and public drunkenness (the *Licensing Act 1872*) (*ibid.*, pp. 194–201), were criminalised as part of what Wiener has referred to as 'the Victorian character-building enterprise' (Wiener, 1994). Yet it would seem there was never a legislative frenzy on a scale anything like what the UK has recently experienced. Indeed, in the 1950s and 1960s there was even a short-lived trend towards the decriminalisation of certain activities, such as homosexual relations in private, abortion under certain conditions, and suicide. The Thatcher and Major governments reversed this trend, creating 500 new offences between 1988 and 1997, yet this figure pales into insignificance when compared with the record of the New Labour administration (Morris, 2006).

One particularly novel feature of the most recent trend towards increased criminalisation has been what may be referred to as 'indirect' criminalisation, meaning the penalisation of certain forms of behaviour via the civil law. Increasingly, new civil penalties, such as the Anti-social Behaviour Order or Penalty Notices for Disorder, are backed up by the threat of imprisonment. These new penalties, many of which are handed down out of court, are dealt with in Chapter 2. For now, however, the focus is on 'direct' criminalisation whereby offenders are sanctioned directly by the courts. The creation of new offences, such as that of causing death by careless driving or while uninsured (*Road Safety Act 2006*) has contributed to a rise in the number of receptions into prison (Ministry of Justice, 2009a, p. 11). In that sense, they are a clear indicator of the adoption of a more punitive attitude towards offenders. But perhaps the most significant indicator of punitiveness is not just the increased resort to imprisonment but rather the fact that certain new offences are defined so broadly that, in some cases, it may not even be necessary for a person to have committed a criminal act to be sanctioned for a criminal offence. For example, although it has always been possible to persecute people for omissions or inchoate offences, the *Serious Crime Act 2007* has significantly broadened the definition of these latter so that a person may be considered to have committed a criminal offence when he or she engages in conduct (whether it is criminal or not) that is capable of assisting or encouraging another person to commit a criminal offence, regardless of whether or not there is a direct causal link between the two acts and whether the other person actually goes on to commit an offence, provided *mens rea* is proved. Consequently, 'there is the stark risk of over-criminalisation' (Ormerod and Fortson, 2009, p. 4).

Similarly, the new anti-terrorist legislation criminalises not just those who commit acts of terrorism but also those who incite such acts. Under the *Terrorism Act 2006*, those who recklessly publish a statement with the intention of encouraging members of the public, either directly or indirectly, to commit acts of terrorism are liable to a sentence of up to seven years imprisonment. The anti-terrorist legislation also effectively permits the indefinite detention without charge or trial of those who have not committed any crime whatsoever but who are suspected of acts of terrorism. The *Anti-Terrorism Crime and Security Act 2001* allowed foreign nationals to be detained indefinitely in prison until the House of Lords ruled the practice unlawful (A [FC] and Others [FC] [Appellants] v. Secretary of State for the Home Department). Following this decision, the *Prevention of Terrorism Act 2005* introduced Control Orders which may require those subject to them to be placed under house arrest for an indefinite period of time. Despite repeated challenges to the orders in both the British and European courts, New Labour governments continued to renew the régime. Since 2007, the Conservative Party has refrained from voting on the issue. Pre-charge detention of terrorist suspects for up to 28 days also continues in the face of considerable opposition from civil liberties groups.

Such exceptional powers are not of course entirely new. Detention without trial – otherwise known as internment – was used against British citizens in Northern Ireland between 1971 and 1975 but the use of such powers in peacetime on the British mainland is entirely novel. It should be noted that such 'exceptional' powers are have not just been invoked against terrorist suspects. For example, police stop and search powers provided by section 44 of the *Terrorism Act 2000* have been used, not just against terrorist suspects, but also against ordinary citizens such as peace protesters (Liberty, 2003). This would suggest that, far from being exceptional, the use of these powers has become routinised. In January 2010, the European Court of Human Rights ruled that section 44 stop and search powers violated human rights (Gillan and Quinton v United Kingdom [2009] ECHR 28), forcing the new coalition government to limit their use. However, the powers may continue to be used to stop and search those who the police 'reasonably suspect' to be terrorists.

Tougher enforcement

Attempts by the courts to keep people out of prison routinely fail. There are currently two main kinds of adult non-custodial sentences available to courts in England and Wales: the Suspended Sentence Order (SSO) and the Single Community Order (SCO). The latter was introduced in 2005 by the *Criminal Justice Act 2003* in an attempt to simplify the system which included a wide range of community penalties such as Curfew Orders, Drug Treatment and Testing Orders and Community Rehabilitation Orders. The SCO allows judges to impose a personalised penalty, adapted to the needs of the individual offender who may be subject to a number of different requirements, such as attendance at drug or alcohol treatment programmes, unpaid work within the community, or restrictive measures such as curfews and electronic surveillance. It is up to the trial judge to select as many conditions as he or she sees fit from a list of 12. When offenders fail to respect the conditions of their order and do not have a legitimate excuse, their probation officer may either give them a warning or take out legal proceedings against them. If this occurs a second time in a 12-month period, the probation officer is obliged to launch legal proceedings. The judge must then either add tougher supplementary conditions to the order or impose a new one. There were initial concerns that judges might 'overload' offenders with conditions which they may find difficult to respect (Dobson, 2003, p. 16).

More recent research has shown that this has not generally proved to be the case: for people commencing SCOs between 2006 and 2008, the majority of them – between 47 and 51 per cent – were only subjected to one requirement (Mair and Mills, 2009, p. 10). The next highest number – between 35 and 36 per cent – were subjected to two requirements, whilst none were subjected to five requirements or more (*ibid.*). Nonetheless, it may be difficult for certain offenders to respect even the simplest of conditions on account of the often chaotic lives they lead. Indeed, although the percentage of orders terminated for breach is decreasing, the figure still remains relatively high compared to breach rates for other kinds of community penalties – 40 per cent in 2008 (*ibid.*, pp. 13–14).

Concerns have also been raised that the new penalty is not serving as an alternative to custody (Mair *et al.*, 2007, pp. 25–6). Given that there has been no overall decrease in the use of custodial sentences between 2006 and 2007 when the new order might be expected to have made most impact, it would seem that is has generally not served as an alternative (Mair and Mills, 2009, p. 15). The fact that half of all orders were made for summary offences which would in most cases not lead to custody in any event would also suggest that this is the case (*ibid.*). Indeed, there has been little overall change in the number of adults receiving community penalties – use increased from just 8 to 9 per cent from 1998 to 2007 (Ministry of Justice, 2010a, p. 33). Rather than acting as an alternative to prison, it might be asked whether tougher enforcement of these penalties has led to an increase in the prison population. The number of people imprisoned for breach of a non-custodial penalty has grown by 470 per cent since 1995 (Ministry of Justice, 2009a, p. 7). However, it is estimated that this has only contributed to a 3 per cent increase in the prison population of approximately 800 people (*ibid.*).

Perhaps more significant when evaluating the punitiveness of these new measures is the fact that the majority of requirements imposed on offenders tend to focus more on the need to punish and control offenders rather than on their rehabilitation. Since the introduction of the new order in 2005, the use of unpaid work and curfews as requirements has increased whilst there has been a decline in the use of accredited programme requirements (Mair and Mills, 2009, p. 11). Requirements to attend alcohol treatment programmes were used on very few occasions, whilst requirements to undergo mental health treatment or to participate in activities at an attendance centre were never used (*ibid.*). It should nonetheless be noted that some clearly punitive measures – exclusion, residence orders or prohibition from engaging in certain activities – were not used either (*ibid.*). Yet, if the judges did not specifically set out to make community sentences more punitive in nature, it would appear that the New Labour government did and that the new coalition government also intends to do so (see Chapter 5). In December 2008, the former government introduced the new Community Payback scheme under which offenders in England and Wales serving SCOs may be required to wear fluorescent orange vests emblazoned with the words 'community payback' whilst carrying out work in the public interest. As part of a campaign entitled, 'Justice Seen, Justice Done', the public themselves were asked to vote for the projects which they considered to be most beneficial to their local communities from a list of five projects per area (Ministry of Justice, 2009d). The philosophy behind such a move is clear – to boost public confidence in the system by ensuring that the penalty is perceived to be tough. Such concerns are not new. Indeed, when community service was first introduced in England and Wales by the *Criminal Justice Act 1972* following the recommendations of the Advisory Council on the Penal System, it was intended to serve a number of different penological functions: reparation to the community, an alternative to custodial sentences, a form of punishment and a means of rehabilitation (Mair, 1997, p. 1209). All of these elements are still present. However, it might be argued that increasing emphasis is now placed on the punitive and reparative elements of the penalty. The deliberate humiliation of offenders by forcing them to wear fluorescent vests marking them out as criminals may perhaps be regarded as a throwback to earlier forms of pre-modern punishment which often relied on public shaming techniques to punish offenders.

The Suspended Sentence Order was also created by the *Criminal Justice Act 2003* and applies to adults over 18 facing a custodial sentence of less than 12 months. It is effectively a prison sentence which is suspended for a period of between six months and two years and is only applied in the event that an offender fails to meet its requirements which are the same as those provided for Community Orders. It represents an attempt to revive the old Suspended Sentence (Mair and Mills, 2009, p. 5) which had been introduced by the *Criminal Justice Act 1967*. Although the old sentence was intended to lead to a reduction in the prison population by making it obligatory for all sentences of less than six months, this requirement was quickly overturned by the Heath government and subsequent legislation ensured that its application was limited (Morris, 1989, pp. 115–16). By 2001, it is claimed that 'the sanction was effectively on life support' (Roberts, 2003, p. 232). The declared intention of the former New Labour administration in creating the new offence was to make it more 'rigorous' and to ensure that failure to comply with its conditions would result in custody (Home Office, 2002, p. 94).

The new penalty has been widely used, far surpassing the initial expectations of the Home Secretary when he introduced it (Mair *et al.*, 2007, p. 17). Whereas the old suspended sentence only accounted for 0.2 per cent of all offences in 1998, by 2008 the new sentence represented 3 per cent of all offences or 9 per cent of all indictable offences (Ministry of Justice, 2010a, pp. 17–18). It has tended to be more punitive than the SCO and more frequently carries two or three requirements (Mair and Mills, 2009, p. 10). In addition, in 2008 breach of the SSO represented 5.8 per cent of all receptions into prison, compared with 4.5 per cent for the SCO (Ministry of Justice, 2009e, p. 67). Although it is likely that it too accounted for only a small increase in the prison population, it is clear that it is punitive in nature and is certainly not particularly effective as an alternative sentence to imprisonment. Indeed, as with the SCO, the SSO has been extensively used to sentence offenders convicted of summary offences which would not have attracted a custodial penalty – summary offences accounted for half of all SSOs passed in magistrates' courts in 2007 (Mair and Mills, 2009, p. 9).

The Scottish Government has also proposed the introduction of a single Community Service Order to replace the existing Community Service Orders, Supervised Attendance Orders and Community Reparation Orders (Drug Treatment and Testing Orders and Restriction of Liberty Orders are to remain in place) and to 'fit better with the public's understanding of what community service involves' (Scottish Government, 2007a, p. 12). The proposal was taken up by the Scottish Prisons Commission in 2008 and the Scottish Government eventually proposed the introduction of what it calls the 'Community Payback Sentence' (Scottish Government, 2008b, pp. 10–11), a proposal which was put before the Scottish Parliament in 2009 as part of the Criminal Justice and Licensing (Scotland) Bill. As in England, the main focus is on reparation (Scottish Government, 2007a, p. 15) and it was envisaged that courts should be able to 'deal robustly with offenders who do not pay back' (Scottish Prisons Commission, 2008, p. 36). However, unlike south of the border, community payback is not intended to be 'stigmatising and shaming' (*ibid.*, p. 37) and the rehabilitative element of the sentence is likely to be boosted by the recommendation that a court-based social worker should play a role in new 'progress courts' which should be set up to review the progress of the offender and his or her compliance with the requirements set out in the order (*ibid.*, p. 36). The Scottish Government also proposed introducing a conditional (suspended) sentence in Scotland for the very first time but it specifically expressed a desire that Scotland should not follow the English example where suspended sentences have not acted as alternatives to custody (Scottish Government, 2008b, p. 12). Indeed, the Scottish Prisons Commission had expressly recommended that the use of custody be reduced in Scotland (Scottish Prisons Commission, 2008). It remains to be seen how these new sentences might work out in practice, yet the dramatic rise in the use of existing community penalties may suggest that that Scotland is also having difficulty ensuring that community penalties are used as alternatives to imprisonment. For example, the use of Restriction of Liberty Orders (RLOs), which sentence offenders to electronic monitoring, has increased by over 75 per cent since they were rolled out nationally in 2002 (Scottish Government, 2009b, p. 30). An evaluation study carried out on the use of the orders during the pilot period between 1998 and 2000 found that 'it was rare for orders to be completed without some violation of their requirements' (Lobley and Smith, 2000). This would suggest that there is a distinct risk that a significant number of RLOs will result in imprisonment for breach.

The idea of community payback has also been examined in Northern Ireland (Northern Ireland Office 2008) but no legislation in this direction has yet been proposed. Courts in Northern Ireland continue to apply Probation Orders, Community Service Orders and Combination Orders which, as their name suggests, combine the first two penalties. Probation Orders, which can place an offender under the supervision of a probation officer for a period of between six months and two years, account for the majority of non-custodial penalties, whilst Community Service Orders for work of between 40 and 240 hours duration account for the second most commonly-used non-custodial penalty (Northern Ireland Office, 2009, p. 89). It should be noted that the latter may only be used for those charged with an imprisonable offence. The increased use of these orders (by 23 per cent between 2007 and 2008) might suggest that they do serve as effective alternatives to prison, unlike their equivalent on the British mainland, although no statistics are as yet available to test this hypothesis.

Nonetheless, in the current punitive sentencing climate in which politicians are constantly concerned with proving the 'robustness' of non-custodial penalties to the public, it will prove difficult to ensure that these penalties are used as *alternatives* to imprisonment and not simply as *supplementary* penalties. As Ashworth has noted, 'History shows that simply adding new non-custodial options has not led to reduced use of imprisonment' (Ashworth, 1989, p. 12). This is exactly what happened in the 1970s, suggesting that there is nothing new about this particular aspect of the punitive turn. Yet, taken together with other sentencing trends which tend to catch increasing numbers of minor offenders in the penal net, community sentences may perhaps be regarded as yet another way in which the punitiveness of British penal policy has been exacerbated.

The prison population explosion is not on its own a sufficient indicator of punitiveness. It is entirely possible for a country to have a low rate of incarceration but to remain extremely punitive. For example, Timor-Leste, formerly East Timor, has the lowest rate of incarceration in the world but has a deplorable human rights record (ICPS, 2010). In the UK, punitiveness is reflected not just in the number of people sentenced to imprisonment but also in the number of people who remain outside prison but who are nonetheless subject to the surveillance of the penal system.

2
Trojan Horses: The Rise of Out-of-Court Justice

The rise of out-of-court justice over recent years is perhaps the most significant way in which increasing numbers of people have become trapped in the penal net. Over the course of its 13 years in power, the New Labour administration created a whole range of new penalties such as Anti-Social Behaviour Orders (ASBOs), Parenting Orders, Dispersal Orders and Penalty Notices for Disorder (PNDs) in order to tackle problem behaviour which does not come under the remit of the criminal law. According to one former Prime Minister, the 'the usual process of the criminal law' was 'hopelessly inadequate' in this respect (Blair, 2006a). These new penalties thus deliberately dispense with due process: they are all civil penalties, applied using the civil standards of proof and procedure, yet they all carry criminal sanctions. Consequently, they act as a form of back-door criminalisation – the ASBO in particular has been described as the Trojan horse of the civil law (Rutherford, 1998, p. 13). It is demonstrated here that these penalties have resulted in the increased criminalisation of some of the most vulnerable members of society.

Anti-social Behaviour Orders

The ASBO is not officially an out-of-court penalty since it is handed down by a magistrates' court in England, Wales and Northern Ireland, or by a Sherriff's court in Scotland. Nonetheless, it might be described as a pre-court order on account of the fact that it is not given as a measure of punishment but rather as a preventative measure. Furthermore, it need not be applied for by a police officer – a local authority, registered social landlord or housing authority may apply for one. Court punishment only results in case of breach, yet in practice an ASBO can, in itself, constitute a form of punishment. Consequently, the ASBO shall be analysed in the context of the general trend towards the imposition of out-of-court penalties which bypass the normal procedures of the criminal law. There has already been a considerable amount of research into the ASBO (Burney, 2005; Matthews *et al.*, 2007; Squires, 2008; Millie, 2008) but it is useful here to rehearse some of the main arguments concerning the penalty in order to highlight in what ways it is indicative of a shift towards increased punitiveness in criminal justice.

Tony Blair first publicly discussed anti-social behaviour in an article published in *The Times* in 1988 (Blair, 1988). At that time, he defined it as violent behaviour, mainly that of gangs. As the years went on, this definition grew wider so that the term may now be understood to include almost all forms of undesirable behaviour. The law which created the ASBO was deliberately widely formulated, leaving it open to broad interpretation. According to article 1(1)(a) of the *Crime and Disorder Act 1998*, an individual may be regarded as having behaved in an anti-social way when he or she behaves 'in a manner that caused or was *likely to cause* harassment, alarm or distress to one or more persons not of the same household as himself' (*my italics*). The list of behaviour capable of falling within this definition is almost inexhaustible, as the application of the law proves. Even the Home Office had difficulty defining exactly what is meant by anti-social behaviour: 'The subjective nature of the concept makes it difficult to identify a single definition of anti-social behaviour' (Home Office, 2004a, p. 3). The Home Office's own typology of anti-social behaviour, based on the perceptions of Crime and Disorder Partnerships, the government and the public, covers anything from carrying out car repairs in the street to kerb-crawling (*ibid.*, p. 38). According to the British Crime Survey from 2008–9, the greatest problems of anti-social behaviour were cited as being 'teenagers hanging around on the streets' and 'rubbish or litter lying around' (Thorpe and Hall, 2009, p. 100), suggesting that the threshold above which behaviour may be considered as anti-social is now considerably lower than it was in 1988 when Blair wrote his article for *The Times*.

Indeed, an Audit Commission report found that almost 30 per cent of ASBOs are imposed for mere 'nuisance behaviour' whilst only 12 per cent are imposed for criminal damage or acts of vandalism (NAO, 2006, p. 9). Given that the conditions of an ASBO can be highly restrictive of liberty, in some cases preventing recipients from frequenting certain people or places, they can be quite disproportionate to the offence actually committed. In addition, penalties for breach are severe: ten to 11-year-olds may be given a community sentence; 12- to 18-year-olds may be given a

Detention and Training Order (see Chapter 3), the maximum length of which is 24 months; whilst adults may be sentenced by a magistrates' court to a maximum of six months' imprisonment and/or a £5000 fine, or by the Crown Court to a maximum penalty of five years' imprisonment. Criminal sanctions for breach are by no means imposed in a minority of cases. Recent statistics have revealed the overall breach rate in England and Wales for adults and juveniles combined to be 54 per cent (House of Commons, 2009, p. 14). Fifty-five per cent of all those who breach their ASBO receive a custodial sentence whilst only 2 per cent are discharged (House of Commons, 2009, p. 15).

Evidence suggests that ASBOs are used disproportionately against some of the weakest and most vulnerable members of society. Particular concern has been expressed about the use of ASBOs against children as young as ten (Gil-Robles, 2005, pp. 36–7). Indeed, 41 per cent of all ASBOs issued between 2000 and 2007 were against children under 18 (House of Commons, 2009, p. 8) and 41 per cent of juveniles who breached their orders were sentenced to custody (House of Commons, 2009, p. 15). The children who find themselves subject to ASBOs generally come from disadvantaged backgrounds. They tend to live in high-crime areas and suffer from a whole host of problems including family breakdown, educational failure, emotional difficulties, bereavement and abuse (YJB, 2006). It is indeed more likely that children living in deprived areas will find themselves subject to anti-social behaviour legislation on account of the fact that they are more often than not obliged to play in the street rather than in the private gardens of chic suburbs. Already in 1968 Barbara Wootton noted, 'One of the deepest and most persistent class divisions in this country is that between children who have to play in the streets and those who have adequate play-space in their homes, or for whom organised recreation is available in school or elsewhere' (Wootton, 1968, p. 468). This statement is particularly relevant today. The Home Office typology expressly cites the playing of games in restricted/inappropriate areas as an example of anti-social behaviour (Home Office, 2004a, p. 38). In one case, a 15-year-old boy was served an ASBO forbidding him from playing football in the street because he was using the bus stop as a goal post and reportedly bothering cars, pedestrians and the users of public transport (Fletcher, 2005).

The former government's initiatives were not, however, wholly punitive with regard to young people. Attempts were made to tackle the underlying causes of anti-social behaviour by attaching Individual Support Orders (ISOs – see Chapter 3) to an ASBO, by requiring young people to sign an Acceptable Behaviour Contract (ABC), or by serving

Parenting Orders on parents or guardians of young people engaged in crime or anti-social behaviour. An ABC is a voluntary agreement, signed by the young offender, his or her parents or legal guardian, the Youth Offending Team and the local authority, under the terms of which the young person undertakes to refrain from engaging in anti-social behaviour and to address the causes of the latter. Breach of the terms of the contract can lead to the imposition of an ASBO. Few statistics are available concerning the use of these contracts on account of the fact that they are voluntary. However, a survey of the ABC scheme in Islington from 1999 to 2001 showed that 43 per cent of youths breached the conditions of their contract (Bullock and Jones, 2004, p. 4). This would suggest that they are not a particularly effective means of tackling problem behaviour or sparing children from ASBOs. ISOs are also unlikely to significantly address the causes of offending behaviour given that they are rarely used: between May 2004 and December 2007, only 9 per cent of all ASBOs issued had an ISO attached (House of Commons, 2009, p. 16).

Parenting Orders, requiring parents of troublesome young people to attend parenting classes, have perhaps proved to be somewhat more successful. Some researchers have suggested that these orders might even represent an opportunity for parents: a study by the Youth Justice Board found that 93 per cent of parents subject to the orders found the courses they attended useful or mostly useful (Ghate and Ramella, 2002, p. 37). Nonetheless, given that failure to respect the order can result in criminal proceedings being taken out against a parent, there is a danger of criminalising yet another category of people who often suffer from a whole host of problems, financial, emotional or otherwise. Goldson and Jamieson see the order as a substitute for welfare and consequently claim that it amounts to 'the criminalisation of welfare need' (Goldson and Jamieson, 2002, p. 91). The situation is likely to be exacerbated by the extension of the use of Parenting Orders under the *Crime and Security Act 2010* which renders them obligatory for the parents of all children under the age of 16 who breach the conditions of their ASBO.

Mentally-ill adults and children are also likely to be disproportionately targeted by ASBOs. In a study carried out in 2004–05, the British Institute for Brain Injured Children (BIBIC) found that 35 per cent of young people aged under 17 who had been served an ASBO suffer from mental health problems (BIBIC, 2005). Many of them had officially-diagnosed learning difficulties and/or suffered from Attention-Deficit Hyperactivity Disorder but it is probable that many more suffered from problems that had yet to be diagnosed (*ibid.*). Such children obviously have particular problems respecting the conditions of their orders: 81 per cent of children who participated in the BIBIC study had signed an ABC, but 74 per cent of them breached the conditions of their contract (*ibid.*). A significant number of adults suffering from mental health problems such as schizophrenia have also been served ASBOs (Statewatch, 2010).

Other marginalised groups find themselves disproportionately targeted by ASBOs: prostitutes, homeless people and those living in social housing. Prostitutes are often served ASBOs in an attempt to force them to leave the trade, yet there is of course a risk that they will be subject to increased criminalisation despite the fact that prostitution ceased to be an imprisonable offence in 1983 (Phoenix, 2008). Homeless people have long been targeted by the criminal law, namely by the *Vagrancy Act 1824*, the *Highways Act 1980* and the *Public Order Act 1986*. Latterly, the *Criminal Justice Act 2003* allows the courts to sentence beggars to a Community Order in an attempt to force them to attend treatment programmes for drug and alcohol addiction. ASBOs are yet another addition to the government's arsenal against the homeless who are increasingly regarded as a public nuisance. As the White Paper, *Respect and Responsibility* put it:

> No one in this country should beg – It is degrading for them, embarrassing for those they approach and often a detriment to the very areas where environmental and social improvements are crucial to the broader regeneration of the community itself. [...] There are places for rough sleepers to sleep at night, there is support and treatment available for their health needs and drug habits, and there are benefits available to pay for food and rent. The reality is that the majority of people who beg are doing so to sustain a drug habit, and are often caught up in much more serious crime (Home Office, 2003a).

Using ASBOs or other disposals to tackle the problem of homelessness is justified by the idea that homeless people are entirely responsible for their own predicament, having made the wrong lifestyle choices. In order to deal with the threat they present to themselves and society at large, it is argued that they must be forced to change their behaviour. As with prostitutes, the help offered is entirely coercive and risks further criminalising the vulnerable.

Those who live in social housing are similarly subject to coercive measures. In an attempt to tackle the much-mediatised problem of 'neighbours from hell', the *Antisocial Behaviour Act 2003* modified the *Housing Act 1996* in such a way as to allow social housing authorities and registered social landlords to apply for housing injunctions (Antisocial Behaviour Injunctions – ASBIs) against the anti-social behaviour of their tenants. Should tenants fail to respect the injunction, they may be immediately evicted. Demotion Orders were created by the same law – they allow social housing authorities to cancel the assured tenancy of their tenants when they engage in anti-social behaviour.

ASBOs are rarely directed against the powerful, such as big business. Indeed, they are more commonly used to protect businesses despite the fact that ASBOs would be particularly well-suited to target the anti-social behaviour they might engage in, notably on account of the fact that there is no need to prove *mens rea* (something which is notoriously difficult to prove in the case of white-collar crime) (Whyte, 2004, p. 1293). ASBOs have been used to protect businesses from protesters: for example, nine people were arrested under the *Antisocial Behaviour Act 2003* for holding a demonstration outside Caterpillar's offices in Solihull, Birmingham, in protest against the sale of machinery to the Israeli army (Statewatch, 2010). According to Peter Ramsay, it was never intended that all behaviour capable of satisfying the criteria laid out in section 1(1) of the *Crime and Disorder Act 1998* would be targeted by ASBOs (Ramsay, 2004). In order to demonstrate his point, he gives the fictitious but entirely realistic example of a big company who decides to relocate a significant part of its production abroad. Such a decision would indeed be likely to cause 'harassment, alarm or distress' to a considerable number of employees but, given that section 1(5) of the same law stipulates that 'for the purpose of determining whether the condition mentioned in subsection (1)(a) above is fulfilled, the court shall disregard any act of the defendant which he shows was reasonable in the circumstances', it is probable that the company could rely on this clause to prove that its behaviour was reasonable. Yet the test of reasonableness itself is highly subjective and likely to discriminate against the vulnerable. Ramsay asks,

> If a prostitute working to feed her thirst for heroin is not reasonable when her conduct is likely to cause harassment, alarm or distress, why are a corporation's efforts to feed its shareholders' thirst for profits reasonable when it too is likely to cause harassment, alarm or distress? This difference can only turn on a strictly political assessment of the motives for their actions, an assessment implicitly

undertaken by the relevant authority long before any court action occurs (Ramsay, 2004, p. 918).

On account of the fact that the ASBO has resulted in the increased criminalisation of marginal groups, it must be regarded as a key indicator of increased punitiveness in the UK. The very notion of *anti-social* behaviour places such behaviour outside its social context and makes it close to impossible to deal effectively with its underlying causes. The European Commissioner for Human Rights has noted that the practice of 'naming and shaming' those who are subject to ASBOs risks violating article 8 of the European Convention on Human Rights which guarantees the right to respect for private and family life (Gil-Robles, 2005, p. 37), whilst the admission of hearsay evidence may constitute a violation of article 5 protecting the right to liberty and security of person and article 6 guaranteeing the right to a fair trial (*ibid.*, p. 36). Yet the collection of hearsay evidence is actively encouraged by some local authorities. Peterborough council, for instance, provided free Dictaphones to local inhabitants to allow them to collect proof of their neighbours' anti-social behaviour (Rowlands, 2005). On account of the dubious legality of the ASBO, Ashworth has commented, 'It is plain that in introducing the anti-social behaviour order – which has since become a model for other orders – the government intended to sail as close to the wind as possible' (Ashworth, 2004, p. 289).

Yet, the ASBO régime has been considerably extended as new kinds of orders have been created. The *Police Reform Act 2002* created interim ASBOs which may be imposed by the court whilst an application for an ASBO is being processed. The person subject to the interim order need receive no notice of the proceedings against him or her and consequently has no opportunity to present a defence, yet once the order is served he or she will be treated as if subject to a full ASBO. The 2002 Act also created Criminal Anti-social Behaviour Orders (CrASBOs), ASBOs served on those who have already been convicted of a crime. They have significantly extended the use of ASBOs (Burney, 2008). Drinking Banning Orders, nicknamed 'booze ASBOs', were introduced in 2009 by the *Violent Crime Reduction Act 2006* to deal with individuals over the age of 16 responsible for criminal or disorderly conduct whilst under the influence of alcohol. Individuals may be banned from entering premises that sell alcohol or from entering specific pubs or clubs for a period ranging from two months to two years. These new orders resemble ASBOs in that they are civil orders which may result in prosecution for breach, although the maximum penalty that can be handed down is a fine of

£2500. ASBOs may also now be used to tackle more serious crime. The *Serious Crime Act 2007* introduced Serious Crime Prevention Orders (SCPOs). Nicknamed 'super ASBOs', these civil orders may be served on those whom a court believes have been 'involved in' serious crime when there is insufficient evidence to prosecute them in a criminal court. Such orders thus allow the court to bypass the usual rules of due process when tackling crime, making mere suspicion of criminal activity grounds for prosecution.

The New Labour administration dismissed criticisms of the ASBO, believing that its benefits outweighed its disadvantages. Rather than seeing it as a discriminatory measure, criminalising vulnerable groups, the former government presented the order as the best way to *protect* vulnerable groups from anti-social behaviour. The idea that the poorest suffer most from crime was recognised long before New Labour came to power, by left realist criminologists such as John Lea and Jock Young who deplored the fact that the Left tended to play down the harmful effects of crime (Lea and Young, 1993 [1984]). Yet, the argument that ASBOs are a good way of protecting disadvantaged communities is fallacious. Firstly, the high rate of ASBO breach proves that the orders are rather ineffective in preventing anti-social behaviour. Secondly, orders which prevent offenders from frequenting certain places risk simply displacing the problem to another area. Thirdly, targeting vulnerable groups such as young people often obscures the fact that they themselves are often victims of anti-social behaviour. Finally, the majority of ASBOs target street crime whilst the crime of the suites is ignored, despite the harm that this may cause. Rather than being an effective crime-fighting measure, ASBOs would appear rather to be a means of criminalising problem populations. In New Labour's Britain, people could be sanctioned not just for what they had done but also for what their behaviour represented.

It must nonetheless be noted that the use of this particular indicator of punitiveness is not uniform across the UK. Within England and Wales alone there are considerable regional variations in the use of ASBOs: the rate of ASBOs issued per head of population is almost seven times higher in Greater Manchester than in Dyfed-Powys, Lincolnshire or Wiltshire (House of Commons, 2009, p. 5). ASBO use is also more limited in Scotland and Northern Ireland. Although the introduction of ASBOs into Scotland via the *Crime and Disorder Act 1998* has been regarded as an example of penal populism and consequently as a move away from Scotland's traditional social work approach to youth justice (Croall, 2006, p. 599), the order has not been applied in such a punitive way as in England. The *Antisocial Behaviour (Scotland) Act 2004* extended the application of ASBOs to children aged between 12 and 15 but children under 16 cannot be detained for breach as they are dealt with via the Children's Hearing System (see Chapter 3). The Commissioner for Human Rights strongly recommended the extension of this limitation on the imprisonment of juveniles to the rest of the UK (Gil-Robles, 2005, p. 37). A Scottish Government report noted that, with regard to young people in Scotland, ABCs and mandatory supervision are generally considered preferable to ASBOs (Scottish Government, 2007b, p. 42). While 96 applications for ASBOs against children were made in 2005/06, only four orders were granted (*ibid.*). Consequently, the Report concluded, 'While the new powers remain relatively recently enacted, it appears highly unlikely that the pattern of ASBO use in Scotland might come to resemble that in England and Wales, where young people account for a substantial proportion of Orders' (*ibid.*, p. 43). With regard to adults, ASBO use has been increasing in Scotland, but not so rapidly as in England and Wales and use has generally been concentrated in five local authority areas (*ibid.*). Breach resulted in imprisonment in less than 10 per cent of cases considered by the Report (*ibid.*, p. 70). All this would suggest that ASBOs have not been applied in such a punitive way north of the border.

ASBOs were only introduced to Northern Ireland by the Anti-social Behaviour (Northern Ireland) Order 2004. As in England and Wales, they may be served on children as young as ten and an even higher percentage of all orders given – 46.2 per cent – are served on children (CJINI, 2008, p. 29). Nonetheless, no child under the age of 12 had been given an ASBO by the end of December 2007 and only one child had been remanded in custody for breach (*ibid.*). Although fewer ASBOs were generally handed out overall in Northern Ireland – 65 by the end of December 2007 – their use is increasing (*ibid.*, pp. 39–40). However, there is one significant difference between Northern Ireland and England and Wales: only 16.7 per cent of all ASBOs breached resulted in a custodial sentence in Northern Ireland, compared to 55 per cent in England in Wales (*ibid.*, p. 43). This might suggest that, as in Scotland, ASBOs may not be having quite such punitive consequences as in England and Wales even if it can be said that the decision to introduce them at all may be indicative of a certain hardening of attitudes towards punishment.

Dispersal orders

Despite the wide powers conferred by the ASBO, it was not considered sufficient on its own to deal with the problem of anti-social behaviour.

Consequently, section 30 of the *Antisocial Behaviour Act 2003* created the Dispersal Order which gives senior police officers the power to disperse groups of two people or more from a public place when he or she has reasonable grounds for believing that *their presence or* behaviour has resulted in, *or is likely to result in*, one or more people being intimidated, harassed, alarmed or distressed. First, the police officer must 'designate' the area, provided that anti-social behaviour is considered to constitute a 'significant and persistent problem' and the local authority agrees to the designation. The designation can last for a period of up to six months during which the police may exclude groups from the area for a maximum of 24 hours. Breach of the order is a criminal offence liable to a fine or imprisonment. The police also have the power to escort young people aged under 16 home if they are found unaccompanied in the street between 9pm and 6am and if an officer considers that they are at risk of either suffering from or engaging in anti-social behaviour.

This latter power reinforces and extends the powers already created by the *Crime and Disorder Act 1998* and the *Criminal Justice and Police Act 2001*. The 1998 Act had given local authorities the power to introduce a local child curfew scheme forbidding children aged under ten from being present in certain areas between 9pm and 6am unless accompanied by a parent or other responsible person aged over 18. The 2001 Act extended the power to children aged under 16. According to the Youth Justice Board, no curfew had been used between 1998 and 2001 but the powers granted under the 2003 Act have been used (YJB, 2010b). A preliminary report published by the Home Office in 2005 found that between the law coming into force in January 2004 and June 2005, a total of 809 zones had been designated in England and Wales and 520 youths aged under 16 had been escorted home by the police (Home Office, 2005a). By the end of March the following year, 1065 areas had been designated although there had been a considerable drop in the number of those designated from the previous year (Strickland, 2008, p. 3).

These new powers are extraordinarily broad, targeting not just those responsible for anti-social behaviour but also those who *might* engage in such behaviour. It therefore targets the risk of future bad behaviour rather than actual behaviour, totally reversing the idea that one is innocent until proven guilty. Again, the interpretation of anti-social behaviour is wide – in 2006 the Court of Appeal ruled that the use of a dispersal order against demonstrators was perfectly legitimate (Pritpal Singh v Chief Constable of the West Midlands Police [2006] 1 WLR 3374). Most frequently, however, the power of dispersal is used against children. A report for the Joseph Rowntree Foundation found that the use of this power against young people who were not actually engaging in anti-social behaviour was likely to be counterproductive and simply result in their stigmatisation. It criticises the fact that 'the power is potentially less concerned with the agency of individuals than the assumptions that are made about what they might do' (Crawford and Lister, 2007). The use of the curfew power against innocent children led the human rights charity, Liberty, to launch a legal challenge against it. The Court of Appeal subsequently ruled that the 2003 Act does not confer an arbitrary power to remove children who are not involved in or at risk from anti-social behaviour (R[W] v Commissioner of Police of the Metropolis and another, Secretary of State for the Home Department [2006] ECWA Civ 458). Yet it is clear that the power to remove 'at risk' children is considerably wide. As with ASBOs, the New Labour government was 'sailing very close to the wind' when it introduced the dispersal power. The legality of the power in European law is questionable as it could easily interfere with article 11 of the ECHR which guarantees freedom of assembly and association.

Dispersal powers were nonetheless introduced into Scotland by the *AntiSocial Behaviour (Scotland) Act*. So far, they have not been introduced into Northern Ireland. As with the ASBO, dispersal powers seem to have been used in a slightly less punitive way in Scotland. Firstly, an area can only be designated for a maximum of three months as opposed to six months renewable in England and Wales. More importantly, the power has been used considerably less than south of the border: between the introduction of the powers in October 2004 and the end of March 2007, dispersal powers had been used only 14 times, compared with 809 uses in England and Wales within 18 months of their introduction (Cavanagh, 2007, p. 7). This difference might be explained by the fact that in Scotland, the power may only be used when problems are considered to be 'serious' in addition to them being 'significant and persistent' (*ibid.*, p. 8).

Penalty notices for disorder

The Penalty Notice for Disorder (PND), created by the *Criminal Justice and Police Act 2001*, gives police, community support officers and other 'accredited persons' (such as neighbourhood wardens) the power to give on-the-spot fines to those responsible for behaviour which is considered to provoke 'harassment, alarm or distress', as well as to those guilty of more specific offences such as criminal damage or the purchase of alcohol for a young person aged under 18. PNDs extend the existing system of Fixed Penalty Notices (FPNs) which were originally created to sanction minor offences such as traffic offences or illegal rubbish dumping. Although PNDs are usually issued against more serious behaviour, the maximum fine which can be imposed is £80 compared to £500 for FPNs.

The former New Labour administration considered on-the-spot fines to be advantageous because they 'offer swift, simple and effective justice which carries a deterrent effect; reduce the amount of time that police officers spend completing paperwork and attending court, while also reducing the burden on the courts; and increase the amount of time police spend on the streets and allow both them and the courts to concentrate on more serious crime' (Home Office, 2006a, p. 2). If they do indeed achieve these aims, it is only by bypassing the normal rules of due process which are regarded as excessively cumbersome. PNDs have consequently been described as a 'fast-track to arrest, prosecution and punishment in, what is effectively, a justice-free zone' (Roberts and Garside, 2005, p. 4). Indeed, the payment of a fine after being served with a PND does not require any admission of guilt, but if a person refuses to pay, he or she must contest the fine in court and risk a criminal prosecution. For Roberts and Garside, this poses two problems in particular: firstly, a person might be led to pay a fine for an offence of which he or she is not even guilty and, secondly, wealthier people are better-placed than poorer people to pay the fine and consequently avoid criminal proceedings (*ibid.*). Furthermore, even if there is no admission of guilt made when a person pays a fine following a PND, the police nonetheless have the right to take fingerprints, DNA samples and photographs from the offender and to stock them on the Police National Computer (*ibid.*, p. 6).

Further criticisms have concerned the use of PNDs against children. Although PNDs were originally only to be used against adults, the *Antisocial Behaviour Act 2003* extended their use to 16- and 17-year-olds. NACRO estimates that between 2004 and March 2009, the use of fines for this age group increased by 407 per cent (NACRO, 2009, p. 6), although the majority of PNDs – 92 per cent – continue to be issued against adults (Ministry of Justice, 2010b, p. 22). In December 2004, a statutory instrument (n°3166) reduced the minimum age for eligibility for a PND to ten. The only difference with regard to under-16s is that parents may be liable to pay the fines, which are lower than those for adults (£40 maximum). Although PNDs for ten to 15-year-olds have so far only been used in pilot areas, research suggests that where they have been piloted, take-up has been high (Amadi, 2008, p. 6).

Another problem with the use of PNDs is the risk of netwidening. The evaluation of the pilot scheme found that PNDs were often used against low-level disorder where no action would otherwise have been taken – this was thought to have been the case for 72 per cent of all PNDs handed out for offences which could be counted as 'offences brought to justice' (*ibid.*, p. 15). Rod Morgan's analysis of recent research confirms this trend (Morgan, 2008a, p. 25). Taking the example of the offence of shoplifting, he explains that between 2000 and 2006 there was a reduction in the number of people being cautioned for the offence, whilst an additional 27 per cent of all those dealt with received a PND (*ibid.*, p. 26). Overall, the total number of shoplifting offenders dealt with in 2006 was 16.5 per cent higher than in 2000, suggesting that more people than before were being brought into the criminal justice system for this offence (*ibid.*).

However, Morgan also notes that, simultaneously, fewer people were being convicted in court for the offence of shoplifting, suggesting that fewer offences are now coming before the magistrates' courts (*ibid.*). This finding would at first appear to support criticisms that the overall increase in the use of PNDs – an increase of over 177 per cent since their introduction in 2004 (Home Office, 2006b, p. 33; Ministry of Justice, 2010b, p. 24) – is diverting crimes from the courts. The British Retail Consortium complained, 'This sends the wrong message to criminals. It tells them they have a licence to steal and won't get any serious punishment' (quoted by Leapman, 2007). It might therefore appear that the PND has been both a sign of increased punitiveness, especially for those who may previously have escaped punishment altogether, *and* a sign of increased leniency with regard to the increased number of offenders who avoid a court disposal in the magistrates' court. However, it might also be argued that the tougher treatment of criminals who do come before the courts (Chapter 1) cancels out the latter trend towards apparent leniency. In addition, the number of court convictions has only declined for certain offences – recent statistics show that the conviction rate for all offences increased between 1998 and 2008 (Ministry of Justice, 2010b, p. 59). This is also true for summary non-motoring offences for which PNDs are most likely to be issued (*ibid.*). This would suggest that the introduction of PNDs has not led to more lenient treatment of offenders – on the contrary, they have simply enmeshed ever more people in the criminal justice system. As Morgan has commented, 'PNDs represent the most recent and fastest growing criminalisation measure introduced by the government' (Morgan, 2009, p. 11).

In Scotland, Fixed Penalty Notices for Anti-social Behaviour were introduced by the *Antisocial Behaviour (Scotland) Act 2004*. However, as with other out-of-court penalties, it would appear that they have been used somewhat differently there. Firstly, fines of a maximum of £40 may only be given out for ten specific offences, thus limiting their application. Secondly, they may only be issued to those aged 16 and over. Yet, as in England and Wales, the new fines have been used extensively – 65,490 FPNs were issued in Scotland between April 2007 and March 2009 (Cavanagh, 2009, p. 17) – and they have had a certain netwidening effect. Police officers interviewed said they had often given FPNs to people to whom they would previously have given a warning or simply ignored (*ibid.*, p. 30). There has been a significant fall in the number of 'no action markings' (where police record an offence but note that they took no action against it) for a number of minor offences since FPNs were introduced: 'breach of the peace', 'vandalism', 'drunk and incapable', 'drinking in public' and 'urinating/defecating in public' (*ibid.*, p. 31). This would suggest that FPNs are also having a punitive effect in Scotland even if this may be slightly less marked than in England and Wales. PNDs have not so far been introduced in Northern Ireland.

Cautions

Cautions have long been used by the police throughout the UK to sanction any summary or indictable offence which would normally lead to prosecution. For young people, cautions have been replaced by reprimands and warnings (see Chapter 3). The use of cautions or their equivalent with regard to both adults and young people fell between 1998 and 2002 but rose considerably between 2002 and 2007 before falling again in 2008 (Ministry of Justice, 2010b, p. 29). The extensive use of cautions has prompted concerns similar to those expressed about the growth in the use of PNDs.

It has been suggested that serious offenders are now increasingly likely to receive a caution, prompting fears that the criminal justice system is becoming too lenient. Consequently, in December 2009, the former Justice Secretary, Jack Straw, announced the launch of a review into the use of out-of-court disposals for serious offences, to be carried out by the Office for Criminal Justice Reform (Ministry of Justice, 2009f). However, as noted above, concerns about leniency appear to be unfounded. While it is true that the proportion of all cautions given out for violent offences (including violence against the person, sexual offences and robbery) in England and Wales increased between 1998 and 2008 – from 9 per cent to 12 per cent (Ministry of Justice, 2010b, p. 33) – the proportion of cautions used for all indictable offences actually decreased from 67 per cent in 1998 to 55 per cent in 2008 (*ibid.*, p. 30). Furthermore, the conviction rate increased for all the violent offences just mentioned (*ibid.*, p. 60), suggesting that cautions have not diverted serious offenders from court.

The significant increase in the use of cautions over the ten-year period may be explained by the rise in their use for summary offences. Indeed, the 14 per cent increase in the use of cautions for all offences can mostly be explained by the 52 per cent increase in cautions issued for summary, non-motoring offences (*ibid.*, p. 30). The conviction rate has also increased for these offences (*ibid.*, p. 59). This would again suggest a certain degree of netwidening.

The introduction of the conditional caution in 2004 in England and Wales by the *Criminal Justice Act 2003* may have contributed to the overall increase in the use of cautions. Although the conditional caution was intended to encourage the rehabilitation of the offender and reparation to his or her victims (these are the conditions of the disposal), it seems that in practice it has had punitive consequences. The introduction of an expressly punitive condition into the disposal, namely the payment of a financial penalty, by the *Police and Justice Act 2006*, is currently being rolled out across England and Wales. Most significantly, a review of an initial pilot of the new disposal found that it could result in 'up-tariffing' on account of the fact that offenders who might have been given a simple caution or discharged completely were actually charged when their cases were refused for a conditional caution (Blakeborough and Pierpoint, 2007, p. 3). Following the *Criminal Justice and Immigration Act 2008*, conditional cautions are currently being extended to youths aged between 10 and 17. Used alongside Final Warnings, Reprimands (see Chapter 3) and PNDs, it is likely that the criminalisation of young people will consequently be exacerbated.

In conclusion, the use of out-of-court and pre-court sanctions would indeed appear to be a significant indicator of increased punitiveness in Britain today on account of the fact that they have, in most cases, resulted in increased criminalisation through the back door. However, the trend is not entirely new. The distinction between the civil and the criminal law, particularly blurred in the case of the ASBO, has not always been clear. In reality, the criminal law has always been supported by the civil law. For example, under section 222 of the *Local Government Act 1972*, local authorities could apply to the County

Courts or the High Court for an injunction to prevent 'anti-social' activities such as prostitution, loitering or the sale of drugs. The injunction was a civil order but breach could result in a criminal sanction. The same is true of a civil injunction applied for under the *Prevention of Harassment Act 1997* (Rutherford, 1998, p. 13).

Similarly, out-of-court 'informal' justice has always existed as part of the exercise of police discretion. Yet, the former Justice Secretary stressed the need to for today's out-of-court disposals to be 'formal' and 'visible' and for data to be collected on them (Straw, 1998). Of course, the formalisation of these essentially informal disposals is necessary for reasons of accountability. However, we might surmise that the New Labour government also wished to record these disposals in order to boost the official number of offences brought to justice (OBTJ). Indeed, the Office for Criminal Justice Reform has noted that the rise in the use of PNDs in particular 'now make[s] an important contribution to the PSA [Public Service Agreement] target to bring 1.25m offences to justice by 2007/08' (OCJR, 2006, p. 2). Morgan has affirmed that the sharp rise in the number of OBTJ can solely be accounted for by the rise in the use of cautions, PNDs, formal warnings for possession of cannabis and a small increase in the number of offences officially recorded as such (Morgan, 2008a, p. 24).

The proliferation of out-of-court and pre-court disposals must also be understood in the context of a wider, more recent, trend towards the bypassing of due process in the name of 'modernisation' and the promotion of 'simple, speedier, summary justice' (DCA, 2006). Indeed, dealing with offences out-of-court is just one part of a package of reforms which include the introduction of 'next day' justice in magistrates' courts, the setting up of 'courts on the move' and the removal of 'unnecessary procedures' in the Crown Court which slow down the legal process (*ibid.*). These reforms could potentially have an extremely negative effect on the quality of service provided by the courts. For example, 'next day justice', which aims to take certain summary offences to court within a maximum of 72 hours of them being committed, would make it extremely difficult for defendants to prepare an adequate defence. Budgetary cuts made to legal aid in the wake of the Carter Review of 2006 are also likely to have a negative effect on the quality of justice delivered (Carter, 2006). Legal aid lawyers, who were already relatively poorly remunerated, are now only paid a fixed amount for each case, rather than an hourly rate and law firms offering legal aid are expected to compete with each other in order to win their legal aid budgets. Commenting on the reform, one retired barrister wrote, 'One fears not only for the adequacy, but also for the quality and independence of criminal defence work in the future' (Soar, 2007, p. 35). In March 2010, further reform proposals envisaged severely cutting the number of legal aid firms by eliminating the least efficient firms through tendering (Ministry of Justice, 2010c). The new coalition government's commitment to public spending cuts and the further privatisation of criminal justice services means that these trends are unlikely to be reversed in the foreseeable future. Indeed, the current government has committed itself to a fundamental review of the legal aid system in an attempt to render it more 'efficient' (HM Government, 2010).

In addition, the legal protections traditionally offered to the defendant in court to ensure that he or she gets a fair trial are being slowly eroded. With the *Crime and Victims Act 2004*, the New Labour government succeeded in restricting jury trial in cases where some, but not all, of the counts included in an indictment may be tried by jury. The use of jury trial was further restricted when sections 44 to 49 of the *Criminal Justice Act* came into force in July 2006, allowing defendants charged with serious indictable offences to be tried in the absence of a jury when 'there is evidence of a real and present danger that jury tampering would take place' and when, 'notwithstanding any steps (including the provision of police protection) which might reasonably be taken to prevent jury tampering, the likelihood that it would take place would be so substantial as to make it necessary in the interests of justice for the trial to be conducted without a jury'. The first ever case to be tried under the new law came before the Crown Court in January 2010 (R v Twomey and Others). Finally, the *Coroners and Justice Act 2009* provides for inquests to be held in the absence of a jury when 'a senior coroner thinks that there is sufficient reason for doing so'. A jury must be present only when there is 'good reason to suspect' that the deceased died in suspicious circumstances whilst in custody or in state detention or if death resulted from an act of omission on the part of a police officer.

Furthermore, the New Labour administration made it possible for previously inadmissible evidence, such as evidence of bad character or hearsay evidence, to be admissible in a criminal court under certain circumstances. Following the enactment of section 99 of the *Criminal Justice Act 2003*, it would appear that the court may not only take previous convictions into account but also proof of simple 'misconduct'. Finally, the rule of double jeopardy, according to which an offender cannot be tried twice for the same crime, was effectively abolished by the *Criminal Justice Act 2003* which permits the Court of Appeal to annul an acquittal and order a new trial when there is 'new and compelling evidence against the acquitted person in relation to the qualifying offence' (section 78[1]) provided that a new trial would be 'in the interests of justice' (section 79). Scotland also has plans to abolish double jeopardy (BBC, 2009). Although the reform is unlikely to affect large numbers of defendants, it represents yet another reversal of legal principle in favour of the victim, symbolic of a more punitive attitude towards the offender. Indeed, for the New Labour administration, there was an assumption that the removal or limitation of legal protections for the offender would automatically confer more rights and protections on the victims of crime, thus helping to 'rebalance' the criminal justice system in favour of 'the law-abiding majority' (Home Office, 2006c). This distorted logic has been a key driver of the move away from a welfare approach towards a more punitive approach to offenders, as being tough on crime translated as being tough on the criminal. Whilst the new coalition government has promised to defend the right to trial by jury (HM Government, 2010), it is likely that its plans to 'reduce time-wasting bureaucracy that hampers police operation' (*ibid.*) will lead to the further erosion of legal protections for offenders (see Chapter 5).

3
The New Welfare Sanction

It is often suggested that a retreat from the 'rehabilitative ideal' – that faith in the capacity of prison to reform offenders which dominated penal philosophy throughout much of the twentieth century – is another sign of a new punitive direction in penal policy (Garland, 2001a). It is argued here, in line with Garland, that it was not so much the abandonment of the rehabilitative ideal in the UK but rather its revival in a different form which has led to increased penal severity in recent years. Rather than the welfarist measures associated with that ideal being abandoned, they have actually been extended and rendered more coercive. In *Punishment and Welfare* (1985), David Garland described the emergence of this combination of punishment and treatment at the end of the nineteenth and the beginning of the twentieth century the 'welfare sanction'. Although it would appear that such a sanction did not lead to significantly increased penal severity in the early part of the twentieth century, it is argued that a proliferation of 'welfare sanctions' has indeed done so at the beginning of the twenty-first. This chapter briefly discusses the rise of the rehabilitative ideal and its mutation into the 'neo-rehabilitative ideal' (Morgan, 1994) before examining how welfare sanctions function in practice in Britain today and how the new rehabilitative philosophy has affected the prison and probation services.

The rise (and fall) of the rehabilitative ideal

Although the earliest function of incarceration was incapacitation (Harding *et al.*, 1985, p. 3), it would appear that it also served a rehabilitative function from at least the sixteenth century onwards. Indeed, the first House of Correction, known as the 'Bridewell', was established in England in 1556 to incarcerate both the able-bodied poor and a wide variety of petty offenders (McConville, 1981, p. 30). Its aim was to punish inmates and to discipline them in the habits of work, whilst providing them with shelter and sustenance (*ibid.*, p. 41). Punishment, welfare *and* reform were thus not seen as incompatible, although the role of punishment remained predominant and very soon the roles of the prisons and the houses of correction became confounded (*ibid.*, p. 44).

It was only in the eighteenth century that the idea of rehabilitation was revived. Influenced by the ideas of the penal reformer, John Howard, the *Penitentiary Act 1779* sought to create a national prison capable 'not only of deterring others from the Commission of [...] Crimes, but also of reforming the Individuals, and incurring them to the Habits of Industry' (cited in Harding *et al.*, 1985, p. 117). But if the main principles of the Act were adopted in practice at local level, namely in the 45 new prisons which had been constructed by 1790 (McGowen, 1995, p. 89), they were already being questioned by the turn of the century. For instance, there was public and official concern about the strict application of the principle of solitary confinement at Gloucester Prison where prisoners were locked in their cells for 22 hours a day (Ignatieff, 1978, p. 100). In addition, Enlightenment thought had begun to question the idea that men could be reformed by coercion. William Godwin, for example, argued that solitary confinement only numbed the mind and rendered reform impossible (*ibid.*, p. 120).

Throughout the nineteenth century, the idea of rehabilitation continued to be controversial. On the one hand, there were concerns about the negative effects of the 'separate system' on inmates, particularly in Pentonville Prison, where prisoners were confined in individual cells and were forced to wear masks whenever they were in contact with other prisoners to prevent them from communicating with each other (McGowen, 1995, p. 101). On the other hand, others criticised what they considered to be excessive leniency towards prisoners. A series of articles published in *The Times* in 1850 portrayed the image of 'pampered' prisoners (Radzinowicz and Hood, 1990, p. 505) and the apparent rise in garottings by convicts released on licence fuelled feelings of disillusionment in the capacity of prison to rehabilitate (Sindall, 1990, pp. 38–9). It was largely in response to these concerns that the Carnarvon Committee was appointed to inquire into discipline in local prisons. Its 1863 report recommended the adoption of more severe disciplinary measures and harsher prison conditions to the detriment of rehabilitative measures (Webb and Webb, 1922, pp. 188–9). The appointment of the intransigent disciplinarian,

Sir Edmund Du Cane, as head of the convict prison system in 1869 and then as Director of the Prison Commission in 1877 seemed to represent the final nail in the coffin for the rehabilitative ideal (Radzinowicz and Hood, 1990, pp. 526–72).

Interest in the ideal was nonetheless revived again towards the end of the nineteenth century when the Gladstone Committee, set up to investigate the penal system, declared that Du Cane's régime was 'deficient on the reformatory side' and recommended that prisons should from that point on 'maintain, stimulate or awaken the higher susceptibilities of prisoners [...], develop their moral instincts [...], train them in orderly and industrial habits [...], turn them out of prison better men and women, both physically and mentally than when they came in' (cited in Forsythe, 1991, p. 27). The Committee's report led to the creation of new prison rules under the *Prisons Act 1898* which replaced the treadmill with more productive work and limited corporal punishment to cases of violence against the person or conspiracy to mutiny (Webb and Webb, 1922, p. 225).

The Report was very much in the spirit of positivist criminology which had by that time become increasingly influential even if it never entirely replaced classical criminology. Positivism favoured the treatment of offenders over their punishment and, in opposition to classical criminology, favoured individualised penalties aimed at different categories of offenders. According to some penal historians, the rise of a new optimism in the possibility of reforming prisoners at the beginning of the twentieth century was inspired by the ideas of T. H. Green, the famous Oxford philosopher, who considered that man had the ability and the will to behave in a responsible manner and to make the right moral choices, if only he was given the opportunity to do so (Bailey, 1997, p. 310; Forsythe, 1995, pp. 259–73). This line of thinking also fitted well with an evolution in Christian thought which tended to place less faith in the redemptive value of suffering (Wiener, 1994, p. 332). Garland, however, has preferred to emphasise the influence of new psychiatric and biological explanations of criminality, such as those inspired by Cesare Lombroso, which focused on innate differences between criminals and the law-abiding majority (Garland, 1985, pp. 81–2).

What is certain is that the New Liberals who dominated British politics at the time believed that the emerging Democratic State had a responsibility to encourage the moral development of all its citizens, prisoners included. Under the leadership of Herbert Asquith, they promoted increased state intervention in an attempt to remove the social and economic barriers which prevented them from doing so. Consequently, the foundations of the welfare state were laid by the *Old Age Pensions Act 1908* and the *National Insurance Act 1911*. It was no coincidence that the return of the rehabilitative ideal coincided with the birth of the welfare state: confidence in the ability of the State to 'cure' the offender went hand in hand with confidence in its capacity to develop policies capable of solving a host of social problems.

Throughout much of the twentieth century, rehabilitation was officially recognised as one of the principal aims of imprisonment and plaques were even affixed at the entrance to prisons declaring their aim of encouraging offenders to lead 'a good and useful life' (Hudson, 2003, p. 19). The rehabilitative ideal reached its highpoint in the 1950s and 1960s. The 1959 White Paper, *Penal Practice in a Changing Society*, was considered as the supreme declaration of the new approach (Morgan, 1979, p. 2). In 1964, a report by the Labour Party Study Group, *Crime – A Challenge to Us All*, recommended 'the transformation of prisons into institutions for social learning, so making a reality of the high aims which have been officially accepted for many years but have so far remained largely unattainable owing to lack of essential resources' (Labour Party, 1964, p. 2).

Yet, despite this optimistic rhetoric, rehabilitative programmes were in practice difficult to set up. This was partly due to lack of resources – indeed, prisons were considered as the poor relation of the welfare state (Lord Allen, 1995, p. 10). Moreover, it was difficult to reconcile the aim of rehabilitation with those of deterrence and retribution, as was starkly demonstrated by a number of high-profile escapes, such as that of the Great Train Robber Ronald Biggs from Wandsworth Prison in 1965. In response to these escapes, the Wilson government set up an inquiry, chaired by Lord Mountbatten (Home Office, 1966), which recommended the creation of a system of classification according to which each prisoner would be classified according to their security risk on a scale of A to D ('A' being reserved for the most dangerous prisoners) (Morris, 1989, pp. 131–4). Rather than 'treatment and training', the key aim of the prison system was from then on to be 'humane containment' (Bottomley and Coleman, 1984, p. 53). Surveillance and control were reinforced to the detriment of work, training, entertainment, the improvement of prison conditions and concern for prisoners' rights (Downes and Morgan, 1997, p. 123). The rehabilitative ideal was thus undermined, contrary to the intentions of Mountbatten (Morris, 1989, p. 135).

The situation was exacerbated by the publication in 1974 of an article by the American researcher Robert Martinson in which he pessimistically concluded that 'nothing works' with regard to the rehabilitation of offenders (Martinson, 1974). Despite Martinson's later attempts to nuance these conclusions and point to the positive outcomes of some rehabilitative programmes, his 1974 article was used to justify the adoption of tougher penal policies (Reiner, 2007, p. 141). In 1978, Stephen Brody, a Home Office researcher, published an article which appeared to corroborate Martinson's conclusions by concluding that most rehabilitation programmes were not particularly effective (Brody, 1978). In addition, the ideal was assaulted by both the Left and the Right. The latter criticised it for its apparent leniency whilst the former criticised the gap between the rhetoric and reality of the rehabilitative project, claiming that it had, in some cases, actually led to more rather than less punitiveness, despite the humanitarian discourse which accompanied it and the good intentions of those who promoted it. Stanley Cohen, for example, claimed that in the twentieth century there had been 'an intensification, complication and extension' of nineteenth century punishment practices, rather than their reversal (Cohen, 2001, p. 37). According to him, as in the previous century, there had been a huge rise in the prison population and more people than ever had become enmeshed in the penal net (*ibid.*, pp. 43–55). He consequently affirmed, 'The warning from history is that benevolence itself must be distrusted' (*ibid.*, p. 21).

Similar arguments have been advanced by David Garland. He claims that the positivist criminology which underpinned the rehabilitative ideal at the turn of the century inspired the 'welfare sanction' (Garland, 1985) whereby penal institutions underpinned and enlarged social institutions (*ibid.*, p. 233). He explains that the new rehabilitative initiatives were even harsher and interventionist than previously: firstly, because classicist principles of proportionality could easily be overridden by the argument that detention could be justified for as long as was necessary to 'cure' the offender; secondly, because the new penalties did not just target criminals but also vagrants, alcoholics and other 'undesirables' (*ibid.*, p. 104). Garland is supported by Michel Foucault who also claims that positivist criminology led to increased penal severity, although he dates the beginnings of this trend to the early part of the nineteenth century (Foucault, 1975).

In practice, however, these new penalties were not as severe as they may have seemed. As we noted above, the indeterminate sentence created for recidivist criminals by the *Prevention of Crime Act 1908* was little-used (Chapter 1) and, rather than more people being imprisoned, there was actually 'a mass movement away from reliance on incarceration' (Radzinowicz and Hood, 1990, p. 778). The 'abatement of imprisonment' was encouraged by the *Probation of Offenders Act 1907*, the *Children's Act 1908* and the *Criminal Justice Administration Act 1914* (Bailey, 1997, p. 319). The first of these acts introduced probation orders, the second diverted children under 16 from custody and the third limited the imprisonment of fine defaulters. In any case, it might be suggested that arguments concerning whether or not welfarism led to more or less punishment are irrelevant. Lucia Zedner has suggested that no matter how much welfarism may have dominated penal discourse throughout much of the twentieth century, there was nonetheless 'a continuing commitment by the courts to classical legalism' as exemplified by the fact that the fine remained the most frequently-used penal sanction throughout the period (Zedner, 2002, p. 344).

Although Garland would seem to be wrong to suggest that positivism resulted in harsher punishment in the first quarter of the twentieth century, it might be asserted that his thesis may be appropriately applied to the early years of the twenty-first century in the United Kingdom. Garland himself recognised in his later work, *The Culture of Control*, that welfarist sanctions were, regardless of their punitive consequences, nonetheless focused on offender welfare, just as the social institutions of the welfare state were concerned with citizens' welfare more generally (Garland, 2001a). Consequently, they served as something of a barrier to the discourse of vengeance which prevails today. Garland argues that welfarist concerns about the offender have today been replaced by utilitarian concerns about risk management and victim protection. Yet, rather than the rehabilitative ideal being abandoned, it has rather been redefined in a way which enables it to be presented as an effective strategy of risk management (*ibid.*, pp. 176–7). Consequently, it can easily sit alongside the concurrent aims of the punishment of offenders, the reduction of crime, public protection and reparation (*Criminal Justice Act 2003*, section 142). It would be wrong to suggest that welfarist concerns have been abandoned altogether. On the contrary, as this chapter seeks to demonstrate, it is the recent massive extension of a welfarist agenda which has actually reinforced the trend towards increased punitiveness.

The neo-rehabilitative ideal

In the wake of the worst prison riots in English history at HMP Strangeways, Manchester in 1990, the '*neo*-rehabilitative ideal' was born (Morgan, 1994, pp. 135–7). The redefined ideal aimed to place more emphasis on the individual responsibility of offenders via, for example, the creation of prisoner 'compacts' between inmates and the prison authorities which outlined the rights and responsibilities of both parties. These compacts were recommended by Lord Woolf (Woolf, 1991) as a way of restoring the balance of power between prisoners and prison officers, the disruption of which he considered responsible for provoking the riots in the first place. It was hoped that a better recognition of prisoners' rights would enable the authorities to demand more responsibility in return. Although these compacts were never adopted as extensively as was originally hoped (*ibid.*), the 'neo-rehabilitative ideal' appears to have become firmly entrenched.

The discourse of rights and responsibilities inherent in this new ideal fits perfectly with New Labour's 'third way' which attempted to reconcile welfare and punitive approaches not just to criminality but to social problems in general. For example, tough action against anti-social behaviour has been presented as a way of tackling the social problems which might lead to such behaviour in the first place. As Louise Casey, the minister formerly responsible for promoting the New Labour government's 'Respect' agenda, declared, 'Many people think Respect is all about ASBOs, but for me it is about a Trojan horse so that we can deal with a lot of other things such as child poverty, repeat homelessness, repeat offending and under-attainment in schools' (Casey, 2006). Yet, as we have seen, those who refuse to accept responsibility for their social problems or their criminal behaviour may be severely punished – in reality such measures are Trojan horses for criminalisation. Although individual responsibility for crime and poverty had never been denied, the rehabilitative ideal of the past did tend to place considerably more emphasis on the role of environmental difficulties in causing crime and other social problems. It might be argued that this increased emphasis on the social causes of crime resulted in a less punitive attitude to offending behaviour than that which prevails today.

The present chapter seeks to demonstrate how a number of new penalties which have sought to combine welfare and punishment have today resulted in increased punitiveness, underpinned as they are by the neo-rehabilitative ideal and its focus on individual responsibility. They are often backed up by the threat of incarceration and frequently result in a considerable degree of netwidening yet, as in the past, they are justified by the need to tackle the causes of crime. Indeed, it is with this aim in mind that the New Labour administration became increasingly interventionist over its 13 years in power. As vulnerable groups such as young people, drug addicts, the homeless and prostitutes are increasingly being dealt with via criminal sanctions when welfare interventions fail, it may be suggested that Garland's notion of the 'welfare sanction' is more readily applicable today than at any time in the past. More than ever before, welfare interventions have become a back door to criminalisation. There are also a number of other parallels with the past, as it was understood by Garland in *Punishment and Welfare*, namely the creation of penalties which dispense with principles of proportionality and which tend to focus as much on 'undesirable' people as on criminal acts themselves. It might even be suggested that the eugenicist ideas which Garland considered as informing penal policy at the beginning of the twentieth century have returned and have a wider application than ever: recent attempts to identify a 'criminal gene' may be seen to represent a survival of Lombrosian ideas (Davie, 2007). If the rehabilitative ideal did not have the punitive consequences that Garland describes at the beginning of the twentieth century, it would seem that the *neo*-rehabilitative ideal is indeed having such effects at the beginning of the twenty-first century. This is evident not just in the penalties handed down to offenders but also within penal establishments and in the Probation Service.

Welfare sanctions

The increased emphasis on responsibility is most strikingly illustrated by the abolition of the principle of *doli incapax* according to which children between the ages of ten and 14 were presumed to be 'incapable of evil' unless prosecutors could prove that they were fully aware that their actions were 'seriously wrong'. Children as young as ten may now be considered to be fully responsible for their actions. Yet, under New Labour, the focus on individual responsibility was combined with a range of social interventions intended to tackle the causes of offending behaviour by young people. This chapter discusses the range of welfare sanctions to which youths and other vulnerable groups in Britain are subject and demonstrate how they have resulted in them being treated significantly more harshly than previously.

i) *Responsibilising youth*

Although children were still treated much like adults throughout the nineteenth century (Gatrell, 1994, p. 294), from the 1830s onwards there were attempts to remove them from the adult penal system in order to protect them from the undesirable influence of hardened criminals. In 1835 the government established HMP Parkhurst as a prison reserved for young offenders who would otherwise have been sentenced to transportation (Radzinowicz and Hood, 1990, pp. 148–55). Then, in 1854, the *Reformatory Schools Act* created specialised institutions to which magistrates could send young offenders aged under 16 (*ibid.*, pp. 177–8). The living conditions in these prisons were not necessarily less punitive than those of adult institutions yet they did nonetheless represent a first attempt to remove young people from the formal criminal justice system. Indeed, whilst young people represented 10 per cent of the prison population in 1857, 20 years later, they only represented 4 per cent (*ibid.*, p. 624).

Following the Gladstone Report which had emphasised the importance of rehabilitation, a significant number of young people were definitively removed from the adult penal system. The Borstal was created in 1900 with the specific aim of rehabilitating offenders aged between 16 and 21 (Bailey, 1987). The *Prevention of Crime Act 1908* stipulated that all young offenders in this age group be sent there whilst the *Children's Act 1908* created courts specifically reserved for young people aged under 16. In the interests of rehabilitation, the education of the offender was meant to be prioritised but the harshness of working conditions and strict discipline remained the predominant characteristics of the régime, leaving borstals open to the criticism that they never managed to significantly differentiate themselves from adult prisons (Radzinowicz and Hood, 1990, pp. 393–5). The personnel, recruited from adult prisons and used to their institutional routine, did not have the necessary skills to put in place a truly innovative system (Forsythe, 1991, p 50) and the borstals failed to provide young people with the education or professional training they needed (Hobhouse and Brockway, 1984 [1922]).

It was only with the implementation of the *Criminal Justice Act 1948* and the concurrent strengthening of the welfare state in Britain that a genuine welfarist approach was adopted with regard to young offenders. The new law 'took a long step forward in giving effect to the view that persons under 21 ought not to be sent to prison if any other course can properly be adopted' and created a number of new penalties aimed at diverting young people from the formal criminal justice system: absolute or conditional discharge; attendance at an attendance centre; fines; probation; detention in a detention centre; committal to an approved school; borstal training; imprisonment (Home Office, 1960, p. 51). Moreover, in order to underline the social character of the borstal, the Act no longer spoke of 'borstal detention' but rather of 'borstal training' (*ibid.*, p. 55). The law had a significant impact, leading to a reduction in the number of young people sent to prison (*ibid.*, p. 63) and giving legislative expression to a welfare-oriented approach to young offending. Lionel Fox, head of the Prison Commission from 1942 to 1960, declared, 'Except in its provisions for the treatment of persistent offenders, it is above all an Act for keeping people out of prison' (Fox, 1952, p. 66).

The majority of official statements, at least until the early 1990s, continued to emphasise the need to divert young people from custody. For example, the 1964 report by the Labour Party Study Group favoured the treatment and social assistance of young people outside the prison system and recommended the creation of a Family Court in which the atmosphere would be 'humane' rather than punitive and where 'the welfare of the family as a whole [would] be a primary consideration' (Labour Party, 1964, p. 23). In stark opposition to current discourse, the report declared,

> We believe that in justice to our children, and for the health and well-being of society, no child in early adolescence should have to face criminal proceedings: these children should receive the kind of treatment they need, without any stigma or any association with the penal system (*ibid.*, p. 24).

Following this report, the Labour government of Harold Wilson published an official report on young people and the penal system entitled *Children in Trouble* which recommended that a series of measures should be put in place to ensure that it was more difficult to criminalise children, except in the case of murder. The *Children and Young Persons' Act 1969* largely applied the recommendations of *Children in Trouble* and gave the court the possibility of choosing between a supervision order which placed the young person under the surveillance of a probation officer or local authority, and a care order which placed the offender under the care of social services (Bottoms *et al.*, 1970, p. 379). However, some commentators feared that young people might end up spending longer periods of time under official surveillance in the interests of rehabilitation (*ibid.*, p. 393). In addition, growing concerns about crime, together with a change of government in 1970, meant that the 1969 Act failed to have the desired effect of diverting young people from custody. The number of young people in prison continued to grow throughout the 1970s (Cohen, 2001, p. 98). Hillyard and Percy-Smith suggested that the *Children and Young Persons Act* had the negative result of encouraging the labelling and categorisation of children, focusing attention not just on those children who had committed offences but also on those that were 'troublesome' or who were socially-disadvantaged in some way (Hillyard and Percy-Smith, 1988, p. 185).

This would suggest that the notion of the 'welfare sanction', whereby 'social' interventions have had the unintended consequence of criminalising increasing numbers of people, existed well before New Labour came to power. It is essential to avoid idealising the past. However, previously, successive governments clearly placed welfare first even if the practical results did not always match intentions. Today, punishment is now expressly advanced as an aim concurrent to that of rehabilitation with regard to young people who are increasingly treated as young adults rather than as children. The punitive consequences of welfarist interventions under New Labour were arguably considerably more far-reaching than similar interventions proved to be throughout much of the twentieth century.

Even in the 1980s, there was considerable diversion of young people from custody, despite Home Secretary William Whitelaw's promises to subject young offenders to a 'short, sharp shock' in prison in order to deter them from reoffending. By 1990, only 1000 custodial penalties were being handed down to young people, representing the lowest figure since 1965 (Prison Reform Trust, 1993, p. 4). This fall can be partly attributed to demographic changes, notably the fall in the number of young people aged between 14 and 16 between 1981 and 1988, and partly to an increase in the use of cautions against young people (Ball, 2004, p. 168). Yet, significantly the Thatcher governments did not completely overturn the welfare approach to juvenile offending. Whilst the Wilson government had pinpointed poor parenting as a cause of criminality, Thatcher accused left-wing teachers and local authorities of having led an anti-police propaganda campaign which glorified crime in the eyes of 'impressionable young people' (Thatcher, 1987a). Importantly, young people themselves were not held directly responsible.

The traditional welfarist approach was to be turned on its head in the 1990s. Even if juvenile delinquency had always worried society (Pearson, 1983), these fears reached their height in the 1990s and the Noughties, symbolised by highly-mediatised events such as the James Bulger killing and a series of knife murders. Correspondingly, the number of young people in prison exploded: in 2002, the number of young people sentenced to custody was 90 per cent higher than a decade earlier (NACRO, 2003). It is surely no coincidence that this population explosion was accompanied by a total change in the rhetoric used to speak of young offenders. In 1996, Jack Straw, then shadow Home Secretary, denounced the practice of police cautioning of young people as 'a waste of time' (Straw and Michael, 1996, p. 4) and declared, 'A new balance has to be struck between the sometimes conflicting interests of welfare and punishment [...]. Young offenders need to be held to account for their actions (*ibid.*, p. 9). The incoming New Labour government's White Paper published in 1997, *No More Excuses*, clearly marked the change of approach to be adopted by the new government. In the preface, Jack Straw declared,

> An excuse culture has developed within the youth justice system. It excuses itself for its inefficiency, and too often excuses the young offenders before it, implying that they cannot help their behaviour because of their social circumstances. Rarely are they confronted with their behaviour and helped to take more personal responsibility for their actions. The system allows them to go on wrecking their own lives as well as disrupting their families and communities. This White Paper seeks to draw a line under the past and sets out a new approach to tackling youth crime. It begins the root and branch reform of the youth justice system that the government promised the public before the Election (Home Office, 1997).

'Root and branch reform' quickly translated as the adoption of a series of hybrid measures which expressly aimed both to responsibilise young offenders and to tackle the causes of their offending behaviour. Despite the punitive rhetoric, it might at first have appeared that a welfare approach to youth justice prevailed and had even been extended. The first New Labour government immediately moved responsibility for youth justice out of the hands of the Home Office and into the hands of the new Youth Justice Board (YJB), created by the *Crime and Disorder Act 1998*. The YJB was charged with working with social services and other actors to develop a joint strategy to prevent crime. Youth Offending Teams (YOTs) were thus established, bringing together local authorities, social workers, probation officers, police officers, health and education workers and members of voluntary organisations. The teams were charged with tackling the causes of crime such as drug abuse, educational failure and family problems. They now intervene at each stage of the youth criminal justice process to prevent offending, monitor youths on community penalties and aid their rehabilitation on release from custody. On account of the emphasis placed on rehabilitation and tackling the causes of crime, this aspect of youth justice reform was initially widely welcomed by criminal justice professionals (Newburn, 1998, pp. 208–9). David Smith, for example, considers that this kind of partnership approach is the best way to guarantee social justice and improve the lot of vulnerable children and young people (Smith, 2003, p. 228).

Yet, in practice, it has been extremely difficult to combine welfarist and punitive approaches. In fact, focus on welfare and tackling the causes of crime has merely served as justification for greater intervention in the lives of children and young people who are finding themselves increasingly likely to be criminalised rather than diverted from the criminal justice system. As welfarist and punitive approaches have been combined, the boundaries separating them have become ever-more blurred, allowing the criminal law to penetrate ever further into social policy. A brief analysis of the different penalties available for young offenders helps to illustrate this point.

Firstly, following the *Crime and Disorder Act 1998*, there was a move from informal to formal justice as the system of informal cautioning was replaced by reprimands and final warnings for offenders under the age of 18. Now, a reprimand is to be officially recorded by the police and can only be used once. If young people commit another offence, they will receive a final warning and, if they commit yet a further offence within two years of receiving the warning, they will be brought before a court (unless exceptional circumstances prevail). It was inevitable that these changes would criminalise a large number of young people who would previously have been dealt with informally (Fionda, 1999, p. 42). However, the final warning is accompanied by a socially-interventionist approach which requires that young offenders who are given a warning be referred by the police to a YOT who will assess their suitability for an intervention programme. Types of intervention range from restorative justice through to mentoring, education, cognitive behaviour programmes, parenting programmes and projects aimed at addressing problems of drug and alcohol abuse. The most commonly-used kind of intervention is restorative justice (Holdaway and Desborough, 2004).

Restorative justice is now considered to be 'an important underlying principle for all youth justice disposals' (YJB, 2010c). It was encouraged by the creation of the Referral Order by the *Youth Justice and Criminal Evidence Act 1999*. Since 2002, all offenders pleading guilty to a first-time offence (except those who have committed either particularly serious or particularly minor offences) have been referred to a Youth Offending Panel composed of volunteers from the local community and an adviser from the local YOT. The panel, along with the young offender, their parents or guardians, and often the victim(s) of his or her offence decide together how the young offender might repair the harm caused by the offence and address the causes of the offending behaviour. A contract is then signed which can last for a maximum of 12 months and might require the offender to apologise to his or her victim(s) or to undertake some sort of work for the community. The Youth Restorative Disposal was also introduced in 2009 to deal with young offenders aged between ten and 17 who have not previously received a caution or any other kind of disposal. It allows police officers to bring victims and offenders together, often in the presence of the offender's parents, to discuss the offence and resolve the matter informally.

The extension of restorative justice principles into the youth justice system might be regarded as a progressive move given that one of the principal aims of restorative justice is to reintegrate offenders into the community rather than to exclude them (Wright, 1996). However, some critics have warned that the coercive nature of some penalties such as the referral order may run counter to the basic principles of restorative justice. Indeed, young offenders may be prosecuted if they refuse to sign a contract with the Youth Offending Panel, if they fail to attend meetings organised by the Panel or if they do not respect the conditions of the contract (Ball, 2000, pp. 213–15). Muncie has consequently concluded, 'Restorative processes simply deal with low level offenders who, through a combination of New Labour's other measures in crime prevention and pre-emptive early intervention, are being drawn into the youth justice system (and thereby criminalized) at an increasingly earlier age' (Muncie, 2006, p. 779).

Other New Labour attempts to promote offender rehabilitation and address the welfare needs of young offenders were also extremely coercive. For example, the new Youth Rehabilitation Order (YRO), introduced in November 2009 following the *Criminal Justice and Immigration Act 2008*, is essentially a juvenile version of the Single Community Order. It replaces a number of other community sentences and enables the courts to oblige young people to accept any number of 18 different conditions. At the time of writing, no extensive evaluation of the new order has yet been carried out, but there is certainly a risk that young offenders may find it extremely difficult to respect the order if its conditions are too onerous. Custody is an option for breach of a YRO but only when the order was originally imposed for an imprisonable offence or when there is 'willful and persistent' non-compliance of the order in the case of a non-imprisonable offence. The risk of non-compliance is high. One of the conditions of the YRO is 'Intensive Supervision and Surveillance' (ISS) based on the current 'Intensive Supervision and Surveillance Programme' (ISSP). Yet, experience with this programme, which obliges young people aged between ten and 17 to be placed under surveillance and to attend educational and/or treatment programmes, showed high breach rates of almost 60 per cent within two years of its introduction (Gray *et al.*, 2005, p. 30). Thirty-three per cent of those who breached the order were subsequently sentenced to custodial penalties. By 2007/08, this figure had increased to 51.9 per cent (YJB, 2009, p. 35). In addition, the penalty was found to have a netwidening effect as it often replaced less intensive community sentences (Gray *et al.*, 2005, p. 40).

Attaching a range of 'welfare' measures to community penalties has not resulted in rendering youth justice any less punitive. On the contrary, the coercive nature of these penalties may have actually increased their punitive potential. Indeed, they have not succeeded in significantly reducing the number of young people entering the young system for the first time, despite YJB claims to the contrary. The increasing use of out-of-court penalties such as PNDs has actually only dragged yet more young people into the system, even if these youths are excluded from the official statistics on first-time entrants (Morgan, 2009). It was this trend towards the increasing criminalisation of young people which eventually led Rod Morgan to resign from the Youth Justice Board which he had chaired from April 2004 to February 2007 (Morgan, 2008b).

Although the number of young people sentenced to custody has dropped slightly over the past two years (YJB, 2010d), the juvenile prison population is considerably higher than it was before New Labour came to power. This trend was particularly marked for offenders between the ages of ten and 14 – 550 per cent more of them were being held in custody in 2006 than in 1996 (Barnardo's, 2008, p. 3). Whilst the Youth Justice Board aimed to reduce the number of young people in custody in England and Wales by 10 per cent, this figure actually increased by 8 per cent between March 2005 and February 2008 (Solomon and Garside, 2008, p. 48). Children aged between 12 and 17 are incarcerated in privately-operated Secure Training Centres whilst those aged between 15 and 21 may be committed to Young Offender Institutions. Young people who have been in the care of the social services or who have mental health problems may be detained in secure children's homes. It is quite revealing that in 2007 the Youth Justice Board spent 64 per cent of its overall budget on custody, compared to just 5 per cent on the ISSP (*ibid.*, p. 22). The most common custodial sentence given to young people is the Detention and Training Order (DTO) (YJB, 2009, p. 5). Introduced by the *Crime and Disorder Act 1998*, it is aimed at young people aged between 12 and 17 who are considered to be recidivists and dangerous. Half of the sentence (which may run from anywhere between four and 24 months) must be served in the community where the young person is required to attend various rehabilitation programmes as part of the ISSP. Paradoxically, it is this very 'welfare' element which may have encouraged the extension of youth custody as judges may be more willing to impose a sentence which specifically aims to rehabilitate the offender (Hazel *et al.*, 2002). In addition, it is easier to apply the penalty to offenders aged between 12 and 14 than the Secure Training Order which it replaced, the use of which had been restricted to those offenders convicted of three or more imprisonable offences and found by a court to be in breach of a supervision order served within the community (Goldson, 2002, p. 394). Consequently, in the first year after the DTO was introduced, more children were locked up in absolute terms and a greater proportion of them received custodial sentences, particularly in the 12 to 14 age group (Hazel *et al.*, 2002, pp. 23–4).

Another way in which an extension of a welfare approach might lead to increased punitiveness is via the creation of new programmes which aim to provide help and assistance to families and young people before they even come into contact with the criminal justice system. For example, Youth Inclusion Programmes (YIPs), created in 2000, bring together all those who participate in local Crime Reduction Partnerships, from police to social services and voluntary associations, to share information about eight to 17-year-olds at risk of engaging in criminal or anti-social behaviour. The young people are then invited to participate in a YIP, which may function as a kind of local youth group, providing social and educational services as well as extra-curricular activities. Although these services may provide much-needed help to young people living in deprived areas and have even succeeded in slightly reducing the number of young people arrested and excluded from schools in the areas in which they have been provided (Burrows, 2003), there is a significant risk that the sharing of information about 'at risk' children in this way will bring young people to the attention of criminal justice services before they have even committed an offence. Of course, it is only children living in deprived areas who are likely to be brought under such attention, providing yet another illustration of the discriminatory potential of the criminal justice system. The recent extension of Family Intervention Projects, first introduced in 2006, which aim to work with deprived families to tackle the causes of their anti-social behaviour, is likely to exacerbate this trend as yet more children are brought to the attention of partnerships which bring together social and criminal justice services.

The portrayal of young people as fully-responsible young adults has greatly undermined the potential of these new socially-interventionist disposals to encourage an approach towards youth offending which concentrates predominantly on the welfare of young people. Youths today are regarded less as an asset to be valued and protected and more as a threat to the moral fibre of society itself. A report published by the Institute of Public Policy Research (IPPR) claims that Britain is suffering from a case of 'paedophobia' whereby British people are more likely than their European counterparts to fear young people, believing them to be responsible for crime and anti-social behaviour (Margo and Dixon, 2006). In 2008, the children's charity, Barnardo's, commissioned a poll which discovered that 49 per cent of British people believe that children are increasingly a danger to each other and to adults, many of them describing children as 'feral' (Barnardo's, 2010). The British press helps to fuel such perceptions of young people, often describing them as 'thugs', 'yobs' or 'neds' (in Scotland). Such discourse has even been echoed by government and certain members of the judiciary. A Liverpool Crown Court judge declared that Britain is 'bedeviled by wild feral youth' (Kirkup and Bunyan, 2008) whilst Tony Blair spoke of the need to tackle 'yob culture' (Blair, 2000) and Jack Straw declared that most young people who are put into custody 'are often large, unpleasant thugs [who are] frightening to the public' (Straw in Hansard, 2008b). For Gordon Brown, many 'kids are out of control' (Brown, cited by Mayer, 2008).

These images do not correspond to reality. Both official and self-report statistics show that young offending rates have remained relatively stable over the past ten years (Ministry of Justice, 2007, pp. 44–5; Roe and Ashe, 2008, pp. 13–14), and the vast majority of youths who offend are as much problem children as criminal children, as a breakdown of the youth custody population confirms. For example, whereas 6 per cent of children in England have been excluded from school, 83 per cent of the youth prison population has been so excluded. Whereas those who have lived in care or had previous involvement with the social services represent 3 per cent of all children, they represent 50 per cent of children in prison (Barnardo's, 2008, p. 4). The fact that such disadvantaged children find themselves in prison at all is testimony to the failure of New Labour's welfare approach to divert vulnerable children from the criminal justice system. Instead, New Labour's participation in the demonisation of children led to increased criminalisation and the effective 'dejuvenilisation' (Pitts, 2001, p. 48) of youth justice as special protections for young people were eroded and the adult penal system has encroached on that of youths. The increasingly interventionist approach adopted by New Labour led only to 'the industrial-scale expansion of the youth justice apparatus'

(Goldson and Muncie, 2006, p. 100) and the trapping of ever-more young people in the penal net. New Labour's youth justice policy ultimately failed to 'respond in a more coordinated, efficient and effective way to children who get into trouble with the law', instead encouraging 'formal criminal justice led responses to children who behave in disruptive and challenging ways' (Solomon and Garside, 2008, p. 52).

This is not, however, to ignore the fact that policy has not been applied uniformly across the UK or even across England and Wales where rates of custodial sentencing vary significantly from one area to the next. Scotland in particular has retained a unique approach to offenders aged under 16, based on the system of Children's Hearings. These specialised panels, composed of social workers and lay people rather than judges, were established in 1971 by the *Social Work (Scotland) Act 1968* with the aim of removing all but the most serious young offenders aged under 16 from the criminal courts. Children of this age group are sentenced to supervision by a social worker rather than to custody. Only children who have committed particularly serious offences, such as rape, arson or murder, can be brought before a criminal court. Consequently, only about 100 youths are prosecuted per year in Scotland, representing 'an impressive level of decriminalisation' (Whyte, 2009, p. 201). However, the system has constantly been threatened by more punitive trends. For example, the *Children (Scotland) Act 1995* stipulated that concerns of public protection could sometimes override those of child protection (Asquith and Docherty, 1999, p. 248). More recently, the introduction of measures such ASBOs, Parenting Orders and electronic monitoring of 12- to 15-year-olds via the *Antisocial Behaviour (Scotland) Act* 2004 have led to fears that there may be increased convergence between English and Scottish policy. McAra has even suggested that there may be a 'detartanisation' of youth justice policy, suggesting that it is losing its distinctiveness (McAra, 2006). McAra suggests that penal welfarism is increasingly having to compete with imperatives of public protection and risk management which have informed the adoption of 'what works' principles into social work programmes (McAra, 2008, p. 491). She fears that the new focus on criminogenic rather than welfare needs may undermine Scotland's traditional welfare approach (*ibid.*).

Yet, it might be argued that the Scottish welfare approach has long been limited in that it excludes young offenders aged over 16 who are treated as adults in adult criminal courts. It is estimated that approximately 5 to 7 per cent of young Scottish males aged between

16 and 17 are prosecuted each year (Whyte, 2009, p. 202). As we noted above, the imprisonment of young offenders in this age group largely accounts for the fact that the number of young people in custody in Scotland is disproportionately high. Local authorities can attempt to keep children in the Hearings System until they reach the age of 18 but they are obliged to fund such interventions themselves which may encourage them to place these young offenders in the hands of the formal criminal justice system which is centrally-funded (*ibid.*).

Pilot youth courts were established in 2003 for 16- and 17-year-old offenders and serious 15-year-old offenders. However, experience has suggested that the youth court is not distinct in any significant way from adult Sheriff Courts in 'culture, process or procedure' (Piacentini and Walters, 2006, p. 47) and that it 'is simply an adult court setting masquerading as a fast-track youth process' (*ibid.*, p. 55). The Scottish Prisons Commission did recommend the creation of a Youth Hearings System for 16- and 17-year-olds (Scottish Prisons Commission, 2008, p. 3) but the proposal was not included in the Children's Hearings (Scotland) Bill 2010 which simply aims to streamline the system by creating a new national body to take control of the recruitment, selection and training of panel members. It might be asked whether increased centralisation of the system may lead to further dilution of welfare principles as has occurred in England and Wales.

There nonetheless remain significant differences between English and Scottish youth justice policies, suggesting that a certain degree of Scottish distinctiveness remains. Unlike in England, where a welfare approach has often served as a guise for the deeper penetration of the criminal law, in Scotland the welfare approach continues to act as a break on punitiveness. Although increasing numbers of Scottish youths are being criminalised via 'back-door measures' such as the ASBO and the PND, these penalties are not being used quite so extensively or in quite such a punitive way as in England (see Chapter 2). There have also been recent attempts in Scotland to raise the age of criminal responsibility to 12 via the Criminal Justice and Licensing (Scotland) Bill, introduced in March 2009. This would mean that even serious young offenders cannot be committed to custodial institutions, unlike in England and Wales.

Although England and Wales are often considered together on account of the fact that they share the same legal systems, we should be wary of assuming that policy and practice are identical in the two nations. Indeed, a distinctive approach to youth justice may be detected in Wales. As in Scotland, a welfarist 'children first' approach has been adopted, even though there remains much to be done to reinforce such a position (Howard League, 2009). That the Welsh Assembly was keen to adopt a social-work approach, different to that of England, is evident in its decision to place youth justice services under the responsibility of the Health and Social Services department rather than that of Crime Prevention and Community Safety (Cross *et al.*, 2002, p. 156). In addition, the All Wales Youth Offending Strategy, developed in 2004 in partnership between the Welsh Assembly and the Youth Justice Board, specifically emphasises the need to promote the welfare of children and young people and to stick to the principle that 'young people should be treated as children first and offenders second' (YJB and WAG, 2004, p. 3). The Howard League for penal reform describes the strategy as 'an impressive document that uses the right language about youth justice' (Howard League, 2009, p. 12).

In practice, it would appear that a child-centred approach has indeed been adopted by Youth Offending Teams who have tended to avoid taking potentially punitive measures such as Parenting Orders except in extreme circumstances and who have adopted a much less coercive approach to restorative justice options (Cross *et al.*, 2002, p. 157). However, whilst law and order continue to be 'reserved powers', there is perhaps only so much that the local Assembly can do to resist punitive trends from the centre, even though welfare services do benefit from regional autonomy. Should control of law and order be devolved to Wales, there may be yet more scope for a truly distinctive approach to be adopted. Yet, it has been argued that devolution in Scotland paradoxically encouraged greater punitiveness in criminal justice by rendering local decision-makers more alert to populist concerns that ministers who worked in the relatively closed environment of the Scottish Office (Cavadino and Dignan, 2006, p. 232).

Northern Ireland has in many ways provided a model for a truly distinctive youth justice approach, based on restorative justice. This approach developed in the specific context of civil war whereby paramilitary groups effectively assumed responsibility for law and order in communities where the legitimacy of the police was often highly contested and/or where paramilitary 'justice' based on brute force and punishment beatings was seen to offer a more expedient alternative than formal justice processes. After the end of the 'Troubles', restorative justice initiatives sprang up in a number of deprived areas as an informal alternative to paramilitary justice, dealing principally with young offenders aged between 13 and 22 (McEvoy and Mika, 2002).

Increasingly these informal initiatives have come to form part of the official response to youth offending in Northern Ireland. Following the

Justice (Northern Ireland) Act 2002, the system of Youth Conferencing was launched by the Youth Justice Agency within the Northern Ireland Office in 2003. A young offender may be referred to a youth conference either prior to or following conviction. As such, it is not solely intended to be a means of diverting offenders from custody, although research has shown that this has been one of its practical effects (Jacobson and Gibbs, 2009, p. 14). A youth conference plan agreed at the conference between the interested parties (youth conference officer, a police officer, the young offender and their parent or guardian and possibly the victim) must be submitted to the court for approval. Although these plans are usually accepted in the majority of cases (*ibid.*, p. 7), there may be a risk that the social-work approach of the conference may be undermined as plans are tailored to meet the approval of the courts. A welfare approach may be further undermined by the prosecution of young offenders who fail to respect the conditions of a plan. Consequently, a recent research paper concludes, 'State-based restorative justice approaches are regularly offered to children and young people not as distinct from, but attached to, the criminal justice system – their processes offering little to assuage the structural contexts in which offending behaviour occurs' (Convery *et al.*, 2008, p. 260). It would seem that informal restorative justice processes have effectively been hijacked by the formal criminal justice process, threatening the distinctiveness of the Northern Irish approach. As elsewhere in the UK, there is a risk that a welfare approach might actually lead to the increased criminalisation of young people, working alongside, rather than as an alternative to, a more punitive approach.

ii) *Responsibilising the vulnerable*

Welfare has become inseparable from the notion of individual responsibility. Indeed, welfare rights have been made conditional on the behaviour of their recipients under programmes such as the New Deal for the unemployed which obliges those receiving unemployment benefit to either accept the help offered to them or risk losing their benefits. The same principles apply to New Labour's approach to offenders suffering from problems such as drug addiction. Offenders were expected to take responsibility for their actions and accept the help offered to address the causes of their offending behaviour, or else risk criminal sanctions. As Blair himself put it,

> We will offer offenders a new deal. Education and training; a helping hand to get you into employment and stable accommodation. A drug

treatment place to help you break that addiction. But in return for those opportunities we expect responsibility in return. A commitment that you will turn away from your old criminal lifestyle and become a productive citizen once more (Blair, 2001a).

Once again, rather than offering an alternative to a punitive approach, welfare is backed up by coercion and the threat of punishment.

Such an approach is clearly visible in measures such as Anti-social Behaviour Contracts and Parenting Orders. It also informed the thinking behind New Labour's Drug Interventions Programme, introduced in 2003 to tackle offending behaviour by drug users. The programme works on the assumption that there is a direct link between drug use and crime. Although the New Labour government recognised that not all drug users are criminals, it nonetheless affirmed that three main types of crime are linked to drugs: organised crime; crime committed to obtain the money necessary to feed a drug habit; and crimes of violence (Select Committee on Home Affairs, 2002). Consequently, drug users are often regarded less as victims of their addiction and more as potentially dangerous individuals who must be forced to take responsibility for turning their lives around.

It was recognised that purely repressive policies are unlikely to succeed: 'If there is any single lesson from the experience of the last 30 years, it is that policies based wholly or mainly on enforcement are destined to fail' (*ibid.*). The Drug Treatment and Testing Order (DTTO), introduced by the *Crime and Disorder Act 1998*, was thus intended to act as an alternative to custody for offenders with drug addiction but the conditions imposed on the offenders were so demanding that breach rates were exceptionally high (NAO, 2004; Hough *et al.*, 2003). The new Drug Rehabilitation Requirement (DRR) was introduced in April 2005 to replace the DTTO. The proportion of offenders completing these orders is significantly higher than those for the DTTO – 47 per cent in 2008–9 (Hansard, 2010) – but the breach rate is still high, exposing more than half of those subject to the order to harsher penalties for breach. Given that the DRR may be made one of the conditions of a SSO or SCO which, as we saw above, are strictly enforced, the new intervention may ultimately fail to divert offenders with drug problems from prison. Once again, a welfare approach may actually lead to harsher punishment as drug offenders can effectively be punished not for committing any further offence but simply for failing to address their drug problem.

Prison: Rehabilitating or warehousing?

In 1992, Malcolm Feeley and Jonathan Simon coined the term 'new penology' to refer to a penal strategy which no longer seeks to reform offenders but simply to 'warehouse' them and thus to manage the risk that they represent to society (Feeley and Simon, 1992 and 1994). The success of penal régimes is measured not by their transformative capacity but rather according to their capacity to meet a series of 'objective' management targets borrowed from the world of business. Consequently, Nils Christie has described the modern prison as nothing more than a modern Gulag (Christie, 2000) whilst Wacquant has described it as a ghetto (Wacquant, 2009, pp. 204–8). Both consider that the prison has simply become a means of containing and controlling surplus populations as welfarist initiatives have been abandoned and ameliorative optimism has faded. In their place, managerialist ideology has thrived.

Throughout the UK, such ideology has indeed penetrated the walls of the prison. Like other public services, the Prison Service is now obliged to fulfil a list of specified Key Performance Indicators (KPIs) under the conditions of the Public Service Agreement (PSA) it has signed with the Ministry of Justice and other government departments. These KPIs concern issues such as prison escapes, the level of drug misuse, the rate of serious assaults, prison overcrowding and the rehabilitation and resettlement of offenders (NOMS, 2009). There is a risk that by striving to fulfil numerically quantifiable objectives, prison authorities will overlook qualitative ones (Bryans, 2000, p. 8). For example, the Prison Service is currently aiming to ensure that at least 35 per cent of offenders are in employment at the end of their sentence, order or licence (NOMS, 2009). However, there is no obligation for that employment to be long-term or appropriately tailored to a particular offender's needs. Already in 2000, Bryans noted:

> Governors are becoming increasingly concerned with process issues, 'box-ticking', efficiency and economy. The approach becomes one of ensuring through administrative and bureaucratic mechanisms that the establishment runs as smoothly and cost effectively as possible. [...] There is a grave danger that adopting a managerialist approach to the running of prisons will ignore humanitarian, ethical and moral principles and concerns (Bryans, 2000, p. 8).

It is certainly hard to see how a KPI might include the aim of prison authorities to 'maintain, stimulate or awaken the higher susceptibilities of prisoners', as was laid out in the Gladstone Report over a century ago. However, it would be going too far to suggest that prisons have abandoned rehabilitation altogether in favour of the warehousing of prisoners. The New Labour government declared that it was 'committed to a strong programme to improve offenders' educational attainment, raise skill levels and secure better employment outcomes' (HM Government, 2005, p. 11). This commitment translated as a significant increase in funding from £57 million in 2001–2002 to £151 million in 2005–2006 (*ibid.*, p. 14). The former government claimed that this led to a significant increase in the number of qualifications obtained by prisoners (*ibid.*, p. 15) but recognised that the quality of education in prison does not meet the standards established by the Adult Learning Inspectorate (*ibid.*, p. 17). It therefore demanded that the Prisons Inspectorate apply the same standards to prisons as to any other educational establishment. However, in 2008 a parliamentary report concluded that 'there is a risk that existing performance incentives do not encourage those delivering the [Offenders' Learning and Skills] Service to tackle the hardest to reach prisoners with serious literacy and numeracy needs' (House of Commons, 2008, p. 3). The report explained that the official Prison Service target to achieve at least 80 per cent classroom occupancy might actually encourage it to fill classes with offenders who are most likely to attend, rather than with those who need education most (*ibid.*, p. 10). So, despite considerable investment in prisoner welfare initiatives, managerialist philosophy has meant that this has had little positive practical effect.

In general, rehabilitation programmes tend to be more concerned with risk management than actually bringing about qualitative change in offenders. These programmes have been renamed Offending Behaviour Programmes, highlighting the fact that they aim to deal more specifically with the risk factors which may lead to criminality rather than with the social, physical or psychological problems that individual offenders might have. Many of these programmes focus on cognitive behaviour, seeking to change the way offenders think and react to certain situations in an attempt to lead them away from crime. The official target for these programmes does not relate to their capacity to bring about significant change in offenders. Instead, it provides a numerical target of 7000 offenders per year completing these programmes (HM Prison Service, 2010b). That these programmes are intended solely to control the risk presented by ex-offenders rather than to tackle the social disadvantage experienced by them, is clearly illustrated in the following statement by Paul Goggins, the Home Office minister responsible for prisons from 2003 and 2006: 'The whole purpose of [the Reducing Offending National

Action Plan] is about reducing reoffending. That has to be the sole purpose. We see education as a means to an end, equipping people with skills to gain jobs that can sustain a life outside of crime' (Goggins, cited in House of Commons Education and Skills Committee, 2005).

So it would appear that prisons do more than simply warehousing offenders – they attempt to change their behaviour. However, the prevalence of managerialist philosophy has undermined attempts at rehabilitation, as has the enduring problem of prison overcrowding. In June 2009, it was estimated that 61 per cent of the prison estate in England and Wales and 79 per cent of prisons in Scotland were overcrowded (Berman, 2009, p. 11; Audit Scotland, 2008, p. 11). The lack of space, the increasing numbers of offenders serving short sentences and the constant moving of prisoners from one penal establishment to another has made the organisation of quality rehabilitation programmes difficult, if not impossible (HC Education and Skills Committee, 2005, p. 11). Lord Woolf has compared prison overcrowding to the AIDS virus since it debilitates the entire penal system and it is extremely hard to find a cure without considerable investment (Woolf, 2001). Overcrowding also exacerbates the 'pains of imprisonment' (Sykes, 1958), having a negative overall impact on prisoner welfare and rendering the sentence of imprisonment particularly punitive: it encourages increased levels of violence in prison; it means prisoners have to be accommodated wherever there is space for them, even if this means isolating them from friends and families; and it means that prisoners' privacy is not respected as increasing numbers of them have to share a cell (Levenson, 2002). In addition, overcrowding is thought to increase the risk of prisoner suicide (Joint Committee on Human Rights, 2004). Consequently, although material conditions in prison might have improved somewhat, with the ending of degrading practices such as 'slopping out', prisoners still have to deal with a whole range of problems which render the daily experience of imprisonment highly punitive. This situation cannot, however, be wholly attributed to the decline of rehabilitative, welfarist philosophy in prison. Joe Sim has argued that it is doubtful whether rehabilitative discourses were ever totally insitutionalised within the Prison Service and claims that 'prisons remained invisible places of physical hardship and psychological shredding throughout the twentieth century' (Sim, 2009, p. 4). Nonetheless, the current managerialist discourse has undoubtedly introduced a new philosophy into prison management which is more likely than ever before to lead to the warehousing of prisoners and to further exacerbate the pains of imprisonment.

Probation: From befriending to surveillance

The impact of managerialist philosophy in terms of undermining a welfarist approach to offending behaviour has been even more striking within the Probation Service. The Probation Service originated as a charitable missionary service in the nineteenth century before being placed on a statutory footing in England, Wales and Ireland by the *Probation of Offenders Act 1907* and, in Scotland, by the *Probation of Offenders (Scotland) Act 1931*. Under the 1907 Act, 'officers of the court', who were later to become known as probation officers, were required to 'advise, assist and befriend' offenders placed on probation orders. Historians such as Radzinowicz and Hood have regarded this development as a sign of humanitarian progress on account of the fact that it represented the first step towards integrating social work into the penal system (Radzinowicz and Hood, 1990, pp. 633–47). Other historians such as David Garland, however, have regarded the creation of probation officers and orders as just another example of the expansion of the penal apparatus which occurred at the beginning of the twentieth century (Garland, 1985, p. 21). Yet it is hard to support the idea that probation resulted in practice in a significant expansion of state control on account of the fact that probation orders were little-used – they represented only 4 per cent of sentences in 1911 (Radzinowicz and Hood, 1990, p. 647). Even in 1966, at a time which is often considered as being the very apogee of the rehabilitative ideal, probation orders (which probably focused more on rehabilitation than any other sentence at the time) were only given to 15 per cent of all male offenders sentenced in England and Wales (Wootton, 1978, pp. 118–19). By 1975, this figure had dropped to 5 per cent (*ibid.*, p. 119) but rose again to 10.9 per cent by 1987 (Prison Reform Trust, 1989, p. 6).

It is only in recent years that the caseload of probation officers has exploded. If the probation order no longer exists, having been replaced by the Community Rehabilitation Order under the *Criminal Justice and Court Services Act 2000* which was in turn replaced by the Single Community Order under the *Criminal Justice Act 2003*, probation officers are now responsible for monitoring the increasing number of offenders who are sentenced to SCOs and SSOs, as well as those sentenced to custodial sentences both pre- and post-release. Young offenders under 18 are now monitored in the community by Youth Offending Teams. Between 1998 and 2008, there was an 18 per cent increase in the total number of offenders starting Probation Service supervision (Ministry of Justice, 2009e, p. 3) but the most significant growth – 55 per cent – was in the number of offenders under pre- or post-release supervision, largely on account of the rise in the number of offenders serving longer sentences who require supervision on release from custody and the increased length of time that all offenders are required to spend under supervision once released from custody (*ibid.*, p. 5).

The increased workload of the Probation Service has not, however, meant that a less punitive approach has spread across the criminal justice system. Rather, as with other 'welfarist' measures introduced under New Labour, the expansion of probation meant the expansion of control. Yet, this development was in no way inevitable. Had probation not been forced to combine its social work approach with the competing aims of risk management and punishment, it might well have succeeded in diverting offenders from prison, addressing their social needs and consequently countering current punitive trends. Although probation officers were always obliged to combine welfare with punishment, it is argued that the toughening-up of alternative sentences and the introduction of managerialist reform into the Probation Service have recently placed punishment in prime position.

The trend towards the toughening-up of probation orders began before New Labour came to power. For example, the *Criminal Justice Act 1982* allowed the courts to add extra conditions to probation orders, resulting in a net-widening effect (Ashworth, 1989, p. 12). It was also under the last Conservative administration that the role of the probation officer was deliberately recentered towards that of punishment and control. The *Criminal Justice Act 1991* declared that his or her role should no longer be to 'advise, assist and befriend' but rather to work towards the reduction of crime, the protection of the public, the rehabilitation of the offender and to administer '*punishment* in the community'. The New Labour government also expressly aimed to place punishment at the forefront of probation services. Home Office minister, Paul Boateng declared, 'We are moving away from a social work type of befriending model, no one should be under illusions about this [...] we intend to form the national probation service on law enforcement' (cited in Ryan, 2005, p. 139). Consequently, in 2000, the *Criminal Justice and Court Services Act* placed a statutory duty on the newly created National Probation Service (previously the Service had been split into regional divisions) to work with the police to develop Multi-Agency Public Protection Arrangements (MAPPAs) designed to manage dangerous offenders outside prison and to inform their victims of their release date when they are sentenced to a prison sentence of one year or longer.

This development reflects an increasing concern for the rights of victims throughout the criminal justice system which, it would seem, has come to permeate the Probation Service as it has the criminal justice system as a whole. As Eithne Wallis, the first director of the new national service explained, her aim was to move the service beyond a social service, centred on the rights of offenders, towards a more 'victim-centred' service (cited in Nellis, 2004, p. 120). The practical consequence of such concerns is that social work with offenders is only valued in so far as it serves the aim of crime reduction and victim protection. Mike Nellis has explained:

> Treatment and education were to be offered to offenders no longer as ends in themselves, but as a means of preventing the next victim. Rehabilitation, once a principal above all others in probation, was merely one means among several to achieving the purpose of public protection, and if the offer was not taken up by the offender, other, more coercive, means would be resorted to (*ibid.*, pp. 120–1).

It is significant that the consultation document, *Restructuring Probation to Reduce Re-offending* (Home Office, 2005b), did not once mention rehabilitation, referring instead to the need to efficiently 'manage' offenders to reduce recidivism. The aim of managing offenders is clearly conveyed by the merging of the Probation and Prison Services into the National Offender Management Service (NOMS) in 2004. The practical result does not, however, appear to have been the more efficient management of offenders. The reform did nothing to reduce the caseload of the Probation Service and has instead resulted in 'a huge increase in bureaucracy, the disappearance of Probation as an entity and a sharp deterioration in the quality of supervision and court report writing' (NAPO, 2010). Indeed, probation officers are currently over-worked and under-funded. There has not just been a considerable increase in the number of offenders monitored by the Probation Service but also in the number of reports staff have to write (Oldfield and Grimshaw, 2008, pp. 13–14). The growing caseload has not been matched by either an adequate rise in the number of trained and experienced officers recruited (*ibid.*, pp. 18–19) or by increases in funding (*ibid.*, p. 12). These problems do not just negatively affect the quality of service delivered to offenders but they have also undermined the New Labour government's stated aim to ensure public protection. Only last summer, the former director of the London Probation Service, David Scott, claimed that the chronic lack of resources provided to his service had been a factor leading to the mismanagement of an ex-offender who was convicted of killing two French students whilst under the supervision of the probation services (Scott, 2009). In addition, rather than NOMS creating a true partnership between the Prison and Probation Services, the latter has become dominated by the former, thus undermining the separate social work philosophy of probation. NAPO has noted that from the moment the merger occurred, probation staff have been outnumbered by those from the Prison Service – consequently, it considers that those controlling NOMS are not 'effective champions for Probation' (NAPO, 2010, p. 2).

The enactment of the *Offender Management Act 2007* has further reformed the Probation Service and arguably undermined its social work philosophy. The Act opened up probation services to tender from the private and voluntary sectors. Only a limited number of probation boards are now allowed to become 'trusts' and to continue to deliver services. They must fulfil certain conditions, defined as the capacity to show local engagement, strong leadership and to demonstrate effective resource use, meaning 'value for money ... economy, efficiency and effectiveness' (Ministry of Justice, 2009g). Boards who do not demonstrate these qualities will have their services competed for on the open market. Although reform and rehabilitation remain a key aim of the Probation Service, such reforms suggest that cost considerations have become paramount whilst those of welfare have been sidelined. Critics of this particular reform do recognise the value of collaborating with the voluntary sector. After all, the service originated out of charitable work (NOMS, 2007) and independent charitable organisations are often better-placed to provide highly specialised services (Morgan, 2006, p. 63). Yet critics fear that this independence might be threatened by the fact that charities will be obliged to compete with other organisations to win contracts for services (Corner, 2006, p. 61). NAPO thus recommended that partnership should be favoured over competition (Fletcher, 2006, p. 72).

There are also concerns that an increasing preoccupation with risk has undermined the welfare role of probation officers. In January 2003, the Electronic Monitoring Unit, the government organisation responsible for providing the electronic monitoring of offenders in the community, was incorporated into the National Probation Service. This development prompted concerns that the dependence on new technologies to monitor offenders could undermine the relationship of trust which needs to be formed between offenders and their probation officers. Increasingly, the probation officer has become a risk manager rather than a social work professional as the extension of yet another apparently welfarist model has contributed to the more punitive treatment of offenders. As Nellis has concluded, 'humanistic values, the only standpoint from which one might resist the onslaughts of managerialism, and the debasements which follow, are ceasing to have credibility in criminal justice' (Nellis, 2004, pp. 16–17). One of the practical consequences of this transformation of the Probation Service into a public protection/risk management agency has been the significant increase in the number of offenders recalled to prison in recent years (Padfield and Maruna, 2006; *cf.* Chapter 1).

Probation in Scotland has followed a somewhat different trajectory from its English cousin. The *Social Work (Scotland) Act 1968* dissolved the probation services created by the 1931 Act and charged social workers with the monitoring of offenders on probation (McIvor and Williams, 1999, pp. 288–90). Probation was thus moved outside the criminal justice system altogether. So far, Scotland has resisted pressure to re-integrate probation into the mainstream criminal justice system by the creation of a single, unified Correctional Service for Scotland based on the NOMS model. Probation remains the responsibility of social workers, even if these last are now obliged to coordinate with the Scottish Prison Service in forming new Community Justice Authorities similar to Crime and Disorder Partnerships in England and Wales. Although concerns about public protection have become increasingly prominent both north and south of the border, it has been suggested that rehabilitation in Scotland is not only seen as a means of managing risk but also as a means of promoting the social inclusion and welfare of offenders, consistent with the approach outlined in the 1968 Act (McNeill, 2005). Once again, it would seem that although Scotland has been affected by nationwide trends, it has nonetheless succeeded in retaining a degree of distinctiveness. In Northern Ireland, too, the Probation Board has remained separate from the Prison Service even if it was never formally incorporated into the social services as in Scotland. Although the Board has been forced to accept an increasingly heavy workload in recent years and a more punitive approach has been encouraged by public protection concerns, the Board seems to have retained a considerable degree of independence and has consequently resisted attempts to make probation officers provide 'prisons in the community' (McCaughey, 2009, pp. 103–4).

In conclusion, it might be argued that although the dominant discourse across the criminal justice system in Britain has become increasingly punitive as government has become more concerned with risk management, a welfare approach to the problem of crime has survived and even been extended. The rehabilitative ideal has often been regarded as the ultimate expression of this welfare approach to the extent that it is concerned with the offender and the causes of offending behaviour rather than exclusively with the offence itself. Historically, rehabilitation aimed at reintegrating offenders into mainstream society. Even if it led to considerable harshness, particularly in the nineteenth century, it was thought to be in the best interests of the offender – it is in this sense that it might be considered to be a welfare initiative. In the twentieth century, confidence in the State's capacity to rehabilitate offenders was matched by its confidence in its capacity to tackle a whole range of social problems. Although the individual responsibility of offenders and welfare recipients was never ignored, just as much emphasis was placed on state responsibility. Today, there has been a shift in emphasis from state to individual responsibility, resulting not in the eclipse of the rehabilitative ideal but rather in its transformation and redefinition. As Robinson has explained, rehabilitation has even enjoyed renewed legitimacy as it has become identified with three new penal narratives which are simultaneously utilitarian, managerial and expressive (Robinson, 2008). Utilitarianism has always been a chief aim of rehabilitation – as we have just noted, it was seen as serving the interests of the offender. Now, however, it is utilitarian to the extent that it is primarily seen as being in the best interests of society as a whole: 'it is no longer offenders themselves who are seen as the main beneficiaries of rehabilitative interventions, but rather communities and potential victims' (*ibid.*, p. 432). In this way, rehabilitation is justified not in terms of its concern for offender welfare but rather in terms of public protection. Rehabilitation also fits with the narrative of managerialism in that it is presented as a strategy of risk management (*ibid.*, pp. 433–5). Finally, whereas rehabilitation was previously regarded as being expressive of welfare concerns for offenders, it is now seen as expressive of punishment on account of the emphasis placed on the responsibilisation of the offender (*ibid.*, pp. 435–9). For New Labour, however, it was important to highlight both punishment *and welfare* in an attempt to position itself in the political centre by offering a 'third way' approach to crime, capable of tackling both crime itself and its causes. However, as we have seen, the renewed emphasis on individual responsibility rendered these welfare initiatives extremely coercive. Consequently, rather than welfare concerns acting as a barrier to punitiveness, the punitive reach of the State was actually extended. It is thus possible to speak of 'punishment *through* welfare'. The reverse process also takes place when the poor find that welfare services such as job training are only offered to them once they are already caught up in the penal net – this is 'welfare *through* punishment' (Scott, 2008, p. 94). In both cases, welfare and punishment become inextricably intertwined. If this did not occur in any significant way with the development of the 'welfare sanction' at the beginning of the twentieth century, it has now become a reality at the beginning of the twenty-first. Rather than fulfiling the traditional function of reinsertion, the 'neo-rehabilitative' ideal has exacerbated the social exclusion of offenders who fail to take responsibility for their reformation.

4
Erecting the Boundaries of Exclusion

The current concern with risk management has not just led to the exclusion of offenders but also of potential offenders from mainstream society. This is perhaps the most potent symbol of the punitive turn. Although offenders have long been banished from society, most strikingly by their transportation to far-off colonies in North America and Australia, the State's current capacity for exclusion has arguably never been greater. As the Neoliberal State has become increasingly interventionist in the lives of the poorest and most vulnerable members of society, its capacity for the control and subsequent exclusion of these same populations has become greater than ever before. It has been greatly assisted in its task by the development of new technologies of surveillance which have enabled it to extend control outside the four walls of the prison and into society at large. The State now has increased capacity to monitor suspicious activities and to try to preempt criminal behaviour before it even occurs, suggesting that the scenario played out in the 2002 film *Minority Report* might not entirely belong to the realm of science fiction. In addition, the rise of the victim as an increasingly prominent character in public discourse about crime has provided the State with the discursive tool necessary to draw ever-starker boundaries between offenders and the fictional law-abiding majority. All of these trends are analysed in turn.

Demonising the offender

From dangerous class to underclass

The term 'dangerous classes' first appeared in the *Oxford English Dictionary* in 1859 (Tobias, 1967, p. 54). It was rapidly adopted by the ruling classes to refer to workers and the poor who threatened the existing social order (Emsley 1996, p. 5; Bailey, 1993, pp. 221–57). The term enabled the Capitalist State to distinguish between those who had to be controlled via the institutions of the workhouse or the prison and those who were considered worthy of the privileges of citizenship. In the course of the twentieth century, there were continued attempts to make such distinctions: for example, the *Old Age Pensions Act 1908*, which created the state pension, deliberately excluded certain 'undesirable' groups such as drunks, paupers and the idle, whilst it rewarded those who made an effort to save for retirement (Mann, 1992, p. 55). The State did gradually adopt a more inclusive notion of citizenship which sought to reintegrate both criminals and certain other excluded groups but, by the 1970s, the gross stereotypes of these groups, which had never really vanished, began to reappear in public discourse.

In the 1980s and 1990s, the notion of the 'underclass' was used to refer to those who might previously have been described as the 'dangerous classes', the 'social residuum' or the 'unemployable' (*ibid.*, p. 140). Although it need not necessarily have such negative connotations (see, for example, Wilson, 1987), the term has most commonly been used in the sense intended by the American sociologist, Charles Murray (Murray, 1990). For Murray, not all poor people are alike – there is a class of the poor who, on account of their lack of respect for traditional moral values, are entirely responsible for their problems. He explains, 'Britain has a growing population of working-aged, healthy people who live in a different world from other Britons, who are raising their children to live in it, and whose values are now contaminating the life of entire neighbourhoods' (Murray, 1996, p. 26). These negative values include a rejection of traditional family values, a lack of respect for the law and a total aversion to work which translates as dependence on the welfare state (*ibid.*).

Such a line of thinking was clearly shared by Britain's political leaders, from Thatcher to Blair. Although they did not regularly use the term themselves, they believed, in common with Murray, that many poor people were responsible for their own state of dependency. Blair defined the members of an underclass as 'people cut off, set apart from the mainstream of society [whose] lives are often characterised by long-term unemployment, poverty or lack of educational opportunity, and at times family instability, drugs abuse and crime' (Blair, 1996, p. 141). Like Murray, Blair defined those who suffer from social exclusion by their particular *culture* which separates them from the rest of society. Indeed, Blair worried that there was a 'sizeable underclass' in Britain that was losing contact with mainstream values (Blair, 1997a). Mandelson and Liddle, key figures in the 'modernisation' of the Labour Party, wrote of the need for strict discipline to break 'the *culture* of hopelessness, idleness and cynicism' which prevailed amongst certain social classes in Britain (Mandelson and Liddle, 2002, p. 101, *my italics*). In an attempt to change that culture, the Blair government launched the so-called 'Respect' agenda in 2006 which aimed to encourage (or force) a greater sense of moral responsibility. As Louise Casey, who coordinated the New Labour government's working group on the subject, put it, 'We will not reach and help that very small number who are most excluded and the most challenging unless we deal with their behaviour or the behaviour of those around them' (Casey, 2006). Unlike Murray, New Labour did nonetheless recognise that the State had a role to play in tackling the problems of the poorest, but it shared the notion that responsibility ultimately lies with the poor themselves.

Given that criminality was often cited as one of the distinguishing characteristics of the underclass, the responsibilisation of the poor was closely linked to the responsibilisation of offenders. New Labour adopted an increasingly unified approach towards social and crime problems as poverty and crime were seen to spring from the same source. Interventionist social policies consequently led to the criminalisation of certain members of large swathes of the socially and economically disadvantaged. Yet it would appear that such strategies were based on an entirely erroneous notion of the criminal underclass. Research conducted by the author at HMP East Sutton Park and HMP Lewes (Bell, 2007) has demonstrated that, just as 'there is no hard evidence to suggest that there are economic or cultural differences between the poor and the rest of society' (Alcock, 1997, p. 35), there are no such differences between offenders and society at large. By analysing prisoners' attitudes to issues such as work, family values and social security, it was possible to prove that Murray was wrong to suggest that 'the habitual criminal is the classic member of an underclass' (Murray, 1996, p. 34). On the contrary, the views of prisoners reflect those which one assumes are shared by mainstream society. Prisoners showed a strong attachment to work which they considered to have an intrinsic moral value, however badly paid it might be. Over 90 per cent of prisoners agreed that it was preferable to have any kind of job than no work at all. Furthermore, most offenders made a distinction between those deserving of benefits and those who were not, with less than 20 per cent considering social benefits as a right. One female prisoner remarked, 'You can't make other tax-payers pay for your laziness'.

Prisoners' views regarding the family were more difficult to interpret. Although a large majority of prisoners – 76 per cent – considered that single-parent families could raise children just as well as two-parent families, a similar percentage also said that both parents should raise their children together. It would appear that the women did not support single-parent families *per se* but believed that in practice it was often better to raise their children alone than with an abusive or otherwise inadequate father. Consequently, considerably more men than women – 83.3 per cent compared to 57.6 per cent – believed that both parents should raise their children together. These men are clearly far removed from the irresponsible, even 'uncivilised', men who form part of Murray's underclass. Just like Murray himself, a majority of them believed that a father figure was necessary to teach a child the difference between right and wrong.

Yet, despite the lack of evidence to the contrary, New Labour repeatedly insisted on the cultural difference between criminals and mainstream society. Offenders were described as 'the selfish minority', to be distinguished from the 'law-abiding majority' (Blair, 2004a). It was claimed that they do not share the values of the 'decent society' (Blair, 1996, p. 247) and that they are 'without any residual moral sense' (Blair, 2004b). When offenders are portrayed as lacking the moral values of mainstream society, it not only becomes easier to demonise them as 'other' but, in linking them to the 'immoral' underclass, it is also more likely that criminal behaviour will be associated only with the poor and disadvantaged whilst the crimes of the powerful are ignored. There is, of course, nothing new in this, but the elision of the behaviour of the poor with that of offenders may have particularly punitive consequences at the present time in the context of an unprecedented wave of direct and indirect criminalisation of merely troublesome behaviour.

Blair made it clear that he considered crime to be almost exclusively committed by the poor and disadvantaged. In 2001, he declared,

> The bulk of crime is committed by a hard core of persistent offenders, around 100,000 in all. Their background is almost universal; truancy; drugs; low employment prospects; often from broken families or having passed through care (Blair, 2001a).

Such a statement ignores the fact that the middle and upper classes may be responsible for crime. Yet, it is estimated that white-collar crime is considerably more widespread than any other form of criminality. Indeed, it has been suggested that the notion of the 'law-abiding majority' is largely fictional: a large proportion of crime is actually committed by those who consider themselves to be 'respectable' (Karstedt and Farrall, 2007). It is estimated that 61 per cent of consumers have committed at least one offence against the government, their employer or businesses (*ibid.*, pp. 3–4). Their offences are minor – what may be referred to as 'crimes of everyday life' – and are not necessarily anti-social, but they are 'anti-civil' in the sense that they reflect a 'considerable lack of civility among citizens and consumers in England and Wales' (*ibid.*, p. 2). Their most common offence is that of accepting payment in cash in order to reduce the amount they pay in tax (*ibid.*, p. 3). Yet, no matter how trivial these crimes may appear, their cost to society is significant. It has frequently been established that white-collar crime as a whole costs much more to society than street crime (Tombs, 2002, pp. 18–20). A report ordered by the Association of Chief Police Officers in 2007 found that the cost of fraud in the UK could be estimated at between £13.9 and 20 billion in 2005 (Levi *et al.*, 2007). Nonetheless, some of the most harmful activities in terms of the social, economic and physical harm they may cause are excluded from the formal definition of criminality. Numerous 'safety crimes', such as those perpetrated in the workplace, are not regarded as health and safety offences (Hillyard and Tombs, 2008, p. 9). Consequently, it is suggested that a 'social harm' approach should be taken to the problem of criminality, whereby attention is focused not just on crime as it is formally defined but also on physical, financial, emotional, psychological and sexual harm (*ibid.*, pp. 14–16).

The problem with identifying crime with a deviant minority is that it becomes easy to adopt an extremely punitive attitude towards offenders: Nils Christie has explained that, as a society, we tend to demonise those whom we know little about (Christie, 1977, p. 8), a view which is supported by David Garland and Zygmunt Bauman. Garland has suggested that the British State is in the process of adopting a 'criminology of the other' whereby offenders are identified as being 'wicked', separate from the mainstream, thus justifying their exclusion and punishment (Garland, 2001a, pp. 184–5). This is to the detriment of policies which seek to reintegrate offenders into mainstream society (*ibid.*). Bauman argues that the spatial separation of the offender from the rest of society leads to a rupture of communication between the two parties, encouraging punitive feelings (Bauman, 2000, p. 208). Exclusion reinforces exclusion when we no longer make any effort to understand difference but rather to eliminate the risk that it represents.

The offender vs the victim

The construction of a metaphorical victim also serves to draw a clear line between the 'good' and the 'bad' citizen, fuelling punitive attitudes towards offenders. Whereas criminality is associated with a minority, victimhood is associated with the majority, justifying the so-called 'rebalancing' of the criminal justice system in favour of the victim as being in the interests of society as a whole. Although the British State has long been meant to play the role of impartial arbiter between the defendant and his or her victim, it would appear that the latter has come to be seen as being more worthy of state protection. As Blair himself declared, 'Our first duty is to the law-abiding citizen. They are our boss. It's time to put them at the centre of the CJS [criminal justice system]' (Blair, 2004b). This preoccupation with victims' rights is relatively new. As Paul Rock has explained,

> [P]ossible changes in the future standing of the victim were being approached gingerly, hedged about with reservations, checks, and doubts, and certainly with no zeal by criminal justice agencies in the 1990s. [...] Conceptions of proper order and procedure seemed to be under threat. Victims were viewed by most with an ambivalence, nervousness and suspicion. They had to be wooed but were nonetheless newcomers, outsiders in the formal world of criminal justice, liable to outbursts of emotion and unreason, undisciplined by the restraints that controlled the professional, and capable of disturbing the balance of forces and proper practice of the trial (Rock, 2004, p. 16).

This is not, however, to say that victims were entirely ignored by the criminal justice system prior to the 1990s. In the 1950s, the social and penal reformer Margery Fry's campaign for the compensation of victims of crime led to the establishment of the Criminal Injuries Compensation Board in 1964 (Walklate, 2001, pp. 204–5). 'Victim Support', a charitable organisation for victims of crime, was founded in the early 1970s and, in the 1980s, the rise of the feminist movement helped to reform the way in which police officers dealt with victims of rape and domestic violence (*ibid.*, pp. 206–7). Yet it was not until the mid to late-1990s that victims started to be placed at the very foreground of the criminal justice system and that the granting of increased rights to victims started to resemble a zero-sum game whereby the rights of offenders were correspondingly reduced.

Despite the problems that their involvement in the criminal justice process might pose to due process, as outlined by Rock, recent years have seen victims accorded an ever-greater role not just in criminal trials but also in the formulation of penal policy. This change has been justified by the need to restore victims' confidence in the criminal justice system – it is estimated that only 38 per cent of British people believe the system to be effective (Thorpe and Hall, 2009, pp. 105–6). In an attempt to alter such perceptions, Jack Straw, when shadow Home Secretary, stated, 'The criminal justice system must give greater attention to the victims of crime. Confidence in the criminal justice system as a whole is eroded when victims are treated in a thoughtless and insensitive way' (Straw, cited by Rock, 2004).

It is the need to protect the interests of victims and all potential victims of crime that has been used to justify the creation of indeterminate sentences for public protection, the increased surveillance of offenders after their release from prison and the abolition of certain procedural protections, such as the double jeopardy rule, designed to protect defendants from miscarriages of justice. Increasingly, government has given in to victims' demands to introduce ever-more punitive policies, the prime example of which is the introduction of an attenuated version of 'Sarah's Law'. Demands for the law arose from the murder of eight-year-old Sarah Payne in 2000 by Roy Whiting, a convicted sex offender. Sarah's mother, supported by the *News of the World*, led a campaign for the introduction of a law which would allow parents to consult the Sex Offenders' Register to find out if any convicted sex offenders are living in their area. This is currently the case in the USA, following the introduction of 'Megan's Law' after the rape and murder of Megan Kanka in 1994, also by a convicted sex offender. The American system, which allows any member of the public to access the national register and view the names, addresses and even photographs of offenders, has been severely criticised. Firstly, it has been suggested that it is counterproductive, forcing offenders underground (BBC, 2006). Secondly, it may encourage vigilante activity such as that which occurred in the Paulsgrove Estate in Portsmouth in Summer 2000 when local residents grouped together to protest against the presence of suspected sex offenders living in their area, following the *News of the World's* publication of 150 names and photographs of convicted sex offenders. The newspaper was forced to stop publishing this information following a spate of attacks against men who, rightly, or wrongly, were identified by members of the public as having appeared in the paper as convicted sex offenders. This suggests that the risk encountered by offenders by the introduction of such a law would be disproportionate to the risk that sex offenders actually present to the public. Indeed, sex offenders show a considerably lower rate of recidivism than most other offenders (Hood *et al.*, 2002, p. 1).

That successive New Labour governments initially resisted public pressure to introduce a 'Sarah's Law', was considered by many as proof that their policy in the field of criminal justice was not uniformly populist and punitive (Randall, 2004, p. 185). Yet, New Labour did eventually give in and introduced a limited form of 'Sarah's Law', despite the fact that a considerable number of measures had already been introduced which aimed to protect the public from sex offenders. For example, the Sex Offenders' Register was introduced in 1997; tougher penalties were created following the *Criminal Justice Act 2003* and the *Sexual Offences Act 2003*, such as 'Risk of Sexual Harm Orders' which monitor those who are simply considered to be at risk of committing a sexual offence; and, in 2006, the *Violent Crime Reduction Act* gave police the right to search the homes of those listed on the Sex Offenders' Register in order to carry out risk assessments.

In June 2007, the UK government announced that it would place a statutory duty on all authorities responsible for monitoring sex offenders to examine whether or not personal details concerning particular paedophiles should be made public in the interests of public protection (Home Office, 2007a, p. 10). Then, in September 2008, a Child Sexual Offender Review Disclosure Pilot was adopted by four police forces in England and Wales. It allows any individual to request the police for information concerning the previous sexual convictions of individuals who are in contact with children (Kemshall and Wood, 2010). Although only 4 per cent of applications for information were granted during the pilot period (*ibid.*, p. 8), the public disclosure of personal information about offenders may set a dangerous precedent, leading to a gradual erosion of their right to protection. The New Labour government's decision to test out such a scheme in defiance of warnings by professionals smacks of populism. As Harry Fletcher of NAPO has stated, 'It is extremely worrying that the Home Secretary has spoken of the need to break the monopoly of information about sex offenders held by professionals. The information is not a commodity; it is highly sensitive and must be kept confidential. This sounds like a sop to the tabloid papers' (Fletcher, cited in *The Independent*, 2007).

Indeed, just like the media, and in ignorance of the full complexity of the problem of sex offending, the New Labour administration reinforced the stereotype of the sexual offender as 'other', as someone who can never be fully 'cured' (Matravers and Hughes, 2003, pp. 51–4). The plethora of laws and measures aimed at tackling the problem give the public the impression that sexual offences are on the increase, despite the fact that they represent a mere 1 per cent of all recorded crime and that the number of people convicted of such crimes has actually been declining since the mid-1990s (*ibid.*, 2003, p. 53). As such, New Labour policy on sexual offences was firmly inscribed in the discourse of 'criminology of the other'.

As offenders have been treated increasingly as objects of, rather than as actors in, the criminal justice system, the victim has come to play a more central role, not just informing penal policy-making, but also playing a more active role in the criminal process itself. In an attempt to ensure that their interests are better-protected, the Brown government appointed the mother of Sarah Payne as the very first 'Victim's Champion', whilst Louise Casey, formerly of 'Respect' notoriety, was appointed as the first 'Victims' Commissioner', notably charged with 'working with local and national victims groups to make sure the voice of victims is fed-back to and impacts directly on Government policy' (Ministry of Justice, 2010d). She was also charged with chairing the Victims' Advisory Panel which was set up in 2003 'to enable victims of crime to have their say both in the reform of the Criminal Justice System and in related developments in services and support for victims of crime' (Home Office, 2007b).

Victims' voices are now also heard more loudly in court via Victim Personal Statements (VPS). Since 2001, victims have been allowed to prepare a written statement for the court, describing the physical, emotional, psychological and financial harm caused by an offence. They were not, however, allowed to speak directly before the court. The 'Victims Advocate Scheme Pilot', on the other hand, which ran from April 2006 to April 2008 enabled relatives of murder and manslaughter victims to tell the court in person about the effect a crime has had on them. The Victim Focus Scheme, based on this pilot, was rolled out nationally in October 2007, despite concerns expressed by judges and barristers that the court is being transformed into an arena charged with emotion, threatening the principles of impartiality and legal rationality (Gibb, 2005). It is to be feared that the State is turning itself into a kind of 'victim-protection agency' (Waiton, 2006) and risks losing its legitimacy as an impartial referee between the opposing parties in a trial. Meanwhile, the rise in status of the victim has been accompanied by the increasing demonisation of offenders.

Erecting the barricades

Once the offender is cast as an outsider, set apart from the mythical 'law-abiding society', the task of excluding and controlling him or her is facilitated. The most symbolic way of doing so is, of course, to place offenders behind the physical boundary of the prison. Whether carceral institutions attempt to reintegrate offenders or not, they have always undeniably remained mechanisms of exclusion *par excellence*. Yet, as Foucault has pointed out, the exclusive power of the prison reaches far beyond the prison walls, targeting not just offenders but also potential offenders (Foucault, 1975). In policing the boundaries between the law-abiding and the rest, the forces of law and order have arguably contributed to reinforcing these boundaries, further extending the exclusive power of the prison into free society.

Realising the Panopticon? Control beyond the prison walls

Foucault argued that the nineteenth century witnessed the spread of the discipline of the prison throughout the social body as its practices were replicated in the factory, the school and the hospital (Foucault, 1975). He claims that the architects of these new disciplinary apparatuses dreamed of submitting their subjects to a constant, all-pervasive gaze which would force them to internalise disciplinary norms. The system was inspired by Jeremy Bentham's Panopticon, first designed in 1787. The Panopticon was to be a prison designed in a circular form, with each cell faced towards a central tower from where the prison governor would be able to monitor all the inmates without them knowing that they were being watched. The idea was that discipline would not be imposed by the prison authorities but rather by the architecture of the prison itself – since prisoners could not know when they were being watched, they would be forced to internalise the system of discipline. In this way, anonymous control of the mind would replace the physical brutality of previous penal régimes.

It is, however, difficult to assert that panoptic control permeated society in the way that Foucault suggests. Even in prisons, Bentham's ideas were not applied to the letter, although his architectural model did inspire the design of the first national prison in England, HMP Millbank, opened in 1816. The nineteenth century State simply did not have the tools necessary to assume such all-pervasive power. However, in the twentieth and twenty-first centuries, the Capitalist State has gradually acquired the technologies which may render the panoptic control described by Foucault possible, if not in practice, then at least in theory. Indeed, in 1994, David Lyon wrote of the existence of an 'electronic panopticon', whereby citizens increasingly found it difficult to avoid the electronic gaze of the CCTV camera (Lyon, 1994). His theory has even wider application in the Britain of 2010 which was described as a 'surveillance society' in a report commissioned by the Information Commissioner, the UK's independent authority charged with controlling access to personal information (Murakami Wood, 2006). Today, with the help of new technologies, the carceral wall is further extended by the development of invisible boundaries which cannot be crossed.

These new technologies include CCTV, 'dataveillance' (the monitoring of individuals' details stored on electronic databases), and other forms of electronic surveillance, all of which are currently tied up with the contemporary practice of governance to order and regulate everyday life (*ibid.*, p. 6). New surveillance technologies have resulted in 'social sorting' whereby personal information is used to identify risky populations (*ibid.*, p. 8; Lyon, 2003). For example, CCTV is used to control access to city-centres, shopping centres and certain residential areas. Certain 'suspicious-looking' people may thus be excluded from defined areas. The Information Commissioner's Report notes how new technologies also allow 'data flow' – the sharing of information between different services and authorities (Murakami Wood, 2006, p. 9). For example, it is now common practice for information to be shared between the different parties to Crime and Disorder Reduction Partnerships. This may result in what the report describes as 'function creep' whereby personal data collected for a specific purpose may be used in a different way from that which was originally intended (*ibid.*, 2006, p. 9). An example may be the way in which data originally collected by social services on young people living in deprived areas may be shared with other members of a CDRP in the context of a Youth Inclusion Programme scheme. Given that these children are already subject to a form of 'dataveillance', there is an increased risk that they may attract the attention of the criminal justice services, resulting in netwidening. Indeed, surveillance technologies may result in the further demonisation and exclusion of those who already live on the margins of society. They may lead to the creation of a climate of distrust (*ibid.*, p. 3) and their very presence may serve as a constant reminder of dangerousness (Lianos and Douglas, 2000, p. 114), creating a climate of fear. This is likely to be especially true of the UK where there are currently 4.2 million CCTV cameras, representing one camera for every 14 people, the highest proportion in the world (Murakami Wood, 2006, p. 19).

Yet some researchers have suggested that surveillance is less invasive than such statistics might lead us to believe (Davie, 2007; Norris and Cahill, 2006). In the course of a study of the London CCTV network, Norris and Cahill found that CCTV cameras do not in reality permit the surveillance of entire populations on account of the fact that the gaze is not the impersonal gaze of the camera but rather the highly subjective gaze of individual camera operators who tend to focus attention on the 'usual suspects'. Moreover, they found that these operators generally lack motivation and are kept busy with a whole range of different tasks, meaning that CCTV footage is not always watched. Consequently, CCTV is rarely proactive: it does not allow the police or private security operatives to intervene to stop crime before it occurs (Norris and Cahill, 2006, p. 108). According to an official report commissioned by the Home Office, CCTV has a negligible impact on crime reduction in general and 'little or no effect' on the reduction of crime on public transport or in city centres (Welsh and Farrington, 2002). This evidence would suggest that, in practice, CCTV works rather badly as a modern panopticon. If discipline is internalised, it would appear that this occurs only amongst those who are generally law-abiding anyway. Given that many people tend to believe that CCTV renders them less powerless (Coleman, 2004, p. 294), they are happy to participate in their own surveillance by accepting the installation of cameras in their streets, towns and workplaces.

But if surveillance is not yet truly panoptic, it does nonetheless have punitive potential, on account of the discriminatory manner in which it is used and its capacity to exclude certain 'undesirables' from mainstream society. Coleman and Sim, taking the case of Liverpool, have noted that these new technologies, although neutral in themselves, are used to control activities which threaten commercial interests and may dissuade potential customers from entering the city centre (Coleman and Sim, 2005, pp. 108–9). For example, CCTV has been used to enforce bye-laws forbidding young people from skateboarding or homeless people from selling the *Big Issue* (Coleman, 2004, pp. 301–2). The development of algorithmic technology may render CCTV an even more effective tool of exclusion as cameras become capable of recognising certain characteristics, including skin colour, which may be considered suspicious (Murakami Wood, 2006, p. 44).

It has been suggested that the indefinite retention (in England and Wales, but not in Scotland) of DNA profiles on the National DNA Database (NDNAD) has also disproportionately affected certain groups. It is estimated that in 2009 just under one million people whose profiles were stored on the NDNAD had no previous record of conviction, caution, reprimand or final warning on the Police National Computer (House of Commons Home Affairs Committee, 2010, para. 13). About 36,000 of these people had never even been arrested (*ibid.*). There is no information currently available about the ethnic or social composition of these people but, on account of the fact that the police have the power to take a DNA sample without consent from anyone suspected of having committed an offence, certain groups of people may find themselves disproportionately represented on NDNAD (Staley, 2005, p. 40). Following the 2008 Strasbourg ruling that such a practice violated article 8 of the ECHR, the recent *Crime and Security Act 2010* has limited the indefinite retention of such data to convicted offenders. However, it is still possible to retain the DNA profiles of those who have been arrested but who have not been convicted of a recordable offence for up to six years. The powers for police to take DNA samples have actually been extended to include the taking of samples retrospectively from violent and sexual offenders who are no longer in prison. The new coalition government has promised to ban the indefinite retention of DNA profiles and to regulate the use of CCTV (HM Government, 2010; see Chapter 5) but it is highly questionable that recent trends will be fully reversed now that the technologies have already been put in place.

With the extension of surveillance technologies, boundaries are no longer drawn simply between the innocent and the guilty but also, increasingly, between the innocent and those who are considered to be merely suspicious. This situation has been exacerbated as the police service has come to be more proactive than reactive, attempting to manage risk as much as to prevent crime. It is helped in these boundary control tasks by a whole host of private security officers and new quasi-police officers such as Community Support Officers and Street Wardens, not to mention the existence of extremely broadly-worded legislation (such as the anti-terrorism Acts) which has led to a considerable extension of police powers.

Policing the boundaries

The London Metropolitan Police, which would eventually provide the model for police forces throughout Great Britain, was established in 1829 by Sir Robert Peel. It was proud to present itself as a public protection agency rather than an agency of the State designed to spy on its citizens (Reiner, 2000; Radzinowicz and Hood, 1990, p. 247). In sharp contrast with the military image of the French *gendarmerie*, the force was unarmed and wore a civilian uniform of top hat and white trousers (Midwinter, 1971, p. 38). It consistently resisted attempts to force it to assume a surveillance role (Radzinowicz and Hood, 1990, p. 249). Yet, over time, its civilian character came to be threatened as it adopted an increasingly proactive role. Some of these changes took place in the nineteenth century, such as the development of the intelligence-gathering role of the police following the creation of Special Branch in 1883, initially to fight against Irish Fenian terrorist attacks on the British mainland. But the most considerable changes took place from the late 1960s onwards as there was a considerable expansion in police powers and police numbers and the service began to borrow tactics from the military (Hillyard and Percy-Smith, 1988, p. 236). All of these trends have been further accentuated in recent years.

Police numbers in England and Wales remained relatively stable throughout the latter quarter of the nineteenth century and the first half of the twentieth century, before expanding significantly in the 1950s and 1960s and then tailing off again in the 1990s (Hicks and Allen, 1999, p. 14). Total police force strength increased significantly between 2002 and 2009, although the number of civilian staff increased more than that of non-civilian staff (Mills *et al.*, 2010, pp. 46–8). In Scotland too, police numbers are at a record high, having increased by almost 17 per cent between 1996/7 and 2008/9 (HMICS, 2010). These figures do not include civilian community wardens which were introduced in 2003 to help with community policing. Only in Northern Ireland did police numbers fall, from 11,480 in 1997 (Barclay and Tavares, 2003, p. 18) to 7280 in 2009 (Berman, 2009, p. 12), but this may be explained by the transition towards normalised policing following the signing of the Belfast Agreement in 1998.

The expansion in police numbers has been matched by an extension in police powers. The widening of stop and search powers has perhaps been most marked. These powers date back to the old 'sus laws', created by the *Vagrancy Act 1924*, which allowed the police to stop and search anyone whom they suspected of intending to commit a criminal offence. The powers were notoriously used against young black men living in Brixton in the early 1980s and were subsequently identified has having been one of the main causes of the deterioration in relations between the police and the local community which prompted the urban riots of 1981 (Scarman, 1981). The *Police and Criminal Evidence Act (PACE) 1984* subsequently repealed the 'sus laws' and authorised the police to stop and search only those whom they have 'reasonable suspicion' to be guilty of a criminal offence. Yet, the law was widely drafted and no definition of 'reasonable suspicion' was provided. To this day, most stops and searches are carried out under PACE (EHRC, 2010, p. 10), although they may also be carried out under section 44 of the *Terrorism Act 2000* which gives police the power to stop and search people for objects which could potentially be used to commit acts of terrorism. On account of the fact that there is no need for the police to prove 'reasonable suspicion' under this latter law, the European Court of Human Rights (ECtHR) recently declared section 44 stops and searches to be unlawful (Gillan and Quinton v the United Kingdom, 12th January, 2010). There are concerns that these powers, the use of which has been increasing annually since 1993 (EHRC, 2010, pp. 13–14) are disproportionately used against ethnic minorities. The most recent statistical analysis concluded that black people are at least six times as likely to be stopped and searched as white people, whilst Asian people are approximately twice as likely to be stopped and searched (*ibid.*, p. 46).

Police powers in terms of controlling public order have, of course, been extended massively by the anti-social behaviour powers discussed above which enable them to arrest, exclude, disperse and fine those responsible for, or likely to be responsible for, such behaviour. Freedom of assembly has also been curbed by a gradual increase in police powers to control public demonstrations. Serious limitations to the right to protest had already been made by the *Public Order Act 1986* which enabled a whole series of legal restrictions to be placed on public meetings. At the time, critics worried that the law could apply to an extremely wide range of behaviour which had not previously been defined as criminal, such as participation in pickets (Hillyard and Percy-Smith, 1988, pp. 261–2). The *Criminal Justice and Public Order Act 1994* further limited freedom of assembly by creating the offence of 'aggravated trespass' which had the practical effect of criminalising those who enter private land 'in the open air' for the purposes of organising a protest. When in opposition, New Labour did not oppose this law, which has been described as an 'authoritarian juggernaut' (Hoyle and Rose, 2001, p. 78). Instead, Blair imposed a three-line whip to ensure that Labour ministers would attend the vote but abstain (*ibid.*, pp. 78–9). Once in power, New Labour used the *Antisocial Behaviour Act 2003* to amend and strengthen the law, extending its application to cover trespass on private property which is not in the 'open air'. The 2003 Act also limits the definition of public assembly from 20 people to just two. Section 132 of the *Serious Organised Crime and Police Act 2005* allowed the government to give police powers to stop demonstrations from taking place in certain specified areas such as the square mile surrounding Parliament Square in London. This same law also modified the *Protection from Harassment Act 1997* to enable it to apply to the harassment of two people or more, thus permitting it to be used against protesters lobbying against the government or a business, for example. Furthermore, the *Terrorism Act 2006* created what the human rights group, Liberty, describes as 'unacceptably broad speech offences' which are capable of criminalising individuals and organisations whose statements risk inciting or glorifying acts of terrorism (Liberty, 2007). The police have not hesitated to use their increased powers against protesters. For example, in

2005 six students were arrested for distributing tracts at the University of Lancaster during a meeting organised between university staff and the representatives of big business such as BAE Systems, Shell and Unilever (Monbiot, 2005). The police have also used article 44 of the *Terrorism Act 2000*, intended to be used against terrorist suspects, to stop, search and disperse peace protesters from in front of Royal Air Force military bases (Liberty, 2003).

Indeed, together with the anti-social behaviour legislation, these most recent anti-terrorism laws have probably done the most to extend police powers over the past decade. Although the anti-terrorism acts of the 1970s gave police extraordinarily wide powers to detain without charge or trial, and to stop and search those suspected of engaging in terrorist activity, these measures were only intended to be temporary and exceptional in the context of civil war. Increasingly, anti-terrorism powers are becoming normalised and are being extended to apply to activities which cannot reasonably fall within the definition of terrorism. The trend towards the militarisation of the police since the end of the 1960s, symbolised by the adoption of special equipment such as plastic bullets, Taser guns and water cannons, and the creation of specialised units such as the armed Anti-terrorist Branch, has also helped to normalise what previously might have been considered as exceptional practices.

The massive extension of police powers is highly problematic in terms of police legitimacy. Much-publicised gaffes such as the unlawful shooting of Jean Charles De Menzes in the London Underground in 2005 have helped to undermine confidence in the capacity of the police to exercise their extensive powers with prudence. The image of the police has, of course, also been severely damaged by accusations that it is 'institutionally racist' (Macpherson, 1999; Rollock, 2009). Consequently, alongside the 'hard policing' tactics outlined above, the police have long been attempting to adopt more consensual policing methods. In the early 1980s, in the wake of a number of scandals involving the police – notably the Brixton riots and the death of Blair Peach, an anti-fascist protester, during a confrontation with the police in 1979 (MPS, 2010) – the police authorities developed the concept of 'community policing' whereby the police would aim to work in partnership with, and with the consent of, local communities. John Alderson, the former police chief of Devon and Cornwall defined the strategy as follows:

> [Community policing] is not primarily concerned with law enforcement but is concerned with social protection and the amelioration of social conditions which lead to the creation of criminogenic cir-

cumstances. It's based on a social contract between police in an area, in a community or neighbourhood, and the people who live there (Alderson, cited in *Marxism Today*, 1982, p. 11).

The emphasis of community policing, therefore, was to be on crime prevention, as opposed to repression. The police were not to be solely concerned with upholding law and order but also with addressing the social causes of crime. Alderson countered accusations that this would render policing more insidious by insisting that increased social intervention was intended to avoid rather than encourage prosecution (*ibid.*, pp. 11–13).

Alderson's good intentions were not, however, respected, and the new model quickly became the focus of serious criticism. The political context of the time was not favourable to its development. Indeed, Alderson's conciliatory discourse contrasted starkly with that of the Thatcher governments with regard to law and order. For example, in 1983, just two years after the Brixton and Toxteth riots, the Thatcher government spoke not of the need to improve relations between the police and the public but rather of the need to reinforce police numbers and to provide them with better equipment (Thatcher, 1983). The government's reliance on the police to suppress the striking miners of 1984–5 also undoubtedly damaged relations between the police and certain communities. The *Public Order Act 1986* was thought to be 'insensitive, damaging to future relationships with sections of the community or the image of a neutral police force' (Wallington, 1987, p. 191). Moreover, the difficult socioeconomic climate of the 1980s in which social inequalities were growing (see Chapter 7) was hardly favourable to tackling the causes of crime identified by Alderson. Consequently, community policing ended up being imposed from above rather than below (Brake and Hale, 1992, p. 78). For some critics, it turned out to be nothing more than 'a method of intelligence gathering enabling police to identify "trouble-makers" and to keep themselves informed of what goes on in the community; a method of "soft" surveillance' (Chatwin, 1981, p. 27).

The failed experience of community policing in the 1980s did not, however, prevent New Labour from taking up the idea when it came to power, under the banner of 'neighbourhood policing'. In its 2004 report on policing, the New Labour government committed itself to ensuring that neighbourhood policing was adopted by police forces throughout England and Wales (Home Office, 2004b, p. 47). For New Labour, neighbourhood policing meant recruiting civilians to 'neighbourhood policing teams', run by police officers, PCSOs, Special Constables (volunteer police officers with police powers), neighbourhood wardens (civilians recruited by local authorities to work in tandem with the police to improve the quality of life of their neighbourhoods) and other experts.

The new PCSOs, support police created by the *Police Reform Act 2002* to tackle minor crime and anti-social behaviour, were at the centre of the New Labour government's strategy. The experience of PCSOs has often been described as positive (Loveday, 2007, p. 28). They work closely with communities, spending most of their time patrolling the streets and talking to members of the public – this has meant that they are often perceived as being more accessible than ordinary police officers (Cooper *et al.*, 2006 p. 18). In addition, they tend to be more representative of the public at large than the police, including greater numbers of women and ethnic minorities (*ibid.*, p. 44). They have, nonetheless, been strongly criticised, notably by the press, members of the former Opposition and by police officers themselves who have referred to them as 'plastic policemen' on account of the fact that they can exercise a significant number of police powers without having followed the same training as regular police officers. Indeed, under the terms of the *Police Reform Act 2002*, local police chiefs can confer up to 40 different powers on PCSOs (*ibid.*, p. 19). Their power to use 'reasonable force' to detain a suspect whilst waiting for a police officer to arrive on the scene has been criticised by the Police Federation who considers that such powers should not be held by what it describes as 'an ill-equipped and ill-trained second layer of law enforcers' (Police Federation, 2010). Indeed, PCSOs themselves worry that their training is inadequate (Cooper *et al.*, 2006, p. 54).

There is a risk that the use of such wide powers by PCSOs may undermine the legitimacy of neighbourhood policing. Such policing tactics may be considered to be discriminatory on account of the fact that they generally target street crime in the most deprived areas of Britain identified as 'crime hotspots' such as Merseyside (Home Office, 2003b). It is likely that this most recent form of community policing may also result in 'soft surveillance' – the New Labour government explicitly declared that it considered 'an essential part' of the role of neighbourhood policing teams to be 'gathering community intelligence' (Home Office, 2004b, p. 50). Paradoxically, it is their quasi-civilian status which simultaneously renders them more legitimate in the eyes of the public and makes them particularly effective surveillance officers.

The guiding principle of neighbourhood policing remains the participation of local communities themselves. The notion of 'active citizenship' was to be placed at the heart of police reform (Home Office, 2004b). The former Home Secretary, David Blunkett, defined this as follows: 'Active citizenship means taking a shared responsibility to prevent crime and to tackle anti-social behaviour – the community aiding the police and not condoning any form of criminality' (*ibid.*, pp. i–ii). There is a significant contradiction at the heart of this definition: Blunkett demands that the local community take responsibility for the crime problem whilst insisting that it accept the official definition of crime and work in partnership with the police. The New Labour government excluded the idea that communities are diverse entities, composed of individuals who may accept different norms. In encouraging a monolithic view of community, there is the danger that those who do not share dominant norms are excluded rather than reintegrated (Beckett and Sasson, 2004, p. 139). As the community defines itself in opposition to those who do not share the dominant value system, it becomes characterised by a 'defensive exclusivity' (Crawford, 1998, p. 245). The community may thus become a mere extended arm of the State, supporting policies which seek to exclude the 'other'.

In such a context, there is a risk that community/neighbourhood policing can translate as a form of 'zero tolerance' policing. What are commonly referred to as 'zero tolerance' strategies of law and order originated in the 'broken windows' theory developed in 1982 by the conservative criminologists James Q. Wilson and George L. Kelling (Wilson and Kelling, 1982). They used the analogy of the broken window to suggest that crime spreads when the police turn a blind eye to minor offences: when one window is left unrepaired, it is only a matter of time before lots of other windows are broken since the unrepaired window sends out the signal that no-one cares about the problem. It is therefore suggested that the police should adopt a very strict, zero tolerance approach to minor offences and 'incivilities'. The aim is not just to deter crime but also to counter the fear which may result from such behaviour. It is considered necessary to sanction all those who might cause such fear – not just serious offenders, but rather 'disreputable or obstreperous or unpredictable people: panhandlers, drunks, addicts, rowdy teenagers, prostitutes, loiterers, the mentally disturbed' (*ibid.*, pp. 1–2).

The theory was most famously translated into practice by William Bratton, the former head of the NYPD. For Bratton, it was only through working in partnership with the community that such a strategy could be successful (Bratton, 1998). Consequently, the idea of community policing became tied up with zero tolerance strategies as the police and communities joined together to exclude from their midst those who openly did not conform to the dominant norms of behaviour. In England, such policies have proved controversial and were only applied in an experimental way by a small number of police forces, notably by Hartlepool Police in Cleveland on the initiative of Detective Inspector Ray Mallon, nicknamed 'Robocop' (Dennis and Mallon, 1998). Charles Pollard, the former Chief Constable of Thames Valley Police criticised Bratton's methods, arguing that such aggressive policies damaged rather than encouraged community cohesion (Pollard, 1998, p. 45). Pollard claims that, although the theory behind zero tolerance policies had always underpinned British policing strategies in the form of the proverbial 'bobby on the beat', the English approach differs greatly from the New York strategy which he considers to be 'dictatorial, inflexible and oppressive' (*ibid.*, p. 59). Indeed, in theory at least, the British have tended to focus more upon 'problem-oriented policing' whereby the focus is on forming local partnerships to tackle not just crime and disorder but also the causes of such problems. This approach was formalised in the *Crime and Disorder Act 1998* which demands that the police work in partnership with the local community to solve crime (Leigh *et al.*, 1998, p. 2). Yet, in practice, the police have remained reluctant to adopt any form of policing which might undermine its traditional function of keeping order (Tilley, 2003, pp. 329–33).

If the police in Britain have so far avoided replicating the New York experience, it might be argued that they have nonetheless found themselves influenced by zero tolerance strategies in the sense that they are now adopting an ever-stricter approach to minor offences and anti-social behaviour. Indeed, the ASBO may be considered to be the typical example of a zero tolerance policy on account of its capacity to sanction an extraordinarily wide range of non-criminal behaviour. Phil Scraton has suggested that the White Paper which preceded the *Antisocial Behaviour Act 2003* (Home Office, 2003a) could have been written by Rudolph Giuliani himself (the Mayor or New York from 1994 to 2001 who recruited William Bratton as police chief) (Scraton, 2003). Indeed, in his introduction to the White Paper, David Blunkett referred indirectly to the 'broken windows' theory:

> We have seen the way communities spiral downwards once windows get broken and are not fixed, graffiti spreads and stays there, cars are left abandoned, streets get grimier and dirtier, youths hang around street corners intimidating the elderly. The result: crime increases, fear goes up and people feel trapped (Blunkett in Home Office, 2003a).

The targets of such policies were clearly enounced by Blunkett: the young inhabitants of the most deprived areas in Britain. Given that zero tolerance policies tend to focus on the 'usual suspects', rarely targeting white-collar criminals, we should rather speak of '*selective intolerance*' (Crawford, 1998, p. 242).

In applying such policies, the police have effectively moved from policing public order and crime to policing people (Hillyard and Percy-Smith, 1988, pp. 270–88). This is not of course an entirely new development. Arguably, the police have always focused their attention not on crime itself but on those who commit it, criminalising people for who they are rather than for what they might have done. In the nineteenth century, the police primarily focused their attention on the poor. In the 1840s and 1850s, working class opinion was quite obviously hostile to the surveillance of their leisure activities by those whom they described as a 'plague of blue locusts' (Briggs *et al.*, 1996, pp. 150–1). In more recent years, police attention has continued to focus on the poor but also, at different periods of time, on black people (Hall *et al.*, 1978), the Irish (Hillyard and Percy-Smith, 1988, pp. 271–5; Hillyard, 1993) and, latterly Muslims (Pantazis and Pemberton, 2009). Consequently, the British police have effectively become agents of 'border control' (Reiner, 1999, p. 181), patrolling the metaphorical and physical divisions which separate the 'respectable' majority and the threatening minority. Perhaps what is new today is the fact that the capacity of the police to fulfil such a role has been enormously expanded, both through the increase in their numbers and the development of new surveillance technologies.

The result is the exclusion of ever-greater numbers of people as the reach of the prison does indeed extend far beyond the prison walls. Jock Young is surely right to note that we are now living in an 'exclusive society' in which a 'cordon sanitaire' has been erected to protect a 'central core' from the 'outgroup' who has become something of a scapegoat for the problems of wider society (Young, 1999). This situation is certainly far removed from what Young describes as the 'inclusive' society of the post-war period which at least attempted to incorporate all members of society in a common social project. It may be suggested that we have simply reverted to a pre-modern period when exclusion was the norm but, as suggested above, the development of new technologies of control have ensured that society's power of exclusion is now greater than at any time in the past.

5
Whither the Punitive Turn?

The UK's 'punitive turn'

The punitive consequences of New Labour's penal policy are indisputable, even though they may vary considerably from region to region. In the UK, increasing numbers of people are now locked up in penal institutions or placed under the surveillance of the criminal law. This trend has been accompanied by the rise of a discourse about the crime problem which tends to demonise offenders and potential offenders, pitting their interests against those of the crime victim and thus exacerbating their exclusion from mainstream society. However, it might be argued that trends in penal policy have not been unidirectional. According to Cavadino, Crow and Dignan, drawing on the work of Andrew Rutherford, punitive and managerialist approaches to criminal justice sit alongside a human rights approach which attempts to ensure fairness and due process within the criminal justice system (Cavadino *et al.*, 1999, pp. 45–8). They recognise that this approach 'has never been central to governmental criminal justice policy' but they consider that it may be embodied in attempts to reform offenders, to involve victims and offenders in restorative justice programmes and in a preoccupation with 'just deserts' sentencing. Successive New Labour governments showed an interest in all three of these policies. As we noted above, there was a continued commitment to offender reform, exemplified by the considerable investment in prisoner education. Yet, the utilitarian managerialist approach to rehabilitation has ensured that reform programmes have often been unsuccessful, leading to the simple warehousing of offenders. Similarly, there was a serious commitment to restorative justice, notably in the youth justice system, but such initiatives were underpinned by coercion, preventing them from serving as a diversion from custody. The principle of 'just deserts' in sentencing has, as Cavadino, Crow and Dignan recognised, the capacity to lead to either more fairness or more punitiveness, depending on how it is applied. In the case of New Labour, as with the Conservative governments of John Major, it translated in practice as greater sentencing severity as the sentencing climate became increasingly punitive.

Nonetheless, some experts still refute the thesis of punitiveness. Roger Matthews has even gone so far as to describe it as a 'myth', arguing that there has been considerable divergence between the rhetoric and the reality of punishment (Matthews, 2005). For him, many apparently 'punitive' penalties have not proved to be particularly punitive in practice. He cites the example of the 'three-strikes' legislation introduced under the *Crime (Sentences) Act 1997* which was little-used in the first few years of its introduction (*ibid.*, p. 193). However, it was noted above that considerably more use has been made of the three strikes sentence for domestic burglary in recent years (see Chapter 1). It was also demonstrated above that the new IPP sentence which replaced the 'two-strikes' sentence for serious violent or sexual offenders has been used so extensively that it is now considered to be a primary driver of the increase in the prison population in England and Wales. Indeed, recent sentencing policy in the UK fits exactly with Matthew's own definition of punitiveness, characterised as it is by 'a disproportionate use of sanctions and consequently a deviation from the principle of proportionality' (Matthews, 2005, p. 179). Matthews is correct to note that material conditions in many British prisons have improved considerably in recent years (*ibid.*, pp. 193–4). However, this is not a sign of less punitiveness: we noted above that problems of overcrowding, caused by the over-use of prison as a sanction, have accentuated many of the psychological pains of imprisonment. Matthews also suggests that the media and political panic over paedophiles, dramatised by events at the Paulsgrove Estate in summer 2000, has 'slipped down the social and media agenda' (*ibid.*, p. 194). Yet, we have noted that the New Labour government eventually gave in to introducing a diluted form of 'Megan's Law' in the UK, proving its willingness to respond to popular punitive sentiment with regard to sex offenders. Matthews noted elsewhere that certain penalties were actually rendered *less* severe under New Labour – he cites the example of the reclassification of cannabis from a Class B to a Class C drug in January 2004 which reduced the maximum penalty for possession from five to two years' imprisonment (Matthews, 2003, pp. 225–6). Yet, in January 2009 the former government reclassified the drug to a Class B drug once again, in defiance of expert advice given by the Advisory Council on the Misuse of Drugs (ACMD, 2008).

It is true that there have been some positive legal and institutional developments in recent years but they have not been so significant as to counter the punitive trends described above. Firstly, although the incorporation of the European Convention on Human Rights into British law following the *Human Rights Act 1998* was widely welcomed, it has not prompted a greater respect for the human rights of citizens targeted by the criminal law. On the contrary, the UK has repeatedly been criticised by the European Commissioner for Human Rights for its low age of criminal responsibility (Hammarberg, 2008), its high rates of detention and the use of civil orders to combat minor offending and anti-social behaviour (Gil-Robles, 2005). One report worried that, 'The United Kingdom has not been immune (...) to a tendency increasingly discernible across Europe to consider human rights as excessively restricting the effective administration of justice and the protection of the public interest' (*ibid.*, para. 3). The British courts have also been critical of government policy in this respect and have ruled certain aspects of recent legislation to be incompatible with human rights, such as the indefinite detention of terrorist suspects under the *Anti-Terrorism Crime and Security Act 2001*. Yet, the New Labour government persisted in sailing as close to the wind as possible as far as human rights legislation is concerned, continuing to impose control orders on terrorist suspects. In so far as prisoners' rights are concerned, it simply ignored the 2004 ruling from the European Court of Human Rights which deemed the blanket ban on prisoners from voting in elections to be in contravention of the ECHR (Prison Reform Trust, 2010a). In general, prisoners have had great difficulty enforcing their human rights, leading one commentator to conclude, 'if the prison service is moving towards a rights culture at all, it is doing so with considerable resistance' (Eady, 2007, p. 268).

It might have been expected that the devolution of powers to Scotland, Wales and Northern Ireland under the constitutional settlement of 1998 would have enabled counter-punitive trends to develop outside England. However, we have seen that this has not necessarily been the case. In the case of Scotland, which has long retained a quite unique, explicitly welfarist approach to criminal justice, particularly with respect to young people and children, devolution has arguably had the contrary result and actually encouraged the development of punitive trends north of the border. Although there has been considerable resistance to punitive trends in Scotland, there has also been increasing convergence with policy in England, as exemplified by the introduction of ASBOs, the increase in the prison population, the lengthening of sentences, the tough enforcement of alternative sentences and the introduction of preventive sentences such as the Order for Lifelong Restriction. It has been suggested that devolution has rendered policy more susceptible to electoral pressure and punitive demands since Members of the Scottish Parliament are now more directly answerable to the public than the distant élites operating from within the Scottish Office (Cavadino and Dignan, 2006, p. 232). Similar punitive trends have been detected in Wales and Northern Ireland, although, as in Scotland, there has been a certain resistance to trends common in England. It remains to be seen whether the devolution of policing and justice powers will enable these nations to develop a truly unique approach to criminal justice or whether this will have the same paradoxical effect of encouraging greater convergence, as has arguably been the case in Scotland.

The novelty of punitiveness

In spite of the existence of certain counter-trends, it is hard to deny the punitive direction taken by penal policy in Britain over the past 15 years and more. It might even be suggested that the nation has been experiencing a veritable 'punishment frenzy' (Irwin *et al.*, 1998, p. 33). However, it might be suggested that there is nothing particularly new about this turn of events. There is much continuity with the past. As ever, the main targets of penal policy are the poor, namely the underclass – that particular category of the poor who may have previously been described as the *lumpenproletariat* – who are sanctioned as much for who they are as for what they have done. In addition, punishment is still intended to serve as a public spectacle. Although hanging, the most spectacular form of punishment, was removed from the public eye in 1868, punishment has always retained its value as a spectacle, as a means of conveying a particular message to both the offender and the wider public about what kinds of behaviour will and will not be tolerated. The judicial homily is often used to send out a particular moral message (Hall *et al.*, 1978, pp. 31–2) and the media reporting of trials, in the press and on television, has ensured that the public remain willing spectators to punishment. Politicians have encouraged public participation, implementing schemes such as 'Community Payback' to ensure that justice is *seen* to be done.

It has even been suggested that there has been a revival of premodern forms of punishment, exemplified most notably by the move away from proportionate sentencing (Hallsworth, 2000, p. 153). Indeed, as noted above, proportionality in sentencing was an Enlightenment invention, contrasting with the sentencing practices of the past which saw the death penalty imposed for what would now appear to be relatively minor offences (Sharpe, 1999, pp. 211–13). The notion of proportionality is a highly subjective one and it has not always led to parsimony in punishment. Nonetheless, the idea that there should be an understandable correlation between offence and punishment became the dominant principle of sentencing throughout the nineteenth century onwards, exemplified by the failed attempt to insert a clause in the Habitual Criminals Bill of 1869 which would have made seven years' penal servitude mandatory for those convicted of a third offence of felony (Radzinowicz and Hood, 1990, pp. 245–6). The recent tendency to impose very severe penalties for minor offences and to base sentencing decisions on criminal history as much as on the present offence would appear to signify a certain throwback to older forms of punishment.

All this would suggest that we are perhaps witnessing a great 'penal leap backwards' (Wacquant, 2005). Yet, despite considerable continuity, recent penal trends in the UK do mark a certain rupture with the past. Firstly, the role played by victims of crime, in terms of their influence over policy-making and the part they may now play in the criminal trial itself, is quite unprecedented. The role played by the media in the publicisation of their cause, as exemplified by the 'Sarah's Law' campaign run by the *News of the World*, is also new. Although in the past newspapers were capable of mobilising opinion against offenders and in favour of victims, as in the case of the garroting panic of the 1860s (Davis, 1980; Sindall, 1990), the reach and influence of the media, particularly the press, is wider than ever before. As Anthony Sampson suggested, 'the fourth estate [has] become the first estate' (Sampson, 2005, p. 241; see Chapter 8).

Perhaps the most significant point of departure from the past is the capacity of the penal arm of the State to penetrate deeper than ever before into civil society. This has been achieved by the extension of welfarist interventions and by the development of new surveillance technologies. Welfarist interventions can act as a barrier to punitiveness, as was long the case in Scotland, at least with regard to youth justice. However, as Garland has pointed out, they can also help to extend the scope of the criminal law by legitimising greater state intervention into the lives of those who are deemed to be socially inadequate. As argued above, this did not lead to greater punitiveness when the welfare sanction was first developed at the beginning of the twentieth century. On the contrary, it might be argued that a welfarist approach which focused primarily on state responsibility for the reformation of offenders (even if individual responsibility was never denied), softened the punitive consequences of penal welfarist interventions. As focus was once again centred on the individual responsibility of offenders themselves and government became increasingly preoccupied with appearing to be 'tough' on crime, welfarist interventions in turn became increasingly coercive. The result has been that social measures aimed at diverting individuals from the formal penal system, such as drug treatment programmes and initiatives aimed at tackling the causes of antisocial behaviour, have had the perverse effect of criminalising ever more people. This is especially true as the boundaries between social and penal policy and between the civil and the criminal law have been increasingly blurred. The development of new surveillance technologies, together with the encouragement of a partnership approach to crime-solving which has united social and criminal justice agencies along a single penal continuum, has meant that it is harder than ever before for individuals to escape the controlling gaze of the State. As criminal justice and social work agencies have become increasingly concerned with risk management, penal and social interventions are no longer simply concerned with bringing offenders to justice or tackling the root causes of crime but also in ensuring that would-be offenders are prevented from committing crime in the first place. Humanistic approaches to the crime problem are consequently sidelined in favour of control measures, the punitive consequences of which are obvious.

In the final analysis, the punitive turn reflects both continuity *and* rupture with the past. To suggest that it is an entirely new development would paint too rosy a picture of a past which is filled with examples of the infliction of extreme pain and suffering on the subjects of the criminal law. One need only examine the nineteenth century attempts at prisoner reform through the separate system (McConville, 1981; Radzinowicz and Hood, 1990) or the degrading prison conditions which prevailed in British prisons before the so-called punitive turn occurred (King and McDermott, 1995). Perhaps, therefore, it would be more accurate to follow Joe Sim and speak rather of the 'intensification' of punishment (Sim, 2009). This conveys the idea that punishment has become particularly severe in recent years whilst acknowledging that penal severity is far from novel.

The development of a punitive consensus?

In light of the 2010 elections, the question to be asked now is whether the intensification of punishment is set to continue. Is there a punitive consensus on law and order? For some time the Conservative Party, having initiated the 'punitive turn' of 1993, certainly appeared to form part of the punitive consensus on law and order. Downes and Morgan wrote of the existence of a centre-right consensus with regard to criminal justice policy in the British general election of 2001 (Downes and Morgan, 2002b). Such a consensus unquestionably prevailed right up until after the general election of 2005 as both Labour and the Conservatives focused on the need for tougher punishment and putting more police on the streets. Yet, the election of David Cameron to the party leadership in 2005 initially seemed to herald a new approach to criminal justice policy, particularly to youth justice. Cameron used a speech to the party's Centre for Social Justice to emphasise the need to understand the causes of crime and anti-social behaviour and to show some understanding, 'compassion and kindness' to troubled young people, arguing that 'hoodies are often more defensive than offensive' (Cameron, 2006a). The speech was mocked by the *News of the World* which carried the headline, 'Hug A Hoodie says Cameron'. Whilst the tabloid headline was grossly exaggerated, the rhetoric used in the speech did nonetheless mark a break from that used in the Labour Party White Paper, *No More Excuses*, of 1997 (see Chapter 3), and indeed from his predecessor Michael Howard's tough approach to youth crime which was based almost exclusively on punishment, notably via the incarceration of juvenile offenders (Newburn, 1998, p. 200).

Cameron has declared his support for an approach which combines tough measures on crime with tough measures on the causes of crime, describing it as 'one of the best things [Tony Blair] ever said' (Cameron, 2006b). Consequently, party policy places emphasis on the need to rehabilitate offenders and to transform prisons 'from unproductive human warehouses where idleness reigns and drugs are rife, to busy, constructive régimes where the environment is clean, and there is purposeful activity' (Conservative Party, 2008, p. 86). However, in light of other policy proposals in the field, it is highly questionable whether this aim is really achievable. Firstly, the Conservatives have promised to increase prison capacity. It is hoped that this will help to address the overcrowding crisis that renders rehabilitation extremely difficult. Yet such a proposal ignores the fact that it is widely recognised that prison is not the best place to rehabilitate prisoners: a recent report by the

House of Commons Justice Committee suggests that money would be more effectively spent on 'prehabilitation' which focuses on tackling crime before it occurs (HCJC, 2010, p. 67). In any case, it is unlikely that the promised increase in prison capacity will offset the forecast increases in the prison population which is expected to rise to as many as 93,900 prisoners by 2015 (Ministry of Justice, 2009b). It is even possible that the prison population will increase at an even faster rate than it did under the last Labour administration given the Conservative proposals to increase the sentencing powers of magistrates' courts from six to 12 months and to introduce 'honesty in sentencing', ending automatic early release from prison and obliging judges to hand down clearly specified minimum and maximum sentences. In addition, there is to be a 'presumption to prison' for anyone convicted of a 'knife crime' (Cameron, 2008). At the time of writing in July 2010 it is unclear how exactly 'knife crime', an unofficial crime category, will be defined by the new government. If defined widely to include offences of simply carrying a knife, there is a distinct possibility that tough new legislation on knife crime will result in the incarceration of increasing numbers of people and the further criminalisation of young people.

Furthermore, the new coalition government's plans to introduce a 'rehabilitation revolution' do not entail significant spending increases but rather focus on the need to pursue the New Labour policy of contracting out rehabilitation services to the private and voluntary sectors. As under New Labour, there is a danger that concerns for offender welfare will be subsumed under concerns about neutralising the immediate risk posed by offenders, particularly since bodies responsible for providing rehabilitation services will be paid on results, namely their capacity to reduce reoffending. This may lead to a situation whereby organisations competing for contracts to provide services only wish to take on the 'easiest' cases involving offenders who are least likely to reoffend in the first place, thus excluding the most 'difficult' cases, i.e. the offenders most likely to reoffend, from certain forms of assistance and treatment. The consequences are serious for both offenders and the wider public.

Conservative attempts to tackle the causes of crime may also founder on account of the party's extremely narrow definition of these causes. The 2010 manifesto focused primarily on the need to tackle alcohol abuse, via changes to the tax and licensing laws, and to pursue early intervention measures such as 'grounding orders' (Conservative Party, 2010). A similar focus is evident in the new coalition government's official policy on crime and policing (HM Government, 2010). Despite the Conservatives' declared desire not to criminalise young people unnecessarily, there is a strong possibility that these grounding orders, which enable the police to circumvent the procedure necessary to have an ASBO imposed and to immediately 'ground' a young person at home for up to one month except during school hours, will lead to even more young people coming into contact with the criminal justice system. Such orders will be even easier to obtain than ASBOs, yet they will have similar consequences: youths who breach their curfews may face prison sentences. Some tabloids have consequently suggested that the Conservative approach has moved from that of 'hug a hoodie' to 'mug a hoodie' (Walters, 2009). Despite the sensationalist headline, it does appear that the Conservatives have indeed moved away from an approach which focuses on the need to tackle the causes of offending behaviour, as exemplified in the 'hug a hoodie' speech (if indeed such an approach was ever dominant), to one which focuses primarily on enforcing the individual responsibility of young people and their parents. Former Shadow Home Secretary, Chris Grayling, echoed such a change in focus, declaring, 'It's time we spent a bit more time worrying about the wrongs in our society, and a bit less about the rights of those who are disrupting it' (Grayling, 2009a). The appointment of Kenneth Clarke as Lord Chancellor and Justice Secretary would also appear to symbolise the new government's desire to adopt a tough approach to juvenile offenders. It was Clarke who initially asked Home Office officials in 1992 to develop tough new measures to deal with persistent juvenile offenders, thus prompting the creation of the Secure Training Order by the *Criminal Justice and Public Order Act 1994* and permitting the incarceration of children aged between 12 and 15 in specialised Secure Training Centres.

For the Conservatives, the causes of crime lie in the 'broken society', characterised by family breakdown, welfare dependency, debt, drugs, inadequate housing and failing schools (Cameron, 2008). The source of these problems is not structural but cultural, grounded in a state which denies personal responsibility and 'a concept of moral choice' (*ibid.*). As Cameron explained, 'Of course, circumstances – where you are born, your neighbourhood, your school, and the choices your parents make – have a huge impact. But social problems are often the consequence of the choices that people make' (*ibid.*). 'Compassionate conservatism' is therefore about enabling individuals to make their own moral choices and to take responsibility for their own lives. Such an approach precludes policies designed to tackle the structural causes of crime, such as social inequalities.

This focus on individual responsibility for crime is clearly reflected in the party's belief in the effectiveness of deterrent sentencing and the need to send 'strong signals' to potential offenders by toughening up sentences and nipping crime in the bud. David Cameron, along with other senior party members such as Chris Grayling, has declared his support for New York-style zero-tolerance policing which clamps down hard on minor acts of anti-social behaviour and crime in an attempt to prevent more serious crime from occurring (Cameron, 2006c; Grayling, 2009b). It is not just individual offenders who are responsibilised here but whole communities who are invited to form part of the 'neighbourly society' in which 'adult members provide their young with a proper start in life' and thereby ensure the continuation of 'a cycle of responsibility' (Letwin, 2002). As highlighted above, a similar approach adopted by New Labour helped to demonise offenders, leading to their exclusion from the community rather than their reintegration. Yet, the Conservative Party has justified its own tough measures on crime as forming an approach to social problems characterised by 'competent authoritarianism' as opposed to the 'incompetent authoritarianism' of the Labour Party (Conservative Party, 2008).

'Incompetent authoritarianism', it is explained, has meant the simultaneous rise in the number of new criminal offences created and in violent crime, as well as the rise in the prison population in the absence of prison places and adequate rehabilitation efforts (*ibid.*, p. 10). 'Competent authoritarianism', on the other hand, presumably effectively cuts crime and recidivism rates. Thus, tough measures with regard to sentencing are justified, as are plans to extend police powers, enabling police to stop and question suspects without needing to make a written record and reducing the number of situations in which the police have to obtain permission for surveillance operations under the *Regulation of Investigatory Powers Act 2000* (Conservative Party, 2010). Such an approach may appear to contradict the coalition government's declared commitment to civil liberties, symbolised by its promise to introduce a 'Freedom Bill', scrapping the previous New Labour government's plan to introduce ID cards and ensuring that only those people convicted of a crime will have their personal details stored on the DNA database (*ibid.*). Yet, whilst respect for the civil liberties of the innocent is considered as sacrosanct, the Conservatives show somewhat less respect for the civil liberties of those suspected of having committed a crime. They have promised to repeal the *Human Rights Act 1998* which they claim has rendered the fight against crime more difficult by protecting the human rights of criminals. For example, Cameron has railed against the fact that Article 8 protecting the right to respect for privacy and family life has prevented the police from publishing 'wanted' posters featuring photographs of foreign ex-prisoners 'on the run' (Cameron, 2006d). More significantly, the Conservatives' plans to toughen up sentencing may restrict the civil liberties of offenders for longer than may be necessary to protect the public from serious harm. 'Grounding orders' may restrict the civil liberties of young people who have not even committed a criminal offence. In addition, rather than repealing legislation which has led to the blurring of the boundaries between the civil and the criminal law and the rise of out-of-court justice, the coalition government plans to extend the arsenal already available to the police, reducing 'time-wasting bureaucracy' and amending the health and safety laws that 'stand in the way of common sense policing' (HM Government, 2010).

In many respects therefore, Conservative policy on law and order would seem to share more similarities than differences with that of their New Labour predecessors. It may even go further towards the intensification of punishment. The prison population is likely to increase as some sentences are made longer and early release is limited. Despite the Conservatives' support for community sentences, they believe that they should not be used to reduce the prison population and they have promised to toughen up enforcement even more than is already the case (Conservative Party, 2008) – this may lead to an increase in the number of receptions into prison for breach. Although Kenneth Clarke has criticised current prisons policy which entails 'banging up more and more people [for longer] without actively seeking to change them' (Clarke, 2010), it is questionable to what extent the promised 'rehabilitation revolution' can be carried through in the context of current spending cuts. It is also to be asked whether rehabilitation programmes can effectively be delivered by the private and third sectors which are henceforth to be paid according to results. The government's commitment to the continued privatisation of criminal justice services is likely to lead to further erosion of welfarist priorities (see Chapter 7). The proposed creation of Prison and Rehabilitation Trusts to unify rehabilitation services in prison and probation may undermine the welfare orientation of probation services. Furthermore, there is every indication that policy will be tailored to meet the interests of victims – this is indeed one of the justifications for introducing 'honesty in sentencing'. Finally, given the Conservatives' emphasis on personal responsibility for crime and social problems, it is likely that welfarist interventions designed to tackle crime before it occurs will end up being coercive in nature, thus continuing the trend towards punishment through welfare.

Where New Labour largely followed the punitive approach of their Conservative predecessors with regard to law and order (Downes and Morgan, 2002a), the Conservatives under David Cameron are likely to follow the approach of their New Labour predecessors, thus formalising a punitive consensus. Hopes that the Liberal Democrats, as policy-making partners in the new coalition government, may challenge this consensus would appear to be rapidly fading. Contrary to the Conservatives, the Liberal Democrats promised to cancel plans to build more prison places, to replace sentences of under six months with community sentences, to move drug addicts and the mentally-ill out of prison and into 'more appropriate secure accommodation', and to prioritise offender rehabilitation (Liberal Democrats, 2010a). However, like the Conservatives, they support 'honesty in sentencing', considering that 'life should mean life'. They also support minimum and maximum sentencing (Liberal Democrats, 2010b). Furthermore, they believe that community sentences need to be made twice as long as custodial sentences and that the work required of offenders should be more arduous (*ibid.*). Consequently, it is likely that those who are sent to prison will stay there for longer and that those placed on toughened-up community sentences may breach those sentences and end up in prison anyway. Rather than representing a sign of progressiveness, the plan to halt the programme of prison building would therefore do nothing more than exacerbate problems of overcrowding. In any case, the plan has not been included in the coalition's new programme for government, nor has the plan to replace sentences of under six months with community sentences (HM Government, 2010). There is a danger that Liberal Democrat proposals to have police authorities directly elected and to involve the victims of crime more closely in the criminal justice process (now included in the coalition's programme for government) will render professionals working in the service more responsive to populist demands, thus making them less responsive to the needs of offenders.

In any case, even if the Liberal Democrats did wish to advance a progressive agenda in criminal justice, it is likely that they would run up against opposition from the Conservative majority. It is uncertain how deep the Conservatives' progressive rhetoric on criminal justice actually runs, as exemplified from the caricatured move from 'hug a hoodie' to 'mug a hoodie' policy on youth justice. Moreover, it is questionable to what extent the party has managed to shed the baggage of the past.

Cameron spent his formative political years under the tutelage of the right wing of the Conservative Party, beginning his political career working for the Conservative Research Department from 1988–1992, briefing John Major during the 1992 election campaign, and then briefly working for the Treasury before joining Michael Howard at the Home Office at a time when the latter was attempting to formulate a crime policy that it was thought would easily 'out-tough' Labour on the question of law and order. Cameron himself helped to draft Howard's infamous 'prison works' speech delivered at the 1993 Party Conference (Elliott and Hanning, 2009, pp. 152–3). He has admitted that he agreed with Howard's message, even though he was more libertarian on issues of personal lifestyle choice and disagreed with Howard's crackdown on raves (*ibid.*). Cameron is also likely to be subject to pressure from the right wing of his own party to 'reclaim' what are considered to be traditional Tory issues, such as crime and immigration. Indeed, throughout his struggle from the party leadership to Prime Minister, such pressure was acutely felt (Bale, 2010, pp. 283–362). Furthermore, in a coalition government characterised by compromise and concession, there is a possibility that the Liberal Democrats will compromise on issues such as criminal justice, which are considered to be less important in terms of defining party identity, whilst concentrating their energies on securing concessions from the Conservatives on the 'big issues' of Europe, defence and climate change. This would suggest that the authoritarian consensus in law and order is, for the foreseeable future, relatively stable.

A global trend?

Our study has so far concentrated on punitive trends in the UK but it must also be asked to what extent these trends are global. A number of researchers have suggested that they are. Loïc Wacquant, for example, has argued that punitive trends in the United States can now be detected in Europe (Wacquant, 1999; Wacquant, 2009). Similarly, Garland has studied the existence of similar penal trends across all Western nations which are affected by 'late modernity', particularly the USA and the UK (Garland, 2001a), whilst Cavadino and Dignan have identified similar punitive trends across countries which they define as 'neoliberal' (Cavadino and Dignan, 2006). Other researchers have rejected such theses, arguing that they ignore significant variations in penal trends both within and between different countries (Zedner, 2002; Lacey, 2008 etc.). It would certainly be surprising if there were not national variations in penal trends, given the significant cultural, institutional and political differences which exist between countries which may, on the surface, appear to be very similar.

Perhaps the most striking difference is that relating to imprisonment rates. Although it is often suggested that punitive trends in Europe emulate those found in the United States, the USA stands alone in terms of its extraordinarily high rate of imprisonment which surpasses that of any other country in the world. Indeed, the United States is often considered as the example *par excellence* of the punitive turn, not just on account of its high imprisonment rates, but also due to its adoption of harsh and disproportionate sentencing policies and its tendency towards the exclusion and public humiliation of offenders (Garland, 2001a; Wacquant, 2009). As noted above, the USA currently imprisons 2.3 million people and has an imprisonment rate of 753 people per 100,000, almost five times higher than the imprisonment rate of England and Wales (ICPS, 2010). These figures should not, however, blind us to the fact that imprisonment rates vary considerably within the United States, with southern states generally resorting to imprisonment more frequently than those in the north and east (Newburn, 2009, pp. 238–9). Similarly, there are considerable variations in imprisonment rates within Europe. The highest imprisonment rate in the European Union is currently to be found in Latvia where there are 319 people imprisoned per 100,000 of the total population, whilst the lowest is to be found in Slovenia where there are just 65 people imprisoned per 100,000 (ICPS, 2010).

It has been suggested that the United States is somewhat exceptional as a Western democracy on account of its continued use of the death penalty (Newburn, 2009). The practice certainly sets it apart from Europe where opposition to the death penalty forms a distinct part of European identity and serves as a reminder of its commitment to human rights (Girling, 2006). Garland, however, argues that capital punishment is simply 'a residual continuation of a penalty that was once standard in every Western nation', suggesting that distinctiveness is down to 'timing not trajectory' (Garland, 2005, p. 356). He argues that public support for capital punishment is no stronger in the USA than in many European nations and that 'the American way of death is recognizably modern and western', based as it is on the minimisation of pain and legitimised by elaborate legal procedures that seek to avoid arbitrariness or mistake (*ibid.*). In addition, the death penalty is in reality little-used – some of those states which have it on their statute books, namely Michigan, Minnesota and Wisconsin, do not actually use it at all (Newburn, 2009, p. 240) – and it is used more in some states than others: since 1977 over one third of all executions took place in Texas (*ibid.*, p. 241). This would suggest that the death penalty is not as strongly anchored in the American penal system as might sometimes be thought to be the case, thus weakening the case for American exceptionalism. Nonetheless, America is alone in having reinstated the death penalty at a time when most other Western nations were turning away from it (Beckett and Sasson, 2004, pp. 173–4).

There are other points of difference between the United States, the United Kingdom and other countries which show that the punitive trend is by no means universal. A major difference between punitive trends in the UK and the USA is the fact that, whereas in the former country, the punitive reach of the criminal law has occurred as much indirectly as it has directly, via the extension of welfarist interventions, this has not been the case in the United States, at least in recent years. Indeed, as is argued in Part II, it is impossible to understand punitive trends in the UK outside the particular cultural and institutional apparatuses in which they operate.

Within North America, there are stark differences in patterns of punishment. Canada, it has been argued, deliberately attempted to steer a different, more socially inclusive, reintegrative direction in penal policy at the very time that the United States was embarked on its 'punitive turn'. In stark contrast to the USA, imprisonment rates have actually fallen in recent years in Canada; the country remains fundamentally opposed to the death penalty; mandatory minimum sentences exist for only a small number of very serious offences; prisoners are to be sent to prison as punishment and not for punishment; the drug problem is seen as primarily a problem deserving of a health and social services response rather than a penal one; and, most significantly, the Canadian public generally appear to support such an approach (Meyer and O'Malley, 2005).

Punitive trends have also been resisted in other Western democracies such as Australia where American-style policies such as three-strikes legislation have been limited to Western Australia and the Northern Territory and have been strongly opposed by the judiciary (O'Malley, 2004, pp. 37–8). It has been argued that whilst Australian sentencing policy has become more severe in recent years, conditions within prisons have become less punitive (Brown, 2005, p. 35). Within Europe, exceptions to the 'punitive turn' have also been identified in Scandinavia, Germany, Italy and France, amongst others.

Nordic countries such as Norway, Sweden and Finland have long been associated with a culture of tolerance which has translated as a relatively lenient attitude towards offenders and correspondingly low rates of imprisonment (Christie, 2000; Cavadino and Dignan, 2006). In order to illustrate this point, Tonry has cited the contrasting public attitudes to child murder by other children in the UK and Norway (Tonry, 2004a). When two six-year-old boys in Trondheim undressed, stoned and battered to death five-year-old Silje Redergard, the case was relatively under-reported in the media, there were no acts of vigilantism and the mother of the victim even stated that she could forgive the young offenders. This reaction contrasts starkly with the public reaction in Britain to the murder of James Bulger. The boys responsible for that killing were demonised and vilified in the media and, when the High Court granted them anonymity on their release from prison for their own protection, the dead boy's mother circulated a petition against the decision.

It has been suggested that Germany has also been relatively unaffected by punitive tendencies, partly on account of the reverence that is still accorded to professional expertise (Tonry, 2004b; Lacey, 2008). Italy, too, is often regarded as something of an exception to penal severity on account of its relatively low rate of imprisonment and its capacity for the forgiveness and reintegration of offenders, as exemplified by the tradition of the *indulto* (collective pardon) (Nelken, 2009). Similarly, it is argued that France's tradition of the presidential pardon and its use of amnesties are indicative of its capacity for penal tolerance (Tonry, 2009, p. 390; Nelken, 2009, p. 298). Yet, in all these countries, experts have also noted a trend towards increased punitiveness in recent years.

In Scandinavia, for example, rising levels of imprisonment, although small compared to Western nations of a similar size such as New Zealand, might suggest that exceptionalism in an age of increasing 'penal excess' is under threat (Pratt, 2008b). In Sweden, harsher penalties have been introduced for drugs and sexual offences, prison conditions have become harsher, parole eligibility conditions have become stricter and new technologies are increasingly employed in the service of crime control (Tham, 2001). There is also some evidence that penal attitudes in Sweden are becoming more punitive (Demker *et al.*, 2008). In Germany, the launch of the biggest prison construction programme in the country's history, together with increasingly austere prison conditions, punitive political discourse and the increased use of preventive detention are regarded as signs of a return to an older era when concerns for public protection overrode those for the social reintegration of offenders (Salle, 2010). Since 2003, preventive detention has even been available for juvenile offenders, although it is only used in a small minority of cases (Kury *et al.*, 2009, pp. 71–2). Both legislation and prison sentences have been toughened up in recent years, although not to such a significant extent as in the USA or the UK (*ibid.*). In Italy, too, the criminal law has been rendered stricter under the administrations of both Romano Prodi and Silvio Berlusconi (Cortellessa, 2008; Cavadino and Dignan, 2006). The case of France has been particularly striking in this respect.

Although a more punitive direction in penal policy in France could already be detected in the 1980s under the left/right Mitterrand/Chirac 'cohabitation' which marked the start of a significant rise in the prison population (Kensey and Tournier, 1999, p. 98), it is only since 2002 that policy has become markedly more punitive. Recent times have seen politicians adopt an increasingly 'tough' line on law and order, reflected in the proliferation of penal legislation. In September 2002, Dominique Perben (Justice Minister from 2002 to 2005) introduced a controversial law (*la loi d'orientation et de programmation pour la justice/ loi Perben I*), the provisions of which extended the use of remand for adults and enabled the courts to remand young people aged between 13 and 16 in custody under certain circumstances. In March 2003, under Nicolas Sarkozy's tenure as Home Secretary, the controversial 'law on domestic security' (*la loi sur la sécurité intérieure*) was passed, creating a number of new offences such as 'passive solicitation' (*raco- lage passif*), meaning that women can now be arrested if they are merely considered to be dressed in a certain way or to behave in a certain manner likely to incite others to enter into sexual relations in exchange for remuneration. The sentence for soliciting was increased from a mere fine to a sentence of two months' imprisonment and a fine. Mirroring anti-social behaviour legislation in France, the 2003 law also notably outlawed the gathering of young people in the hallways or staircases of buildings and the use of children for the purposes of begging. Legis- lation in 2005 and 2007 toughened up penalties for recidivists: 'life' sentences for these offenders were increased from 15 to 22 years; 'danger- ous' offenders were subjected to electronic surveillance outside prison; minimum sentences were created for all recidivists aged 13 or over who have committed an offence punishable by more than three years' impris- onment. In an attempt to reduce reoffending, all 'particularly dangerous' offenders may now be subject to additional sentences of preventive detention once they have served their original sentence. Most recently, a new justice bill, nicknamed 'LOPSI II' (*la loi d'orientation et de program- mation pour la performance de la sécurité intérieure*), proposed introducing curfews for minors aged under 13, increasing sentence lengths for crimes committed against vulnerable people, and further widening police powers.

The parallels with current sentencing trends in the UK and the United States are striking, not only in terms of the legislation which has been enacted but also in terms of the practical effects it has had. The prison population in France, although significantly lower than that of many Western nations, has increased dramatically since 2001 (by 33.7 per cent – ICPS, 2010). As in Britain and the States, offenders are increasingly seen as fully responsible beings, whatever their age or mental capacity. This approach is reflected in the increasingly harsh approach adopted towards juvenile offenders who are, significantly, now officially referred to as 'minors' rather than 'children' (Varinard, 2008). In 2007, President Sarkozy went so far as to suggest that the law should be changed to ensure that even mentally-ill offenders can no longer be deemed to be 'criminally irresponsible'. However, this proposal was never adopted and many punitive measures may appear to be more symbolic than anything else. For example, although there are certainly signs that the welfare model is being eroded in France with regard to young offenders, especially following the creation of specialised penal institutions for children aged between 13 and 17 (*Établissements Pénitentiaires pour Mineurs*) (Lazergues, 2008), the model remains largely intact. In 2002, the *Conseil Constitutionnel* reaffirmed the constitutional status of the welfare approach embodied in the 1945 edict according to which juvenile delinquents should be dealt with by specialist tribunals which must take into consideration the age and personality of each offender in order to determine the measures which are best adapted to their particular needs. Proposals to fix the age of criminal responsibility at 12 in a new juvenile penal code to replace the 1945 edict proved so controversial that the Justice Minister was forced to withdraw the proposal (Varinard, 2008). One expert has thus concluded, 'In France, an ideal of solidarity and consideration of life inequalities still prevail over punitiveness. A commitment to youth re-socialisation endures despite doubts about the efficacy of rehabilitation programmes' (Genderot, 2006, p. 55).

It would therefore seem that despite the punitive direction taken by penal policy in France in recent years, it cannot yet be asserted that the country has taken quite such a definitive step in a punitive direction as its English neighbour. However, it must be borne in mind that punitiveness is a relative concept. Thus, even though a country has not demonstrated such punitive tendencies as another, this does not necessarily mean that it has not experienced an 'intensification of punishment', as has been the case in the UK. Consequently, it might be asserted that the punitive trend is indeed widespread, if not global, despite differences in punitive intensity within and across different countries. What may be regarded as punitiveness in one country may be regarded as leniency in another and *vice versa*. When determining the extent of punitiveness, it is therefore necessary to examine the cultural context in which penal trends occur. For example, UK penal trends may not seem to be particularly punitive from an American perspective, particularly from the perspective of a state such as Texas which still applies the death penalty and experiences extremely high rates of imprisonment. However, in a European context, particularly a Western European context, in which the tradition of human rights is strongly anchored, recent trends are indeed likely to appear to be highly punitive. The widespread intensification of punishment has led a number of commentators to attempt to explain punitive trends by wider global trends. It is to these explanations that the second part of this book shall now turn.

Part II
Explaining Punitiveness

A multitude of explanations for punitive trends in penal policy have been provided in recent years. Governments and conservative criminologists have tended to focus on rising crime rates (Murray, 2005) or the need for politicians and decision-makers to respond to public demands for punitiveness, whilst the majority of academic experts have concentrated their attentions on international trends such as globalisation (Baker and Roberts, 2005), the arrival of late modernity (Garland, 2001a), the rise of neoliberalism (Beckett and Sasson, 2004; Reiner, 2007; Wacquant, 2009), and/or on more local factors such as peculiar cultural and institutional norms (Whitman, 2003; Tonry, 2004c; Gottschalk, 2007; Lacey, 2008; Green, 2009; Newburn, 2009). We have argued above that the link between crime rates and punishment levels simply cannot be proved (see Chapter 1). As Tonry has put it, 'crime does not cause punishment', nor does punishment cause crime (Tonry, 2004c, p. 14). The idea that punitiveness is driven by politicians' desire to respond to public opinion is more plausible. However, as is demonstrated below (Chapter 8), it cannot explain punitive trends on its own. It is necessary to determine why public opinion is resisted by politicians at certain points in time and not at others. It is argued that the role of public opinion can only be fully understood in the context of political economy.

Studies which have focused on the influence of international trends such as globalisation and late modernity tend to highlight the way in which the loosening of international boundaries has facilitated the transfer of punitive ideas between different countries (Baker and Roberts, 2005) and led to the development of a 'risk society' in which individuals faced with new 'ontological' insecurities and uncertainties, such as those created by an increasingly flexible labour market, changes to family structure, immigration or environmental threats (Beck, 1992; Giddens, 1998), tend to become more intolerant of the risk posed by crime. For Garland, the spread of insecurity amongst the middle classes has meant that they have been drawn into a 'culture of control' in which they are more likely to demand that government protect them from crime risks (Garland, 2001a). In a similar vein, Pratt has argued that the 'civilising process' which Norbert Elias (1939) identified as having characterised Western society since the Middle Ages, is today matched by a 'decivilising process' whereby popular fears and insecurities coalesce around demands for harsher punishment (Pratt, 2005). The problem with theories such as these, as Zedner has pointed out in relation to Garland's theory (Zedner, 2002), is that they tend to make sweeping generalisations which may overlook variations in penal trends and penal cultures. They also tend to suggest that punitive penal policies are widely supported by the public, overlooking the fact that public opinion is notoriously difficult to interpret and is not necessarily as punitive as it may appear to be at first sight (see Chapter 8).

Other theories have concentrated more specifically on the link between penal policy, particularly imprisonment, and political economy. In 1939, Georg Rusche and Otto Kirchheimer argued that the prison was developed with the aim of controlling the 'surplus population' that is no longer subjected to the formal controls of the workplace (Rusche and Kirchheimer, 2003). Consequently, when the offer of work is higher than the demands of the market, penalties become harsher, and *vice versa*. The theory was criticised on account of its simplicity, advancing as it did a direct causal relationship between unemployment rates and imprisonment rates (Box, 1987). More recently, Downes has shown that the imprisonment of large numbers of unemployed people has conveniently enabled the United States to reduce its official unemployment rate by between 30 and 40 per cent since the beginning of the 1990s, but he does not suggest that this link is capable of explaining precisely why mass imprisonment occurred in the first place – political and social factors must also be factored in (Downes, 2001, p. 72). De Giorgi has analysed the link between political economy and punishment in the post-Fordist world (De Giorgi, 2006). Importantly, he also goes much further than the Rusche and Kirchheimer theory and includes cultural and structural factors in his analysis (*ibid.*). Indeed, political economy cannot be reduced to an examination of economic indicators, such as the unemployment rate. It is, in reality, inextricably linked to cultural, institutional and political factors, all of which may help to explain punitive trends.

There are many aspects of culture which may determine how a society reacts to those who offend against its accepted norms. Whitman, for example, has suggested that differences between the severity of punishment in the United States and Europe can largely be explained by the different historical experience of the two countries (Whitman, 2003). He explains that whereas countries such as France and Germany consciously rejected bloody, 'uncivilised' forms of punishment in the wake of the Enlightenment in an attempt to construct a more ordered, 'civilised', even democratic society, America, as a young nation, never felt a similar need to build a society based on humane punishment which could help to define it against a more barbaric past (*ibid.*). Tonry has noted that whilst this theory usefully explains trends in punishment since 1975, it does not correspond to the reality of the less recent past in America from 1870–1975 which was actually characterised by the very kind of moderate and humane punishment which Whitman identifies with Europe (Tonry, 2004c, pp. 57–9). For Tonry, recent punishment trends in America can essentially be explained by the harshness of prevailing cultural sensibilities to crime which politicians have responded to out of a desire for pure electoral gain (*ibid.*). He argues that these sensibilities can partly be traced to the dominance of protestant fundamentalism and intolerance (Tonry, 2009, pp. 382–4). Melossi, however, has questioned this link, noting that Italy, where a culture of catholic forgiveness is prominent, has only had significantly lower imprisonment rates than America since the 1950s (Melossi, 2004, p. 92). The question of prevailing cultural sensibilities was also addressed by Pratt when explaining differences in levels of punitiveness between Scandinavia and other Western nations (Pratt, 2008a) and by Newburn when explaining the same differences within the United States and between the US and the UK (Newburn, 2009). For Pratt, the egalitarian traditions of Scandinavia help to explain why these countries were for so long considered to be 'shining light[s] of Western liberalism' (Pratt, 2008a). For Newburn, there is not one single 'culture of control' sweeping across all Western nations, as Garland suggests (Garland, 2001a), but rather different 'cultures of control' which are mediated according to the degree to which a society adheres to individualistic, moralistic or traditionalistic cultures and the capacity of judicial and political cultures to resist punitive demands (Newburn, 2009). Yet, as Garland has pointed out, 'culture' is not an immutable concept – cultural norms are not passed down from one generation to the next (Garland, 2005). In any case, the capacity of these norms to influence policy depends on the extent to which the political process can translate them into action (*ibid.*).

Importantly therefore, whilst focusing on the cultural, Tonry, Pratt and Newburn also emphasise the importance of institutional factors in determining punitive trends. Indeed, it is these factors which evidently determine the extent to which cultural norms may impact on policy-making. For Tonry, it is 'obsolete constitutional arrangements' in the United States, together with cultural and historical factors, which have allowed punitive sensibilities, fuelled by protestant fundamentalism and political paranoia, to influence the direction of penal policy to such a significant extent (Tonry, 2009). These peculiar constitutional arrangements have two notable features which Tonry sees as encouraging populist politics (assuming that populism equates with punitiveness – see Chapter 8). These are the election of public prosecutors and the adversarial political system (*ibid.*, pp. 384–6). Tonry claims that there are 'prosecutors who run for office on the basis of emotional and sometimes demagogic appeals' (*ibid.*, p. 385). Evidently, they may be reluctant to take unpopular decisions. Gottschalk has noted that the election of public prosecutors has made them more likely to be co-opted into responding to the demands of certain interest groups on the peril of being voted out of office (Gottschalk, 2007, pp. 97–8). It should not, however, be thought that judges who are not directly elected by the public are immune to public pressure – this has certainly not been the case in Britain (see Chapter 8). Tonry suggests that a conflictual rather than a consensual political system in America also encourages politicians to give vent to punitive sentiment on account of the fact that major policy decisions are likely to be defined in opposition to those of government rather than as a result of broad-based consult-ation and consent as may be the case in more consensual political systems (Tonry, 2009, p. 385). This is indeed what happens in the adversarial political culture of the UK where the major parties have, since 1993, been engaged in an ongoing battle to 'out-tough' each other on law and order (Downes and Morgan, 2002a). Yet, adversarial political systems alone do not necessarily lead to populist decision-making. Prior to the early 1990s, the majority of decision-making with regard to criminal justice was made within the Home Office which was dominated by a much more 'cautious' and 'conservative' political cul-ture that was mistrustful of new causes such as those of victims' rights groups (Gottschalk, 2007, p. 103). It is argued that these institutional and cultural changes can only be explained in the wider context of political economy.

Wacquant has criticised what he describes as the 'narrowly material-istic vision of the political economy of punishment' in favour of an approach which can 'capture the reverberating roles of the criminal justice system as cultural engine and fount of social demarcations, public norms, and moral emotions' (Wacquant, 2009, p. xviii). Wacquant is certainly correct to argue that recent punitive trends cannot simply be understood in the context of the transformation of the labour market but rather in the wider context of the reconfiguration of the Capitalist State as it moves from the social to the penal management of poverty. Indeed, as Foucault pointed out long ago, penal trends must be seen in the context of governmentality (Foucault, 1975). The notion of political economy, as it is understood here, does not preclude such an analysis. Rather, it is argued that the current model of 'political economy' which has affected most Western nations to differing degrees over the past 30 years is that of neoliberalism and, as Wacquant himself argues, this is a concept which goes far beyond the purely economic to include cultural, political and institutional dimensions. It is therefore a particularly useful starting point from which to attempt to explain recent punitive trends in Britain.

6
Defining Neoliberalism

The term 'neoliberalism' is polysemous. As Gamble has pointed out, 'There has never been one neo-liberalism' (Gamble, 2009, p. 71). The term was initially used in the 1930s by the German economist, Alexander Rüstow to describe the liberal thought which was emerging at the time which was hostile to the state interventionism that had become common in the early decades of the twentieth century (*ibid.*, pp. 70–1). The original use of the term was therefore intended to distinguish economic liberal thought from the 'new liberalism', so popular in Asquith's Britain or Bismarck's Germany at the turn of the century, and from all forms of collectivism, be they Soviet, Nazi or Keynesian (Dixon, 1998, pp. 6–7). It was in 1938 that a Paris conference brought together a group of intellectuals, including the Austrian economists Friedrich von Hayek and Ludwig von Mises, to discuss their ideas. It was suggested that an international centre should be established to promote the renewal of classical liberalism (*ibid.*, pp. 7–8). The idea was put on hold once war broke out the following year but it was revived in 1947 when von Hayek brought together key economic liberals at another conference held near Montreux in Switzerland and the Mont Pèlerin Society was founded (*ibid.*, pp. 7–8). The Society was to be the nursery of neoliberal ideas in the twentieth century, spawning such well-known neoliberals as Milton Friedman of the Chicago School of Economics and Lionel Robbins of the London School of Economics (*ibid.*, p. 9).

The version of neoliberalism promoted by the intellectuals of the Mont Pèlerin Society and those working for the think tanks which it inspired, such as Antony Fisher, Arthur Seldon or Ralph Harris of the Institute of Economic Affairs (founded in Britain in 1955), was essentially a form of nineteenth-century classical liberalism, in the intellectual tradition of Adam Smith, which favoured minimal state interventionism in economic and social affairs. Neoliberalism was seen as an antidote to the welfare state which, as Hayek had argued, could only lead to totalitarianism (Hayek, 2001 [1944]). As Seldon explained, 'There is no constitutional or moral justification for imprisoning people in the hands of government which has not been subject to the test that the market might have done more things better' (Seldon, 2001, pp. 58–9). Neoliberals therefore argued that the role of the State should be drastically reduced so that it may 'concentrate on those things it has to do, to maintain order, to enforce contracts, to help look after those who cannot live in a free-market state because of a permanent disability' (Harris, 2001, p. 63). It was therefore considered necessary to 'roll back the frontiers' of the State, reducing its role to these core functions.

The contradictions of neoliberalism

However, neoliberal politicians found it extremely difficult to translate theory into practice. Margaret Thatcher, for instance, for all her talk of rolling back the State, largely failed to do so. Despite introducing radical cuts to the education and health budgets and reducing the real value of social benefits, public spending as a percentage of GDP continued to rise in real terms throughout her tenure (Gamble, 1994, p. 122). She recognised that radically reforming the welfare state was simply electorally unacceptable (Harris, 2001, p. 54). Ironically, her most successful effort to promote market freedom – the reduction of trade union power – was accomplished, not by rolling back the frontiers of the State, but rather by rolling them forward, increasing the legal power of government to criminalise their activities. In practice, Thatcherism, just like other forms of neoliberalism across the globe, entailed a simultaneous rolling forwards and backwards of the State, resulting in the paradox of what Gamble has described as the 'free economy and the strong state' (Gamble, 1994). Indeed, in order for market freedom to be protected, the State is obliged to step in and provide the necessary institutional structure. Hence, neoliberalism as it is actually practiced rarely corresponds to its most fundamentalist strands which advocate the privatisation of all state functions. Indeed, it would be a serious mistake to reduce neoliberalism to the mere practice of *laissez-faire* (Dardot and Laval, 2009). Neoliberalism is in practice much more than that – it is a *system*, an entire *raison d'être* which reserves an active role for the State as promoter of market solutions and facilitator of competition between rational, free-thinking individuals (*ibid.*).

Under New Labour governments, neoliberalism mutated, chameleon-like, into an even more interventionist form, different from that which had been practiced by the Thatcher and Major administrations. It has been described as the 'social market strand' of neoliberalism (Gamble, 2009, p. 71). It was, to borrow a concept developed by Peck and Tickell, 'roll out neoliberalism' whereby the State assumed a more creative function in order to consolidate the reforms of the destructive, 'roll back' phase (Peck and Tickell, 2002). Hence, there was *increased* state intervention in many areas, most markedly in the labour market and in social policy in a vain attempt to manage the problems resulting from the social dislocations of the first phases of neoliberalism. Yet, given that the power of the State to manage these problems is severely circumscribed in the absence of any political will to control the excesses of the market, government efforts were reduced to those which aimed to make public services more 'efficient' by subjecting them to market logic. This is not so much about reducing the role of government but rather about making it govern more 'effectively' (Gamble, 2009, p. 83). The Capitalist State has ironically become all the more interventionist as it came to see its chief role as that of imposing market discipline and facilitating market solutions which principally benefit the old economic élites. The role of the State has not been reduced but rather radically transformed as its chief function has moved from that of provider of public services to that of facilitator of market solutions (Leys, 2003). In order to ensure that new market disciplines are respected, the State has come to play an increasingly interventionist role as regulator. The professional élites and civil servants who were previously entrusted with considerable discretion in the running of public services and the making of public policy, have been displaced in favour of a new cadre of 'experts', appointed by government to ensure that these services comply with a plethora of narrowly-defined objectives designed to measure 'efficiency'. The 'rise of the regulatory state' (Moran, 2007) has involved a diffusion of state power beyond the centre and further into civil society. The consequence has been a shift from 'government', under which state power is exercised by the State alone, to 'governance', whereby the State now governs in collaboration with a whole new variety of actors from the world of business and finance (Harvey, 2007, pp. 76–7).

Yet, none of this conforms to neoliberal theory with its profound mistrust of the State and of the influence of special interest groups on government. In addition, for all the rhetoric of freedom, the individual is arguably less free than at any point in the history of modern democracy. In practice, the Neoliberal State is 'an unstable and contradictory political form' (*ibid.*, p. 64). It is therefore essential to be aware of the difference between neoliberal theory and 'actually existing neoliberalism' (Brenner and Theodore, 2002) and to avoid conferring too much coherence on the concept. Although neoliberalism is now recognised as being hegemonic and has variants stretching across the globe, from the United States to South America and Asia, it is applied in different ways in different places (Harvey, 2007). This is true even within the United Kingdom. But whatever these variations, all strands of neoliberalism are recognisable by their belief that a free economy needs a strong state (Gamble, 2009, p. 72). So, what is described as 'the chief hallmark of neoliberal thinking' is 'also one of the main sources of its contradictions' (*ibid.*). It is the extent to which the strength of the Capitalist State has grown in recent years, so presciently predicted by Foucault in the 1970s (Foucault, 2004 [1978–9]), which is perhaps also the main source of the novelty in neoliberalism.

Finally, as highlighted above, any attempt to define neoliberalism must recognise it as a complex *system* which does not simply have an economic dimension but also social, political, legal, cultural and intellectual dimensions (Dardot and Laval, 2010; Christoph, 2010). It is to an analysis of these dimensions in the case of the UK that we now turn before attempting to determine to what extent neoliberalism as it 'actually exists' may help to explain British punitive penal trends.

'Actually existing neoliberalism': The case of Britain

Neoliberal economics

The first attempts in Britain to apply neoliberalism as an economic doctrine were made under the Thatcher governments of the 1980s, even though the key tenets of Keynesianism had already been abandoned by Callaghan's Labour government of 1976–79. Thatcher's first term of office was principally marked by her attempts to apply monetarism by imposing strict controls on the money supply, but monetarism was largely a failure, as was made clear by the doubling of inflation by 1983 (Keegan, 1985, p. 208). Thatcher was to be more successful in turning other aspects of neoliberal theory into practice, even if these had not initially formed part of her strategy. Jessop has identified these as liberalisation, deregulation, privatisation, re-commodification, internationalisation and reduced direct taxes (Jessop, 2007). He argues that all of these strategies were pursued, and even extended, under the New Labour administration

Although, as highlighted above, there has been increased government regulation in many areas, namely in the running of public services, deregulation has advanced unbounded in the financial sector, as New Labour embraced the inheritance of the 'Big Bang' of 1986. The power of the financial sector has grown to such an extent that it now represents almost 30 per cent of the British economy (OECD, 2008). This has undoubtedly been helped by the process of internationalisation, which has allowed capital to flow freely across borders in the absence of international controls. One of the very first policies introduced by the New Labour government in 1997 was the granting of independence to the Bank of England, thus allowing interest rates to be fixed by the independent Monetary Policy Committee. This enabled the new administration to abandon the Keynesian policy of fiscal fine tuning, which had enabled post-war governments to promote a policy of 'full' employment, and to concentrate instead on macroeconomic policies which respect the NAIRU (non-accelerating inflation rate of unemployment) – an 'acceptable' unemployment rate intended to keep inflation down. This allows the government to follow the neoliberal Holy Grail of low inflation as opposed to the Keynesian Holy Grail of unemployment. Indeed, although the rate of unemployment was historically low for much of the period over which New Labour was in power, the labour market was rendered increasingly insecure in the name of flexibility and competitivity. The UK government obtained opt-outs from important pieces of European legislation concerning issues such as maximum working time and paid leave. Although Tony Blair signed the UK up to the Social Charter of the Maastricht Treaty and adopted the Working Time Regulations in 1998, derogations from these regulations remain. In addition, in June 2007 the New Labour government negotiated an opt-out from the European Charter on Fundamental Rights, chapter IV of which protects workers' rights concerning negotiations between unions and employers, working conditions and protection against unfair dismissal. The introduction of a minimum wage in 1999 following the *National Minimum Wage Act 1998* did little to reverse the trend towards labour market flexibility on account of the fact that it remains very low at £5.80 per hour for workers aged 22 years and older.

New Labour extended the corporatisation and commodification of the state-owned sector initiated by the Thatcher governments' privatisation programme (Jessop, 2007, p. 283). Significantly, the rewriting of clause IV(4) of the Party's constitution removed the commitment to the 'common ownership of the means of production'. Since then, the private sector has played an increasingly significant role as a government partner in the provision of public services, with the extension of the Private Finance Initiative (PFI), initially introduced by the Major government in 1992. In conformity with neoliberal orthodoxy, PFI enabled New Labour governments to liberalise public markets and, significantly, to finance public spending without significant tax increases on account of the fact that most of the initial investment under PFI contracts is provided by the private sector. Indeed, the whole *raison d'être* of this particular reform was to deliver economic efficiency. As the Treasury itself declared, 'The decision to undertake PFI investment is taken on value for money grounds alone' (HM Treasury, 2003, p. 1). PFI contracts are now widespread: in March 2006, it was estimated that they represented between 10 and 15 per cent of all investment in public hospitals and that there were 500 contracts underway in England alone (HM Treasury, 2006, p. 15).

Yet PFI exposes yet another contradiction between neoliberal theory and neoliberalism as it actually exists. Although PFI contracts have encouraged market liberalisation, enabling the private sector to play a significant role in the delivery of public services, they have not delivered value for money or reduced public spending in the long run. Even in the short term, public spending as a percentage of GDP has been rising since 2000 despite considerable investment from the private sector (Public Spending, 2010). Some studies have shown PFI investment to be more costly than public investment. For example, a report published by the Certified Accountants Educational Trust found that new hospitals financed via PFI cost at least £45 million per year more than those financed directly by the public sector, partly on account of the fact that the trusts which manage them are obliged to pay a premium of approximately 30 per cent of the total cost of construction to ensure that they are delivered on time and in budget (Edwards *et al.*, 2004). In the long term, government is committing itself to continue paying for services under PFI contracts long after they may have served their useful purpose. It is the State which continues to assume the risk of these contracts whilst the private sector picks up most of the profits (Harvey, 2007, p. 77). Nonetheless, PFI has allowed the State, in conformity with neoliberal doctrine, to introduce market forces into the public sector to an unprecedented extent.

The main beneficiaries of all these policies have of course been the economic élites. They have received significant financial gains and been allowed to reassert their power and influence. Successive New Labour governments ensured that income tax rates remained low for top earners. Although the Brown government introduced an additional tax rate of 50 per cent in the 2009 budget, this only applied to those earning over £150,000 a year, and income tax remains considerably lower than the top tax rates of the 1970s (83 per cent). The main rate of corporation tax also remains low at 28 per cent. Indeed, despite criticism from some business leaders, New Labour did what it could to prove that it was acting in their interests. As Tony Blair declared before an audience at the Confederation of British Industry in 1997, 'There is great commitment and enthusiasm right across the Government, for forging links with the business community' (Blair, 1997b). In practice, New Labour forged extremely close links with business representatives such as David Simon, the former Managing Director of BP and Alec Reed of Reed recruitment agency (Anderson and Mann, 1997, p. 41), and business people were regularly consulted on government policy and were even invited to draft government reports. Patrick Carter, for example, founder of Westminster Health Care, a private health provider, authored two key reports on legal reform (Carter, 2003; Carter, 2007).

Meanwhile, the power and influence of the trade unions, already circumscribed significantly by the Thatcher governments, remained severely limited. As a significant step on the road to party reform and modernisation, New Labour reformed the voting system for party leader in 1994, introducing 'One Member One Vote', thus reducing the percentage of votes allocated to trade unions from 40 per cent to 33 per cent. The party also refused to reverse the restrictive trade union legislation of the 1980s which had severely limited the conditions under which trade unions and their members may benefit from legal immunity when they go on strike. The deregulation of the labour market and the negotiation of opt-outs from European legislation on workers' rights helped tip the balance of power further in the favour of employers and away from the workers and their representatives. Successive New Labour governments kept the trade unions at arm's length in the policy-making process, leading Jon Cruddas, Labour MP and former adviser on trade unions to Tony Blair, to comment that there was 'an in-built hostility to organised labour and labour-market regulation from some of those within the Labour government' (cited by Cohen, 2003, p. 232).

In direct correlation with the rise of the economic élites, the fortunes of the poorest declined. The growth in income and earnings inequalities under the Thatcher governments was not reversed under New Labour (Hills *et al.*, 2010, p. 385) and the richest 10 per cent of households are

146 Criminal Justice and Neoliberalism

now 100 times better off in terms of their total wealth than the poorest tenth (*ibid.*, p. 387). It would appear that the introduction of a minimum wage and tax credits for low-paid workers has done little to improve the lot of the poorest people in Britain. The minimum wage remains too low to enable workers to escape from poverty (Toynbee, 2003). Since its introduction in 1999, it is estimated that the number of households in which one person is in work but which continue to live in poverty has actually increased from almost six in ten to more than seven in ten (Cooke and Lawton, 2008). There is a risk that tax credits may simply encourage employers to continue to pay low wages in the knowledge that these will be subsidised by the government (Toynbee and Walker, 2005, pp. 62–3). Although the number of British people living in poverty – defined as having a net income of below 60 per cent of the national median – decreased between 1994–95 and 2004–05, it has been on the rise again since then and now stands at 18.3 per cent of the total population compared to 19.4 per cent in 1994–95 (Hills *et al.*, 2010, p. 46).

'Actually existing neoliberalism' in the UK over the past 30 years has therefore entailed the restoration of power to the economic élites – a defining characteristic of neoliberalism according to Harvey (2007, p. 19). New Labour also followed the key tenets of neoliberal economic policy as defined by Jessop, doing what it could to encourage market freedom. Nonetheless, some experts have suggested that the policy was not neoliberal at all but rather constituted a form of 'privatised Keynesianism' whereby individuals rather than governments were encouraged to take on extraordinary amounts of debt in order to stimulate the economy (Crouch, 2008). In continuity with Keynesianism, governments played an important role in the economy but, rather than assuming debt, their role was reduced to ensuring that individuals would take on debt. The Thatcher governments, for example, encouraged consumer debt via its policy of council house sales, whilst New Labour did what it could to ensure that consumer lending was encouraged (*ibid.*). The most dramatic illustration of such a policy in action has been the recent rescue packages for banks drawn up by British and American governments to ensure that they can continue transferring debt to individuals. Yet, such interventions may also be interpreted simply as the reverse side of neoliberalism, as another example of the Neoliberal State becoming strong in order to ensure market freedom. For all the discussion of the need to regulate the financial sector, very little has in reality been done to limit its freedom, unlike under the heyday of Keynesianism when UK governments imposed extremely strict controls in an attempt to ensure full employment. What Britain experienced under New Labour may perhaps be better regarded as a new phase of neoliberalism rather than as a new phase of Keynesianism – what Crouch has elsewhere described as a form of 'social neoliberalism' (Crouch, 1997). Actually existing neoliberalism under New Labour has entailed not just decreased regulation in the economic field but also increased regulation in the social field in an attempt to restore the legitimacy of neoliberal economics that had been severely undermined by the time the Thatcher experiment came to an end.

Neoliberal social policy

The Thatcherite project to discredit the post-war consensus and to forge a new neoliberal consensus had not become hegemonic by the time she left power, even if a certain number of policies, namely privatisation, financial deregulation and the decline in trade union power, had become so entrenched that it had become impossible to simply turn the clock back to 1979 (Jenkins, 1989; Gamble, 1994). Indeed, many people remained attached to the old politics, 'torn between the old welfare ideal and the new enterprise ideal, rejecting socialism but not yet at ease with the new order' (Jenkins, 1989, p. 378). On account of the formidable opposition mounted by powerful interest groups against the deleterious effects of her version of neoliberalism, her government was suffering from 'a sizeable legitimacy deficit' by 1987 (Gamble, 1994, p. 219). Thatcherite policies were criticised from the very heart of the Establishment, by the Church of England (Archbishop of Canterbury, 1985) and by the universities. It was shown that she had deliberately pursued a 'strategy of inequality', creating a society that was scarred by social divisions (Johnson, 1990; Novak, 1984; Jones and Novak, 1999; Hudson and Williams, 2000; Walker, 1997). Alan Walker explained, 'Rather than seeing inequality as potentially damaging to the social fabric, the Thatcher governments saw it as an engine of enterprise, providing incentives for those at the bottom as well as those at the top' (Walker, 1997, p. 5). Given that neoliberal conservatives, in Britain as in the United States, considered poverty as a rational choice, the threat of poverty was used as a tool to encourage the development of a spirit of enterprise. Yet, far from creating such a culture, Thatcherite policies had rather created an 'underclass' dependent on the State for its very survival (Gray, 1996, pp. 42–3). The introduction of more stringent qualifying conditions for benefits created a poverty trap whereby recipients risked losing benefits as soon as they started earning even small amounts of money (*ibid.*).

By 1990, it had become clear that the riches at the top had not 'trickled down' to the bottom. Instead, the gap between rich and poor had widened significantly. In 1979 the top 20 per cent of earners were taking home 37 per cent of national income, whilst the poorest 20 per cent were taking home 9 per cent of national income (Pugh, 1994, pp. 312–14). By 1988, these figures were estimated at 44 per cent and 6.9 per cent respectively (*ibid.*). Geographical divisions had also emerged once again between the prosperous south and the declining industrial cities in the north and west of Britain (Dean and Taylor-Gooby, 1992, p. 16). Social inequalities were exacerbated by fiscal policy, privatisation, the decline of trade union power, wage policies, high unemployment and reductions in certain forms of public spending (Johnson, 1990). The tax burden for the highest earners was lightened as income tax was slashed by more than half and inheritance and capital gains taxes were reduced, whilst the poorest found themselves negatively affected by VAT increases (*ibid.*, p. 28). Privatisation helped to deepen wealth inequalities between shareholders in privatised industries and those without shares dependent on public services (*ibid.*, p. 32). Meanwhile, the wages of the lowest-paid workers remained low, especially on account of the limitation of the powers of wage councils, culminating in their abolition in 1993 (*ibid.*, pp. 28–9). For the increasing numbers of people without work – the unemployment rate more than doubled between 1979 and 1986 – the situation was even worse. The value of unemployment benefits as a percentage of average wages fell from 36 per cent in 1983 to 28 per cent in 1994 (Lund, 2002, p. 180) and eligibility conditions were made particularly strict. Some beneficiaries – namely young people aged between 16 and 18 and university students – lost their right to claim altogether (Howard, 1997, p. 86) and a concerted campaign was launched against benefit fraud (Andrews and Jacobs, 1990, pp. 164–9).

The aim was not simply to save money, as was made clear by the fact that no similar attempt was made to tackle tax fraud which costs the State considerably more money (*ibid.*). Rather, the aim was to stigmatise welfare claimants and push them towards self-sufficiency (*ibid.*). This was an ideological project as much as anything else: it sought to generalise the neoliberal dogma that individuals, as rational economic calculators, must be left 'free' to maximise their own interests according to cost-benefit analysis. Just as the market was to be subjected to free competition, so were individuals who, it was argued, should be left to compete with each other for access to social and economic goods. The 'responsible' and 'deserving' would succeed whilst the 'irresponsible' and 'undeserving' would naturally and justifiably fail. Just as 'lame duck' industries should be left to go bankrupt, so these 'inadequate' individuals should be left to sort out their own problems. The main function of neoliberal government is to create the conditions in which free competition can thrive in both the public and private spheres, thus ensuring market freedom and facilitating the accumulation of wealth. To the extent that public assistance to the middle classes via *fiscal* and *occupational* welfare (Titmuss, 1976) helps to encourage such accumulation, it is considered desirable. But the limitation of *social* welfare *for the poorest* is considered by neoliberal governments as the best way to help them, firstly by helping them to help themselves and, secondly, because the creation of wealth at the top will eventually trickle down to them.

In order to ensure that the Thatcherite project did not alienate these classes, it was necessary to spread 'popular capitalism'. By allowing more and more people to have a stake in private enterprise and to access home ownership, the Thatcherites hoped that they would themselves become popular. Indeed, the Thatcher and Major governments were acutely aware of the social disorder which could result from their policies and eventually threaten their very legitimacy. Consequently, they attempted to forge a new consensus built on common sense around which the nation could unite. Harvey notes that a similar strategy was adopted by the majority of neoliberal governments at the time (Harvey, 2007). Following Karl Polanyi (1944), he explains that once the concept of freedom is reduced to that of the market, negative freedoms, such as the freedom to make huge profits without giving anything back to the community, are given free rein. In order to avoid the social chaos which might ensue and to guarantee their popularity before the electorate, neoliberal governments aim to forge new social solidarities along different lines, based on religion and morality or on the revival of older political forms such as nationalism or even fascism (Harvey, 2007, pp. 80–1). This may paradoxically entail increased intervention in the social field. In the United States, this has taken the form of neo-conservatism which promotes a very narrow definition of morality, opposing sexual freedom and the right to abortion, for example. In Britain, it took the form of a call for a return to 'Victorian values' and 'common sense'.

The neo-conservatism of the American New Right never dominated the political scene in Britain (Durham, 1991). The Thatcher governments did adopt a highly moralistic approach to certain issues, such as homosexuality, and called for a return for Victorian values in order to discredit the 'permissiveness' of the post-war consensus. However, they often ran into conflict with those who opposed state funding of family planning and moralists who wished to see media pornography and violence more strictly controlled (*ibid.*). The second Major government (1992–1997) also attempted to pursue a programme of moral renewal, calling for the nation to go 'back to basics', to 'the values of common sense', 'to self-discipline and respect for the law, to consideration for others, to accepting responsibility for yourself and your family and not shuffling it off onto the state' (Major, 1993, cited by Ward, 1996). The morality that is meant to underpin these 'common sense' values was never elaborated in detail: it was simply promoted as being self-evident, as something that everyone understood. In fact, these values of 'common sense' were also the values of neoliberalism – as such, they represented an attempt to unite the nation around the neoliberal project and to demonise those who refused to share these values. In this way, the promotion of moral values was intended to serve as a kind of 'social glue' (Harvey, 2007, p. 82).

Yet, this social glue, if it had ever really existed, was clearly coming apart by the mid-1990s. Many of those who had initially supported the Thatcherite project turned against it. John Gray, once an ardent Thatcherite, argues that the project was self-defeating as the middle classes, the very groups that were intended to benefit from it, came to experience the social insecurity that they previously believed was the reserve of the working classes (Gray, 1996). Thatcherism had generated 'middle class pauperdom' (*ibid.*, p. 11). Indeed, Will Hutton explains how the spread of social and economic insecurity during the Thatcher years had, by 1995, created a 30/30/40 society whereby only 40 per cent of the population was living in relative security (Hutton, 1996). The most disadvantaged 30 per cent was unemployed whilst a further 30 per cent was employed in low-paid, insecure jobs (*ibid.*). The resulting social divisions meant that it had become increasingly difficult to find the right social glue capable of uniting the population. Hutton suggested that British society by the mid-1990s was glued together by a 'fundamental amorality' rather than by a sense of morality (*ibid.*, p. 24).

Consequently, when New Labour came to power, it attempted to forge a new common sense, capable of countering this amorality and uniting society together around a common moral purpose. Indeed, in his first speech as Prime Minister, symbolically made at the impoverished Aylesbury Estate in London, Tony Blair raged against the values of the 'who cares' society and promoted an alliance between the 'haves' and the 'have-nots' based on a new sense of morality (Blair, 1997a). This morality was defined as follows:

> What we need is [a morality] grounded in the core of British values, the sense of fairness and a balance between rights and duties. The basis of this modern civic society is an ethic of mutual responsibility or duty. It is something for something. A society where we play by the rules. You only take out if you put in. That's the bargain (*ibid.*).

This notion of reciprocity, of mutual responsibility, lies at the very heart of 'third way' politics which were presented by New Labour as an antidote to 'the wreckage of our broken society' (Blair, 1996, p. 68). In opposition to Thatcher's assertion that 'there is no society' (Thatcher, 1987b), New Labour promoted the idea of a strong society in which individual citizens are linked to one another and to government via a new social contract which requires them to accept duties and responsibilities in return for certain rights. This was intended not just to mark a rupture with Thatcherism but also with the post-war consensus and the culture of 'anything goes' (Blair, 1997a). However, in practice, New Labour's acceptance of its neoliberal inheritance has meant that any efforts to repair the deleterious social effects of that same inheritance have turned out to be little more than what Jessop has described as 'flanking measures' designed to deaden the impact of neoliberalism rather than to counter it (Jessop, 2007). Rather than promoting mutual responsibility, it is individual responsibility which was encouraged first and foremost. This is most clearly illustrated by New Labour's failed attempts to promote social inclusion.

The redefinition of the problem of poverty by the concept of 'social exclusion' allowed New Labour governments to offer a more socially responsible alternative to Thatcherism without challenging the neoliberal consensus. The concept, as it was used by New Labour, focused on the need for the State to responsibilise the poor, thus conveniently glossing over the links between poverty and neoliberal economics. Rather than adopting what Levitas has described as a 'Redistributive Discourse' (ReD) with regard to the problem of social exclusion, the New Labour government tended to invoke a mixture between a 'Moral Underclass Discourse' (MUD) and a 'Social Integrationist Discourse' (SID) (Levitas, 2005). This means that rather than considering that social exclusion results from structural inequalities (ReD), New Labour held that it was the result of personal failings (MUD) and exclusion from paid work (SID). Hence, policy focused on the need to change the culture of the socially excluded and to get them into paid work. Work was valued not only as a means of alleviating poverty but also as a means of instilling certain moral values in the poor. Those who 'refuse' to work were regarded as culturally different from those who work and held responsible for their own exclusion. For New Labour, 'good citizens' were those who work and save in order to provide for themselves and their dependants (Hewitt, 2002, p. 189). In this sense, there was much continuity with the Thatcher governments who sought to reduce citizenship to the ability of individuals to provide for themselves without relying on the State (Andrews and Jacobs, 1990, p. 29). Welfare reform from the 1980s onwards has focused on the promotion of work rather than the simple alleviation of poverty (Becker, 1997, p. 87). This trend is set to continue under the new coalition government: Iain Duncan Smith, the Work and Pensions Secretary, has stressed the need to further reinforce the conditionality of benefits and poverty is mainly understood in the context of worklessness (Duncan Smith, 2010). This ignores the problem of the working poor, thus rendering any policies to address poverty and social exclusion severely short-sighted. As Jock Young has suggested, badly paid and degrading work might actually exacerbate social exclusion as people are simply 'dragoon[ed] from one category of social exclusion to another' (Young, 2002, p. 474). Under New Labour, benefit levels as a percentage of income for those out of work fell from 13 per cent in 1997 to just 10 per cent in 2008, compared to 19 per cent in 1970 (TUC, 2009). It may thus be suggested that New Labour policy in this area was more concerned with responsibilising the poor than with alleviating poverty.

Whilst the Thatcher governments were particularly influenced by right-wing think tanks, such as the Institute for Economic Affairs, in adopting such a policy, New Labour was rather influenced by new left-wing think tanks, such as Demos, and by intellectuals, such as Anthony Giddens, who sought to reconcile a traditional left-wing concern with social problems with neoliberal economics (Dixon, 1998). Giddens claims that few people experience poverty as victims (Giddens, 2000, p. 110) and argues, 'To be excluded is not always the same as being powerless to influence one's circumstances' (*ibid.*, p. 109). Norman Fairclough, specialist in the semantics of New Labour discourse, notes that the same logic can be detected in its rhetoric concerning social exclusion (Fairclough, 2000). He explains that in the language used by the Social Exclusion Unit (which ran from 1997–2006, before being replaced by a smaller task force based within Cabinet Office) and by Tony Blair to discuss the problem of social exclusion, the noun 'exclusion' appeared much more frequently than the verb 'to exclude'. This means that exclusion was presented as a result rather than a process: the omission of the subjects and objects of verbs which might identify the causes of exclusion means that it was presented as a situation people find themselves in rather than a situation which is imposed upon them (*ibid.*, pp. 53–4). The expression, 'to tackle the problem', was used more often than verbs such as 'prevent' which might have suggested that the government could have done something to stop social exclusion from occurring in the first place (*ibid.*, p. 55). Moreover, moralistic undertones are present, even if they are veiled (*ibid.*, p. 58). Just like Charles Murray (see Chapter 4), New Labour clearly adhered to the notion that those who form the ranks of the socially-excluded are culturally different from the rest of the population. Although New Labour never directly referred to Murray, his ideas were incorporated via think tanks such as Demos. As one Demos tract explained, 'There is a place *in changing cultures* for the more powerful tools of regulation and incentives. The proper role of time-limited benefits and tight conditions of active job search and duties to accept certain kinds of offers is *cultural'* (Demos, 1997, p. 62, *my italics*). As noted above (Chapter 4), New Labour largely accepted the idea that an underclass exists that is culturally different from the rest. Hence, the focus of its social policy was on the remoralisation of the underclass, using coercion if necessary. New Labour was essentially attempting to create a particular culture which would allow society to reconcile itself to the market.

Neoliberal culture

The Thatcher governments had already attempted to forge a cultural change which would enable the British to turn their back on social democracy and to embrace a 'culture of enterprise'. As Thatcher herself put it, 'Economics are the method; the object is to change the heart and soul' (Thatcher, 1981). The change was largely to be brought about using carrots and sticks. The carrot was the chance to participate in 'popular capitalism' whilst the sticks entailed punishing those who continued to remain wedded to the 'dependency culture'. The whole project was based on the promotion of 'Victorian' values of enterprise and thrift and the family values that underpinned such a culture.

New Labour's attempt at remoralisation differed from those of previous conservative governments to the extent that it was considerably more tolerant of alternative forms of family lifestyle and of homosexuality. Whereas the Thatcher government banned the 'promotion' of homosexuality by local authorities or maintained schools via section

28 of the *Local Government Act 1988*, New Labour did much to grant equal rights to homosexuals. The *Sexual Offences (Amendment) Act 2000* lowered the age of consent for homosexual relations to 16; section 122 of the *Local Government Act 2003* repealed section 28 (repealed in Scotland in 2000); the *Civil Partnerships Act 2004* allowed homosexual couples to benefit from the same legal status as heterosexual couples; and the *Equality Act 2006* made it illegal for goods and service providers to discriminate against clients on grounds of their sexuality. Nonetheless, New Labour also supported the traditional family, with one Labour peer declaring that marriage offers 'the most reliable framework for bringing up children' (BBC, 2001). Blair once described the family as 'the fountain of morality' (Anderson and Mann, 1997, p. 264). Yet it was a particular version of morality that New Labour tried to instill in families via programmes such as Family Intervention Programmes, Parenting Orders and Sure Start. Sure Start projects, for example, which offer a range of services to families with children under four living in the most deprived areas of Britain, focus on parental behaviour, encouraging parents to stop smoking or to follow programmes to help them to become better parents. The similarity between the philosophy which lies behind these programmes and the moralising discourse of the 'cycle of deprivation' promoted by the monetarist conservative Keith Joseph in the 1970s is striking (Welshman, 2006, pp. 183–203). According to Joseph's theory, physical, emotional and intellectual problems which hold people back are reproduced from one generation to the next regardless of the material conditions in which people live. A similar term, 'cycle of disadvantage', was used on several occasions by New Labour, suggesting that the party also considers social deprivation to result from individual failings rather than structural problems. Nevertheless, New Labour's moralising discourse must be understood not just in the context of its neoliberal inheritance with its focus on individual responsibility but also in the context of its inheritance from ethical and Christian socialism.

In reality, the Labour Party has emphasised individual responsibility throughout its history, even if it has also placed considerable emphasis on the State's responsibility for social problems. It is something of a myth that the Labour Party was ever in favour of 'permissiveness'. Even the reforms of the 1960s which legalised homosexual relations, abortion and divorce in certain circumstances were not particularly radical and merely reflected changes that were already underway in society at large (National Deviancy Conference, 1980). From its earliest days, the party promoted individual morality as a means of moving towards social progress (Nuttall, 2003, pp. 136–7). Just as religious non-conformism helped inspire the Liberals in the nineteenth century, Christianity helped to give the Labour Party its moral focus in the twentieth, leading to the development of 'ethical' rather than revolutionary socialism (Leach, 2002, p. 5). Yet, Christian socialism was to lose its influence as the century wore on, only to be revived by John Smith when he rose to the leadership of the party in 1992 (*ibid.*, pp. 7–9). Smith was a member of the Christian Socialist Movement (an affiliated organisation founded in 1960 which attempted to influence Labour Party policy), as is Tony Blair, Gordon Brown and a number of other important members of the former Cabinet, such as Jack Straw and Tessa Jowell (Seldon, 2005, p. 520). Tony Blair's faith in particular has attracted much commentary, with his biographer noting that 'few Prime Ministers have been so influenced by their faith' (*ibid.*, p. 515). Blair himself expressly tried to link policy to religious belief, declaring, 'We are trying to establish in the public mind the coincidence between the values of democratic socialism and those of Christianity' (*ibid.*, p. 517). It was through the idea of community that Blair attempted to realise this aim and to counter the rampant individualism of the Thatcher years. His Christian socialism was essential to the idea of the 'third way', an alternative means of uniting a society torn apart by the effects of neoliberalism, but one which differentiated itself from a form of socialism which relies on state control. This version of socialism was to be founded on a series of values, organised around a core belief in the importance of society and local communities. 'Communitarianism' thus became essential to New Labour's remoralisation project.

'Communitarianism' is defined by Amitai Etzioni as 'a call to restore civic virtues, for people to live up to their responsibilities and not merely focus on their entitlements, and to shore up the moral foundations of society' via the restoration of strong and united local communities (Etzioni, 1995, p. ix). Implicit in communitarianism is a Christian ethic of brotherhood, capable of encouraging consideration for others (Beech, 2006, p. 189). Etzioni is correct to note that Tony Blair 'speaks communitarian' (Etzioni, 1995, p. ix). Indeed, following Etzioni, Blair and then Brown encouraged 'active citizenship' underpinned by a social contract based on rights and responsibilities. Blair explained his values to the Christian Socialist Movement in 2001:

> Our values are clear. The equal worth of all citizens, and their right to be treated with equal respect and consideration despite their differences, are fundamental. So too is individual responsibility, a

value which in the past the Left sometimes underplayed. But a large part of individual responsibility concerns the obligations we owe one to another. The self is best realised in community with others. Society is the way we realise our mutual obligations – a society in which we all belong, no one left out. And Parliament and government, properly conceived, are the voice and instrument of the national community (Blair, 2001b).

Individualism is thus redefined as a positive value since, it is argued, it is only via the acceptance of individual responsibility as part of a social contract that citizens can best live in society with others.

Yet, with its focus on individualism, communitarianism under New Labour revealed a rather negative underbelly. Whilst some forms of communitarianism may be progressive, New Labour's communitarianism tended to favour 'conditional, morally prescriptive, conservative and individual communitarianisms [...] at the expense of less conditional and redistributional socioeconomic, progressive and corporate communitarianisms' (Driver and Martell, 1997, p. 27). Communitarianism under New Labour was conditional in the sense that those who refuse to fulfil their obligations with regard to the community may be excluded (*ibid.*, p. 37). These duties are widely interpreted and may include anything from the duty of the unemployed to find work to the duty of local citizens to do what they can to help prevent crime in their community. New Labour's communitarianism also showed itself to be extremely conservative on account of its promotion of traditional values such as respect for the traditional family (*ibid.*, p. 38). Despite the fact that the moral values of the community were supposed to emanate from the community itself, these values were in practice imposed from above, using legislation where necessary (*ibid.*, p. 40).

Consequently, rather than promoting inclusion, communitarianism has rather promoted exclusion. In practice, it runs counter to the values of ethical and Christian socialism such as those promoted by the Christian Scottish philosopher, John Macmurray who Blair often cited as a source of inspiration. Whereas Macmurray believed in a right to public welfare, regardless of whether or not rights were assumed in return, New Labour favoured conditionality and reciprocity (Hale, 2002, p. 195). Furthermore, although Macmurray considered individual responsibility as the precondition of freedom, he thought that it should never be *imposed* on individuals (*ibid.*). Such a viewpoint obviously clashes with New Labour's attempts to promote individual responsibility through coercion.

Yet, just like communitarianism, there are several versions of ethical and Christian socialism, some of which are more authoritarian than others. That which is promoted by New Labour seems to have been more influenced by Frank Field (1996) or Amitai Etzioni (1995), who emphasise conditionality over universality, than by John Macmurray or R. H. Tawney. Tawney, who is often considered to be the founding father of ethical socialism, would have been radically opposed to neo-liberal economics on account of the tendency of the market to undermine social solidarity (Tawney, 1920; Tomlinson, 2002). New Labour, on the contrary, considers that the free market is capable of generating prosperity for society as a whole, thus strengthening social solidarity. When in power, it aimed to create what Michael Freeden has referred to as the 'moral market', capable of reconciling market interests with social values (Freeden, 1999, pp. 47–8). The notion that these two sets of values are compatible is expressed in the revised clause IV (4) of the party's constitution which declares the aim of forging 'a dynamic economy, serving the public interest, in which the enterprise of the market and the rigour of competition are joined with the forces of partnership and cooperation'.

Yet, it is precisely this conviction that citizens must be helped to better adapt themselves to the free market (rather than protecting them from its excesses) that rendered it extremely difficult to develop a spirit of 'partnership and cooperation' and to pursue progressive communitarian politics. Paradoxically, it is the focus on individual responsibility which made irresponsibility towards others all the more likely and ultimately doomed the project of social inclusion to failure. Consequently, despite the difference in rhetoric between the Thatcher and Blair eras, a similar culture of exclusive individualism was in practice encouraged. Although the promotion of individual responsibility is evident in the traditions of both the Conservative and Labour parties, the adoption of neoliberal economic policies made this a priority as never before as the extent to which any political party might address the structural problems which give rise to poverty has been severely circumscribed. As Lister and others have suggested, the failure to address the question of the redistribution of wealth rendered any attempt to tackle social exclusion entirely futile (Lister *et al.*, 2003, p. 139). In the face of such impotence, New Labour, like the Conservative governments before it, promoted the values of work and self-sufficiency as the panacea to all social problems. The result has been the further erosion of social solidarity and the exacerbation of social exclusion as what may be described as a neoliberal culture came to hold sway. Although this culture has common features wherever it prevails, promoting rampant individualism at the expense of social solidarity, it should be noted that it has developed differently in different places, like all other aspects of neoliberalism. For example, whilst in the United States it has led to what Wacquant describes as the retraction of the State's 'social bosom' (Wacquant, 2009), in the UK it has rather led to an extension of the social arm of the State. This probably has something to do with the stronger tradition of individualism and mistrust of the State in the United States than in Britain. No matter how individualistic British society may have become in recent years, it still remains culturally wedded to the notion that the State ought to provide a residual safety net for those in difficulty, as evidenced by continued support for institutions such as the National Health Service. Yet neoliberal culture has come to profoundly transform the British State and the very culture of government in a way that has profoundly altered its relationship with its citizens.

Neoliberal governance

The political and cultural transformations which the British State has undergone over the past 30 years did not initially result from neoliberalism. Rather, it was a crisis in the welfare state which initially challenged the legitimacy of the post-war consensus and cleared the way for the development of neoliberal alternatives (Clarke and Newman, 2006). Whilst a number of left-wing critiques were made against the welfare state, focusing mainly on the racialised and gendered nature of the social settlement, it was a two-pronged attack by the forces of neoliberalism and the New Right which eventually won the political and ideological argument. Whilst proponents of neoliberal solutions focused on the financial inefficiency of the welfare state, the New Right seized on demoralising effects of the dependency culture (*ibid.*). Together, these forces successfully argued that the only solution to the problem would be a profound restructuring of the welfare state itself: 'Welfare' and 'State' would have to be decoupled (*ibid.*). Essentially, this entailed stripping the State of the principal function which it had assumed throughout the post-war period – that of providing social and economic security to its citizenry. Henceforth, it was to assume the new role of facilitator of market solutions to both social and economic problems. Rather than politics being driven by social concerns, they instead became primarily 'market-driven' (Leys, 2003). In order to render such reforms democratically acceptable, the institutional change was accompanied by a cultural change which sought to demonstrate the benefits of competition, flexibility, efficiency and public choice (Clarke and Newman, 2006). Indeed, the idea that state power should be delegated beyond the State seemed to resonate with the cultural revolution of the 1970s which demanded greater individual freedom and choice.

By the time New Labour rose to power in 1997, these transformations were already so entrenched that it would arguably have been difficult for any incumbent party to reverse them. In any case, the discourse of financial efficiency and individual responsibility appealed to a reformed Labour Party which had reconciled itself to the market and was determined to forge a new partnership between individuals and the State, based on reciprocal rights and duties. It might be argued that these political changes were not the direct result of neoliberalism at all but rather the result of changes in the nature of democracy itself whereby citizens were demanding to play a greater role in political decision-making. However, these demands did not result in the delegation of state power to civil society but rather in the dispersal of that power throughout society. As is explained in Chapters 7 and 8, democratic demands were rather co-opted in the service of a neoliberal agenda which placed the interests of big business and state legitimacy above all others. Power was not transferred from government to the people but rather into the hands of capital (Leys, 2003).

The transformation of the Capitalist State from provider of welfare to facilitator of market solutions has taken several forms. Firstly, it has entailed various forms of privatisation; direct privatisation involving the sale of public assets to the private sector; the blurring of the boundaries between the public and the private sectors via, for instance, the creation of public-private partnerships; and the shifting of state responsibilities to the private domain of the family and the community (Clarke and Newman, 2006, pp. 27–9). These changes have profoundly altered the institutional framework of the British State as power is now exercised by a diverse range of public, private and voluntary institutions. Rather than the State offloading its power, there has instead been a 'rolling forward' of the institutional architecture of the State in an attempt to consolidate neoliberal forms of government (Jessop, 1997). Indeed, it was essential for government, particularly one which positions itself on the centre-left of the political spectrum, to *attempt* to manage the social fallout of neoliberal reforms by reasserting its role as provider of security. In the British case at least, the Neoliberal State has consequently extended its intervention into the social sphere at the same time as it has been reducing its control over the economic sphere. Deregulation in the market has been accompanied by 'the rise of the regulatory state' as the State has sought to manage the political crisis following the collapse of 'club government' (the term is borrowed from David Marquand, 1988) at the end of the 1970s (Moran, 2007). The rise of regulation permitted government to replace the increasingly illegitimate informality of this system of government with a more formal, standardised and accountable structure which could be sub-mitted to auditing (*ibid.*). Although the lines of accountability have in fact become more rather than less blurred, the power of the Capitalist State has been in no way diminished. The restructuring of the State has merely enabled it to develop new forms of governance which appear more legitimate but actually help to diffuse power deeper into civil society (Foucault, 2004).

Yet, if the power of the State was in no way diminished, the collapse of 'club government' entailed the involvement of an increasing number of partners in governance. This explains the rise of managerialism, exemplified by the contemporary obsession with evaluating perfor-mance in terms of outcome rather than process, and the increasing con-cern on the part of government to respond to popular fears and concerns. The consequence has been the 'deprofessionalisation' of public services and government decision-making as the old public sector élites, namely career civil servants and academics, have been replaced by management consultants. Members of the public have also come to play an increas-ingly important role in informing government policy. Yet, rather than making the institutions of the State more democratic, the collapse of club governance has made them less so as they are increasingly in thrall to capital. It is argued that a 'de-democratisation of the state' occurred under the Thatcher and Labour governments so that politicians could be left relatively free to adapt policies to the needs of the markets (Leys, 2003, pp. 71–3). Indeed, even the legal framework within which state institu-tions operate was modified in order to favour the interests of capital. For example, legislative changes designed to protect private and intellectual property and to limit the powers of state monopolies and trade unions helped to create the right structural conditions for market competition (Christoph, 2010).

Although other aspects of neoliberalism had a significant impact on patterns of punishment, it is argued in the next chapter that the rise of punitiveness in recent years can only be understood in terms of these fundamental transformations of the Capitalist State. In the case of Britain, these transformations profoundly altered a highly deferential culture of government which, until the early 1990s, had been very well-insulated against the cold winds of punitive sentiment. Furthermore, as the interests of capital were accorded ever-greater priority, government became less concerned with providing social security for the population at large and more concerned with providing economic security for a small élite. In an attempt to compensate, it has tended to focus on providing the population at large with security from the risk of crime. Yet, only some forms of crime and anti-social behaviour have been the focus of government interventions, especially as government has joined forces with business in the fight against crime. Finally, as government's responsibility in the social sphere has diminished, the responsibility of individuals, be they criminals or welfare dependants, has been reinforced. Yet, paradoxically, this has been attempted through increased intervention in the social sphere as the Neoliberal State has aimed to coerce citizens into accepting responsibility for their actions. The punitive consequences are evident.

7
Neoliberal Punishment

Although it is advanced in this chapter that the neoliberal transformation of the British State can help to explain its recent turn towards punitive crime policies, it should be noted that there is no inevitability about the link between these policies and neoliberalism. Indeed, some countries, such as Russia and South Africa, have moved towards neoliberalism at the same time as they have reduced their prison populations, whilst other countries, such as China, have arrived at extremely punitive penal policies without embracing neoliberalism (Nelken, 2009, p. 297). Similarly, the rise of neoliberalism in Britain did not immediately coincide with increased harshness in criminal justice policies. Under the first phase of neoliberalism in Britain, implemented by the Thatcher governments, tough law and order rhetoric did not always translate as tough policy measures – indeed policy continued to follow a similar trajectory to what it had done pre-1979 (Faulkner, 1996; Faulkner, 2001). Attempts to restore the death penalty failed, despite them having the strong support of the Prime Minister herself (see, for example, Thatcher, 1987c); young people were increasingly dealt with via cautions rather than in court despite Whitelaw's original promises to provide 'short, sharp, shocks' for young offenders (Prison Reform Trust, 1993, p. 4); and the prison population actually began to fall towards the end of the 1980s (Downes and Morgan, 1997, p. 87). Margaret Thatcher personally granted two prison amnesties which led to the liberation of thousands of prisoners before they had served the entirety of their sentences (Matthews, 2003, p. 226). The *relative* lack of penal punitiveness under the Thatcher governments was partly due to the fact that it took a certain period of time to dislodge the old policy-making élites and consensus politicians who tended to resist punitive trends (Faulkner, 1996; Faulkner, 2001; Ryan, 2003; Loader, 2006a; Farrall and Hay, 2010), partly due to the delayed social impact of Thatcherite policies (Farrall and Hay, 2010), and partly due to budgetary concerns (Windlesham, 1993). It evidently took some time to change government culture and to implement neoliberal policies across the board, especially as such policies did not have the universal support of all members of government or even of the Cabinet (Farrall and Hay, 2010). New influences, such as those from the world of business, were not immediately able to penetrate into the policy-making process. Furthermore, the crime issue could only be mobilised as a means of addressing the deleterious social effects of neoliberal policies once these same policies had had time to take effect. The New Labour Party was obviously better-equipped than the Conservatives to present itself as an antidote to the worst excesses of Thatcherism and it was to be less ideologically constrained by the need to reduce the role of the State in the social sphere. This might help explain why the most punitive policies only emerged after 1997, even if the 'punitive turn' can be dated back to 1993. As explained above, it was eventually through welfare that the impact of punitive crime policies was most acutely felt. This would suggest that it was not neoliberalism itself which led to punitive crime policies in Britain but rather successive governments' attempts to manage the social and political consequences of neoliberal policies without calling them into question. This is not, however, to deny that there are a number of ways in which neoliberalism can directly contribute to punitiveness. The aim of the present chapter is to examine the 'punitive' characteristics of neoliberalism itself before we turn to a discussion of how punitive crime policies in Britain represent a rather unsuccessful attempt by government to manage social, political and, more recently, economic crisis. The influence of the private sector on crime policy is also examined.

Neoliberal economics and penal rationality

It might have been thought that the Thatcher governments' attempts to adhere to neoliberal economic rationality would have helped to counter trends towards costly crime-fighting policies, such as those which rely heavily on imprisonment. Indeed, as noted above, the prison population fell towards the latter years of her premiership, partly because her governments were under considerable Treasury pressure to reduce public spending on law and order (Windlesham, 1993, pp. 28–9). Yet, in practice, such spending actually increased steadily in real terms throughout a 20-year period running from 1978–9 to 2008–9 (Crawford *et al.*, 2009). But these increases only led to a significant escalation in the severity of punishment from 1993 onwards, suggesting that spending levels on law and order cannot alone explain punitive trends. Perhaps it is more plausible to argue that it is the way in which neoliberal economic rationality influences thinking about crime that leads to increased punitiveness.

Neoliberal economists such as Gary Becker (1968) and Joseph Stigler (1970) argued that all criminals are rational individuals who choose to commit crime depending on the relative costs and benefits incurred. Consequently, should society wish to reduce crime levels, it must increase the relative costs of criminality by rendering punishment more certain and severe (Becker, 1968; Zedner, 2009). Such logic may, at first sight, enable us to explain recent trends towards harsher and disproportional punishment. However, as Stigler has pointed out, disproportionality in punishment, such as we are witnessing today, is not necessarily desirable since 'the marginal deterrence of heavy punishments could be very small or even negative' (Stigler, 1970, p. 527). For example, if the death penalty is applied both to those who commit murder and to those who commit minor assault, there is no marginal deterrence to the crime of murder (*ibid.*). For this reason, and to keep the economic costs of enforcement down, 'overenforcement' should be avoided. Similarly, Becker argued that 'optimal policies' to combat illegal behaviour should be directly proportionate to the gains an offender may hope to receive in choosing to 'risk' criminality (Becker, 1968). He claimed to be resurrecting the ideas of Bentham and Beccaria who, as we noted above, advocated the development of rational, proportional punishment (*ibid.*, p. 209).

Nonetheless, Becker and Stigler's economic analysis of crime may have encouraged excessively punitive crime policies to the extent that it treats offenders as rational, responsible actors. As Becker explained, such an approach 'can dispense with special theories of anomie, psychological inadequacies, or inheritance of special traits' (*ibid.*, p. 170). Such an assertion was essentially a rejection of the theories of criminality which had been dominant in the United States, Britain and other Western nations throughout much of the twentieth century and which tended to focus on the structural causes of crime whilst seeking to enforce the individual responsibility of offenders (Reiner, 2007). Yet, the most influential of these theories, that of anomie, developed by Robert Merton, explicitly presents crime as a rational choice (Merton, 1938). For him, once society conceives of success in strictly pecuniary terms, those who are economically deprived find themselves in a situation of anomie – demoralisation and deinstitutionalisation – on account of their inability to achieve their aims by legitimate means (*ibid.*). The only pathway open to such people who wish to conform to dominant conceptions of success and thus to reintegrate themselves into society is, paradoxically, to adopt illegitimate but ultimately effective strategies, namely crime (*ibid.*). Turning to crime is thus considered to be a strictly rational response to social need. The social-democratic criminologies which were largely inspired by this theory argued that government had a role to play in addressing not just the problem of crime itself, punishing offenders and enforcing individual responsibility, but also in tackling the structural causes of crime. The conservative criminologies which displaced them, on the other hand, have tended to focus almost exclusively on the individual responsibility of offenders.

The most influential advocates for conservative criminology across the Western world have undoubtedly been the former Harvard professors, James Q. Wilson and Robert J. Herrnstein (Wilson, 1975; Wilson and Herrnstein, 1996). Wilson and Herrnstein went beyond a purely economic explanation of crime, arguing that the decision to engage in criminality is determined by more than mere calculation, but also by conscience (the degree of anxiety offenders might feel when violating rules), by sympathy (the capacity of offenders to put themselves in the place of their potential victims) and by a sense of justice (the belief that we get what we deserve) (*ibid.*, pp. 517–18). These three characteristics which determine human nature cannot be totally divorced from their environment since human nature 'develops in intimate settings out of a complex interaction of constitutional and social factors' (*ibid.*, p. 508). Yet, the focus on these 'intimate settings', i.e. familial and social settings, and on 'constitutional factors', means that structural explanations for criminality are sidelined in favour of cultural factors (Currie, 1998, pp. 57–8). Despite the fact that these ideas proved controversial (see, for example, Currie, 1998; Irwin *et al.*, 1998), they have been influential and were readily welcomed by politicians seeking to dissociate themselves from social democratic criminology (Irwin *et al.*, 1998, p. 36). They first proved most influential in the United States, where Wilson served as a senior advisor on crime under the Nixon, Reagan and Bush Jnr. governments, but they quickly migrated to the United Kingdom.

Margaret Thatcher clearly had a preference for conservative criminology, discrediting the criminological theories of the post-war era as being 'soft on crime' (see, for example, Thatcher, 1979). Yet, as is explained below, these new criminological theories did not influence policy to any significant extent until at least the early 1990s. It was under New Labour that the most far-reaching attempts were made, not just to responsibilise offenders as rational actors, but also to address the *cultural* causes of crime via social interventions designed to remoralise the underclass (see Chapter 6). For Tony Blair, it was necessary to break with the 'social' and 'liberal' consensus of the post-war period which, according to him, placed too much emphasis on the rights of offenders and on the need to understand the social causes of crime (Blair, 2004b). Henceforth, he argued, the focus should be on the promotion of responsibility, using coercion where necessary. Both crime policies and social policies which were aimed at tackling the causes of crime therefore focused on bringing about cultural changes which would force offenders and potential offenders to take responsibility for their actions. The State was no longer to be expected to tackle the structural causes of crime but rather to *manage* the crime problem. Here again, neoliberalism impacted upon penal rationality as managerialist logic began to permeate government culture to the extent that government became more concerned with meeting quantifiable objectives than with effecting the reformation of offenders or addressing the structural causes of crime. The punitive consequences of such rationality have been discussed above in relation to the transformation of the prison and probation services. The way in which managerialist logic, allied with conservative criminology, displaced the old is analysed in more detail below in our discussion of the neoliberal transformation of the Capitalist State. For now, however, we concentrate on how exactly the promotion of neoliberal culture, with its stress on individual responsibility, may have helped to inform punitive crime policies.

Neoliberal culture and punishment

Whilst it is correct to note that neoliberal culture emphasises individual as opposed to state responsibility, one should avoid the suggestion that individual responsibility was ignored under social democracy. Indeed, we noted above that social democratic explanations of criminality never sought to deny the responsibility of offenders themselves. However, as Reiner has noted, social democracy promotes a different kind of responsibility to neoliberalism (Reiner, 2007, p. 18). Whereas the 'reciprocal individualism' that underpins social democracy focuses on *mutual* responsibility, the 'egotistic individualism' of neoliberalism focuses on *individual* responsibility (*ibid.*). It might be argued that New Labour favoured mutual responsibility over individual responsibility in an attempt to heal the social divisions resulting from Thatcherism: such a philosophy might appear to be inherent in its promotion of communitarianism. Yet, in practice, the Party's embrace of neo-liberalism whilst in government meant that it was unable to tackle the economic and social divisions which undermine social solidarity and to favour the formation of a culture of mutual responsibility (*ibid.*, p. 153). The failure of the New Labour governments' programme of social inclusion is noted above (Chapter 6). Rather than promoting inclusion, they instead promoted the exclusion of those who do not conform to dominant norms, using the criminal law if necessary. The responsibilisation of individual communities in the fight against crime and anti-social behaviour has exacerbated this process of exclusion as communities have become defined by a 'defensive exclusivity' (Crawford, 1998, p. 245; see Chapter 4).

Neoliberalism can also encourage punitive sentiments by creating a society characterised by a 'chaos of rewards' whereby financial rewards are distributed in what appears to be an entirely arbitrary way, with those who work the hardest often earning the least (Young, 1999). The feelings of resentment that result are directed not only at those who are placed at the top of the social ladder but also towards those who are placed at the very bottom (*ibid.*). This can help to explain punitive sentiments towards 'undeserving' welfare recipients and offenders who are seen to benefit unjustifiably from the proceeds of crime (*ibid.*). These sentiments are likely to be exacerbated in the context of the 'risk society', characterised by uncertainty and insecurity (Beck, 1992; Giddens, 1998), the formation of which is likely to be greatly aided by the advance of neoliberalism.

In such a context the Managerial State is often expected to perform the role of 'risk manager' (Woollacot, 1998), ironically called upon to manage the very insecurities which it may have helped to create. Whilst neoliberal governments remain relatively powerless to address most forms of social and economic insecurity, they may, however, attempt to address the insecurity caused by crime. As Garland suggests, 'A willingness to deliver harsh punishments to convicted offenders magically compensates for a failure to deliver [economic] security to the population at large' (Garland, 1996, p. 460). Similarly, Bauman notes the tendency of harsh penal policies to raise the popularity of governments which adopt them on account of the fact that they enable them to show that they are 'doing something' about risk (Bauman, 2000, pp. 214–15). Consequently, rather than calming public fear of crime, it is in government's best interests to fan it (see Chapter 8). Yet, this is not simply an electoralist strategy, even if governments do indeed regard punitive penal policies as a way of ensuring their popularity. It must also be seen as a strategy of governance itself resulting from the neoliberal transformation of the State.

Punishment in the neoliberal state

'Governing through crime'?

As the State came to see its principal role as that of guarantor of market freedom rather than as guarantor of social and economic security, it was forced to seek new ways of governing. Jonathan Simon has suggested that the American State came to 'govern through crime' (Simon, 2007). He argues that the collapse of the mode of governance which dominated American politics from Roosevelt's New Deal in the 1930s to the 1960s forced government to carve out a new role for itself (*ibid.*). He explains that whilst America's constitutional structure is unfavourable to the creation of a fully-developed European-style welfare state – notably on account of the separation of powers between regional and national governments and the existence of powerful interest groups – the State's power to punish remains uncontested (*ibid.*, pp. 26–9). Thus, as New Deal-style government was increasingly called into question by those on both the left and the right of the political spectrum in the 1960s, crime emerged as a new area in which government could legitimately exercise power (*ibid.*). He explains: 'Each prison cell built by the state adds to the capacity of the state to provide [a] public good in a way that is beyond any "program failure" of the sort that haunted the projects of the New Deal, such as public housing, school desegregation, and so on' (*ibid.*, p. 157). Simon dates the beginning of an intensification of crime control policies in America to the enactment of the *Omnibus Crime Control and Safe Streets Act 1968* (*ibid.*, pp. 89–94). Importantly, this law was enacted under the Democratic government of Lyndon B. Johnson, *before* neoliberal ideas rose to prominence. Indeed, Simon rejects neoliberalism as an explanation for punitive crime policies in favour of cultural, political and institutional explanations. Nonetheless, it is argued here that it is the rise of neoliberalism in the UK which ultimately led British governments to 'govern through crime'.

'Governing through crime' essentially entails the redefinition of social problems as crime problems. Social problems are thus addressed by government not through welfare and social policy but rather through crime policy. To illustrate his point, Simon cites the continued intervention of government in schools, in families, in work and in healthcare via crime control policies. In schools, for example, metal detectors have been installed, compulsory drug testing has been introduced and students are regularly searched (*ibid.*, p. 208). There has thus been a considerable blurring of the boundaries between social and penal systems. In Britain too, crime policies have come to replace, or at least to underpin, social policies. The *Violent Crime Reduction Act 2006*, for instance, granted teachers in England and Wales the right to search pupils without their consent when they have reasonable grounds for suspecting them of carrying a knife or other weapon. The criminal law has also been invoked to tackle the problem of children who play truant from school: their parents may be subject to a series of laws which may see them punished with a parenting order, a fine or even a prison sentence. As noted above, penal sanctions also underpin social interventions to tackle drug and alcohol abuse and the problem behaviour of young people, as people are increasingly punished through welfare (see Chapter 3). The trend has been exacerbated by the development of partnerships between crime control and social work agencies.

Yet, there is a significant difference in the way that American and British governments 'govern through crime'. Whereas Simon sees the State's role in the social sphere as being increasingly contested in the USA, this has not been the case in Britain. Indeed, whilst neoliberal governments in Britain may have largely renounced their role as providers of social and economic security, they have continued to legitimately intervene in social affairs in an attempt to counter the social fallout of neoliberalism. This tendency was, of course, particularly marked under New Labour, as penal interventions underpinned rather than displaced social interventions. Whilst state intervention in the social sphere has, in practice, been extended in both nations as they govern through crime, there has not been a disengagement of the British State in welfare in the way that there has been in the USA. Although the British State has increasingly seen its main function as securing market freedom by reducing state intervention in the market and adapting workers to a neoliberal marketplace rather than cushioning them against it, the welfare state has been transformed rather than seriously retrenched. Unlike in the United States where it has been demonstrated that low levels of social spending are matched by high levels of incarceration (Beckett and Western, 2001), social spending in the UK has actually increased along with high levels of incarceration and increased spending on law and order (HM Treasury, 2009). Welfare reform in the UK has tended to focus on making receipt conditions more stringent than on eliminating public assistance programmes altogether, as occurred in some American States in the 1990s (Wacquant,

2009, pp. 50–1). If the British State has ended up 'governing through crime', it is not so much because its capacity to govern is contested in the social sphere but rather because reliance on increasingly coercive interventions which focus on individual rather than state responsibility for social and crime problems have enabled it to attempt to manage these problems without challenging the neoliberal policies which may lead to these problems in the first place.

Indeed, no longer can neoliberal governments of whatever political hue resort to the redistributive policies which might enable them to tackle social inequalities, or to the Keynesian economic policies which would allow them to promote full employment. Instead, they can effectively do little more than put sticking plasters over the wounds in an attempt to stop them from festering. As we saw above, New Labour's attempts to tackle the problem of social exclusion amounted to little more than a 'flanking measure' (Jessop, 2007), designed to encourage participation in the workforce rather than to attack the underlying causes of inequality. Similarly, attempts to tackle the causes of crime have been focused on behavioural rather than structural measures, despite the fact that many criminologists cite inequality as a principal cause of crime (Merton, 1938; Young, 1999; Wilkinson, 2005; Dorling, 2006). Neoliberal states can do little more than 'manage' the consequences of social and crime problems. According to Wacquant, the American State has adopted a single strategy for managing these problems, as crime and social policies come to form part of a single 'carceral–assistantial continuum' (Wacquant, 2009).

Governing through welfare?

For Wacquant, punitive crime policies are a response, not to crime and the insecurity which it entails, but rather to the social insecurity exacerbated by neoliberalism. Both crime and social policies therefore target the same populations – the poor and marginalised – in an attempt to control them and to neutralise the threat which they pose to society at large. The 'penal management of poverty' must be understood in the context of the triple transformation of the Neoliberal State which has entailed 'the amputation of its economic arm, the retraction of its social bosom, and the massive expansion of its penal fist' (Wacquant, 2009, p. 4). These first two transformations have meant that poverty can no longer be managed by welfarist measures – consequently, the penal arm of the State has been extended in an attempt to regulate the poor. Wacquant argues that poor, usually black, women have been subjected to increasingly harsh 'workfare' measures which have attempted to force them off benefits and into work, no matter how degrading and poorly paid that work may be, whilst their menfolk have been targeted by 'prisonfare', warehoused in prison rather than assisted by the State. Both strategies form part of the same continuum of control, directed at the casualties of economic deregulation. Meanwhile, those at the top of the social ladder escape control altogether. Wacquant argues that such a strategy is central to what he describes as a 'centaur state' which is 'guided by a liberal head mounted upon an authoritarian body', applying the doctrine of *laissez-faire* to the wealthy whilst the poor are dealt with via 'brutally paternalistic and punitive' interventions (*ibid.*, p. 43).

Such 'brutally paternalistic' interventions are also evident in the UK. Policies adopted to tackle social exclusion may be described as such on account of the fact that they attempt to coerce the poor into assuming responsibility in return for assistance. This is evident in UK-style 'work-fare' in the form of 'New Deal' programmes (there is indeed considerable irony in the application of this term to contemporary Britain) which seek to force the unemployed into the labour market, often condemning them to a life of working poverty rather than a life of dependent poverty whereby they rely on state assistance. Although state aid has always contained an element of conditionality, it is increasingly intended to be seen as a privilege rather than as a right as the very notion of citizenship itself becomes founded on the notion of conditionality (Dwyer, 1998). Only those who 'play by the rules', who accept to assume the duties of citizenship, are to be included in society. For the rest, their exclusion is justified, whether in the ghettoes of inner cities or in prison. Wacquant is right to describe these policies as 'paternalistic' since, although they might appear to have little in common with the paternalism of social democracy on account of their emphasis on conditionality over universality, they do nonetheless imply a considerable amount of state intervention. As explained above, it is through welfare that state coercion has been applied. Perhaps then, we should refer to 'governing through welfare' rather than governing through crime.

Those who are targeted by the criminal justice system are often also the subjects of the welfare system. As noted above, the prison population is made up of whole swathes of the most disadvantaged people in society (see Chapter 1) and it is often the poor and vulnerable who are the targets of penal interventions outside the prison walls (see Chapter 3). White-collar criminals rarely find themselves the target of penal interventions, despite the fact that its social and financial costs to society are considerable (see Chapter 4). There are nonetheless some problems with regarding the criminal justice system as a mere extension of the welfare system, as Wacquant does. Firstly, whereas the welfare system generally aims to remodel citizens in order to adapt them to flexible wage labour, the prison system fails spectacularly in this task (Piven, 2010, p. 115). Prisoners face extreme difficulties finding work on their release, not just on account of their lack of qualifications, but also due to employer discrimination (JRF, 2001). This situation is likely to have been exacerbated by the right given to British employers under the *Police Act 1997* (the provisions of which entered into force in 2006) to determine whether or not job applicants have a criminal record. Even if the prison is intended to serve as nothing more than a warehouse for those who cannot be 'remodelled' under 'workfare' programmes, it again fails in its task. Since the majority of sentences are relatively short – 16 months for indictable offences (Ministry of Justice, 2010a, p. 29) – prisoners are only contained for relatively short periods of time and, once released, they are likely to be even more of a burden on the welfare system on account of the difficulties they encounter when attempting to find employment and accommodation. A second problem with Wacquant's argument, as Barbara Hudson has pointed out, is that it is not only the poor who form the ranks of the incarcerated, but also considerable numbers of sex offenders – something Wacquant himself discusses (Hudson, 2010). This would suggest that the criminal justice system is not only designed to target the poor, as an extension of the welfare system, but rather to target the most visible forms of crime which stir up the most public fear – street crime and sex crime. Wacquant is, however, correct to note that the system does in practice primarily affect the poor whilst practicing *laissez-faire* at the top. This is clear in the failure of governments to effectively invoke the criminal justice system to target white-collar crime.

This failure may be understood in three ways. Firstly, there is no particular public demand to do so. When people are asked what kind of crime worries them most, they tend to cite theft and burglary, violent crime and anti-social behaviour (Thorpe and Hall, 2009). Secondly, it is generally more difficult for governments to tackle white-collar crime: such crimes usually take place behind closed doors; the laws governing business and commercial life are complex and make it difficult to establish a chain of causation between the criminal act and its perpetrator; many such offences are dealt with internally; the burden of proof required for crimes such as tax evasion is usually much higher than that for social security; and the regulatory agencies charged with detecting white-collar crimes are often under-resourced (Cook, 1997, pp. 70–4). It is of course, also possible that there is a lack of commitment on the part of government to tackle such crimes. It is suggested that whilst there has been increased penal regulation of ordinary criminals, there has been decreased regulation of the activities of white-collar criminals, particularly evident in the failure of state agencies to effectively regulate breaches of health and safety regulations in the workplace (Tombs and Whyte, 2010). Sim refers to this as the 'non-governance' of social harms (Sim, 2009, p. 88). This occurs despite the fact that the Health and Safety Executive estimates that two thirds of accidents at work are caused by companies breaching their duty of care with regard to health and safety regulations (Tombs and Whyte, 2008, p. 5). New Labour governments' attempts to address this problem were half-hearted at best. The *Corporate Manslaughter and Corporate Homicide Act 2007*, intended to facilitate the prosecution of companies who breach their duty of care in this way, specifically ensured that company directors would not be made personally liable. Monbiot has suggested that the timidity of the law might be explained by the refusal of New Labour to offend powerful business interests, such as those represented by the Confederation of British Industry or the Institute of Directors (Monbiot, 2006). So, rather than penal policy being used to control the poor as Wacquant argues, it was in practice used by successive New Labour governments to gain legitimacy in the eyes of the business community and amongst the public at large. The new importance accorded to the views of both these groups to the detriment of the old 'experts' of the social democratic era goes a long way towards helping us to understand the intensification of punishment in the UK.

The corrections-commercial complex

It has been suggested, with reference to the United States, that a 'corrections-commercial' complex is emerging whereby a 'sub-government' represented by private interests (such as the construction industry and suppliers of services to prisons), federal agencies (such as the Bureau of Justice Assistance and the Office for Victims of Crime) and professional organisations (such as the American Bar Association) has come to exercise considerable influence over the development of penal policy (Lilly and Knepper, 1993). Schlosser has used the term 'prisons-industrial complex' to describe a situation whereby 'a set of bureaucratic, political, and economic interests [come together] that encourage increased spending on imprisonment, regardless of the actual need' (Schlosser, 1998). The term is inspired by the notion of the 'military-industrial complex', first used in 1961 by President Eisenhower to describe the harmful influence that the defence industry can have on government.

The idea of the corrections-commercial or prison-industrial complex is dismissed by Wacquant who considers that recent developments have little to do with the market and much more to do with the institutional apparatus which binds social and penal institutions together in an 'assistantial-correctional mesh' (Wacquant, 2009, pp. 106–7). However, this notion does not suggest that punitive policies are exclusively driven by economic forces. Although economic forces are important, they are not the only reason for the development of a corrections-commercial complex. The great majority of penal interventions, whether in prison or in the community, continue to be paid for by the State and there is so far no evidence of prisons in the UK having deliberately been sited in economically deprived areas in order to boost the local economy, as has been the case in the United States (Schlosser, 1998). Ideological reasons also play a role and the influence of managerialist logic carried over from the private sector is just as important a reason for increased punitiveness as the part-privatisation of criminal justice services themselves.

Nor does the idea of the corrections-commercial complex suggest that government agents are merely the puppets of interest groups representing business. The theory is not one of conspiracy, as Wacquant argues. Rather, as Sim suggests, following Hall and Scraton (1981, pp. 474–5), the notion of the existence of such a complex allows us to see punitive policies as a 'correspondence of interests' between those in dominant positions of power who share a similar class background (Sim, 2010). Governments in post-war Britain tended to share commonality of interest with civil service and academic élites, both of whom tended to see themselves as the 'platonic guardians' of the public interest, entrusted to govern the country as they saw fit (Loader, 2006a). These élites tended to share a common view that the science of government demanded the application of highly-specialised professional (meaning academic) expertise to specific social and economic problems: politics was above all to remain neutral, impervious to the high emotions of public opinion or to personal whims (Loader, 2006a, pp. 568–70; Clarke and Newman, 2006, pp. 4–8). These élites shared a common interest in preserving their (relatively privileged) professional status.

With the 'rise of the public voice' (Ryan, 2004) and the crisis of legitimacy experienced by the welfare state, this peculiar way of conducting politics imploded (Clarke and Newman, 2006, pp. 8–13). The old élites were gradually replaced by a whole range of new 'experts', ready to apply managerial rather than technocratic solutions to social problems. As the Neoliberal State came to see its primary role as that of facilitator of market solutions rather than as guarantor of social and economic security, it welcomed business representatives into government as decision-making partners. Both parties shared an interest in applying market solutions wherever possible. For example, the commodification of public services provided a significant financial opportunity for private business whilst enabling government to preach the discourse of modernisation and to claim to be reducing the cost to the public purse (even if this did not actually occur). In terms of criminal justice, both parties benefited in this way when criminal justice services were opened up to contestability. In addition, tackling the highly visible forms of crime and anti-social behaviour which are perceived to threaten business both helped to protect business interests and enabled the New Labour government to be seen to be responding to the kind of behaviour which most worries the public. It should not be forgotten that a key plank of the Labour Party's transformation from 'old' to 'new' Labour entailed the forging of close links with the business community in an attempt to gain a wider support base and to prove its competence in economic matters. We shall now examine precisely how the increasing 'correspondence of interests' between business representatives and government helped punitive ideas to be translated into practice. Our penultimate chapter focuses on the role played by other actors in the policy-making process: the public, the media and the judiciary.

i) The decline of the 'experts'

The experts who dominated penal policy-making up until the early 1990s were concentrated in a tightly-knit circle, concentrated within the Home Office itself, in academic institutions (such as the Cambridge Institute for Criminology, founded in 1959), in a number of advisory bodies (such as the Advisory Council on the Penal System which ran from 1966 to 1980) and in 'moderate' pressure groups for penal reform such as the Howard League (Morgan, 1979; Ryan, 2003). They formed 'a relatively small, male metropolitan élite' (Ryan, 2005, p. 16), the members of which shared a common view of both how policy should be formulated and the detail of policy itself. The 'liberal' consensus they formed tended to promote a progressive view of criminal justice aimed principally at encouraging the rehabilitation of offenders. It certainly did not deny the importance of reinforcing individual responsibility and those who supported it were deeply worried about the weakening of moral controls at all levels of society (Reiner, 2009, pp. 11–14). Nonetheless, the consensus reflected a profound optimism in the capacity of the State to tackle the social problems of which crime was but one manifestation. It was a cross-party consensus, generally supported by both the Labour and the Conservative parties. Although the experts sometimes ran into conflict with government, with the Howard League for example seeing its proposals for shorter sentences for young people rejected (Ryan, 1978, p. 49), disagreements tended to focus on methods rather than objectives and on the speed of change rather than its direction (Morris, 1989, p. 162).

This consensus was soon, however, to run into difficulties as such an elitist way of decision-making was gradually discredited in favour of more open forms of decision-making which appeared to be more receptive to public opinion (Ryan, 2003; see Chapter 8). Yet, the consensus remained in place right up until the early 1990s with the arrival of Michael Howard at the Home Office. The 'punitive turn' of 1993 coincided with the distancing of the old decision-making élites. Stephen Shaw, the former director of the Prison Reform Trust, commented,

> There was a period between 1979 and 1981, with Willie Whitelaw as Home Secretary with an agenda of opening up the prison system, when there was a feeling that one could achieve something. However, the high point of the lobbies' influence was from the late 80s [...] when Douglas Hurd went to the Home Office, through Strangeways, the Woolf Report, the 1991 White Paper, up to Kenneth Clark. When Michael Howard was Home Secretary he would have happily towed the prisons lobby out to sea and sunk us, if he thought we were important enough to sink [...] which he didn't (cited in Wilson, 2001, p. 141).

Indeed, following the Strangeways riots in 1990, the penal reform lobby contributed to a considerable extent to the drafting of the Woolf Report but, as the 1990s wore on, they found themselves increasingly excluded from the policy-making process. For example, their opposition to the construction of private prisons was entirely ignored.

Although the 'rise of the public voice' was undoubtedly important, this sudden u-turn in policy-making can also be partly explained by the rise of the 'managerial state' in which concerns for costs and efficiency had become paramount (Clarke and Newman, 2006, pp. 34–55). The new State required a whole new army of experts trained specifically for performing tasks such as auditing. Consequently, the old experts were either displaced in favour of new ones or forced to adapt to accept the new managerialist culture which regards 'progress' not as the capacity to 'solve' social problems but rather as the capacity to respond to customer needs, to empower staff and to deliver quality services (*ibid.*, p. 37). In the criminal justice system itself, the career civil servants were replaced by professionals seconded in from the world of business. Perhaps the most striking example of this change was the appointment of Derek Lewis, former Chief Executive and Chairman of the Board of Management of the media group Grenada Group Plc., as the first director of the Prison Service when it became a 'Next Steps Agency' of government (this meant that the Service would henceforth be headed by a director general chosen by open competition who would look after its day-to-day operation, whilst government would remain responsible for policy). As mentioned above, those with experience of the private sector were also invited to develop policy, as was the case of Lord Carter. Of course, the old experts were not forced out completely, but their influence significantly declined from this point onwards as managerialist concerns came to dominate the policy-making process.

ii)   *The influence of managerialism*

Managerialism, with its emphasis on measuring performance results against objectives, should in theory go hand-in-hand with evidence-based policy-making. Indeed, when New Labour came to power it declared itself to be in favour of evidence-based policy-making. It spent more money than ever before on criminological research: between 1998/99 and 2000/01, the budget of the Research Development and Statistics Department was increased by 500 per cent from £2,754,000 to £17,013,000 (Hillyard *et al.*, 2004, p. 372). The Crime Reduction Programme, described as 'the most comprehensive, systematic and far-sighted initiative ever undertaken by a British government to develop strategies for tackling crime' (Maguire, 2004, p. 214), was established to develop a series of crime-fighting initiatives based on rigorous scientific evaluation. Many researchers hoped that the new government would once again give them a privileged place in the policy-making process (Hope, 2004). They were soon disillusioned. Whilst the Home Office ordered numerous studies, it seems that it only chose to publish those which came out in favour of government policy (Maguire, 2004, p. 229). For example, Tim Hope, a university researcher appointed to carry out an assessment of the New Labour government's Reducing Burglary Initiative, explains how his conclusions were manipulated by the Home Office (Hope, 2004). He notes that only the conclusions which showed that government initiatives had contributed to a reduction in the number of burglaries were published whilst those which showed the reverse were suppressed (*ibid.*). Rod Morgan has recounted the difficulties he encountered in having Youth Justice Board research published which did not show government programmes in a wholly favourable light (Morgan, 2008b). Perhaps the most striking example of government attempts to take control of the research agenda was former Home Secretary, Alan Johnson's decision to dismiss Professor David Nutt, chairman of the Advisory Council on the Misuse of Drugs, after he publicly claimed that alcohol was more harmful than many illegal drugs such as LSD, Ecstasy and cannabis and accused the Brown government of distorting and devaluing the research evidence on the matter.

According to Mike Maguire, academic experts now find themselves up against a performance culture which favours short-term solutions (Maguire, 2004). Consequently, more fundamental questions, such as those which address the underlying causes of crime, do not attract government attention. Reece Walters confirms that experts other than criminologists find themselves more welcome in Home Office circles: economists, physicists and psychologists, who are considered better qualified to carry out statistical and quantitative analyses (Walters, 2005, pp. 6–7). There was a clear preference on the part of New Labour governments for 'administrative criminology', which treats criminals as rational actors and seeks to manage the crime problem rather than to search for the underlying causes of crime, over 'critical criminology' which tends to focus more on the structural context in which crime occurs (Young, 1988; Walters, 2003). Zedner notes that much of the literature produced by the Home Office under the New Labour governments 'declares itself singularly uninterested in why people turn to crime in the first place', thus reflecting an economic analysis of crime which treats criminals as rational actors (Zedner, 2009). Literature which focuses on the structural causes of crime is considered to be largely irrelevant, as David Blunkett, the former Home Secretary has complained (Blunkett, 2010). He criticises the academic community as a whole for producing research that 'doesn't have clear and implementable conclusions' (*ibid.*). Critical criminological research is considered in this light. Blunkett describes the Centre for Crime and Justice Studies, an independent research group which contributes much to the current debate about crime, as being 'more like a think tank', 'like a propaganda unit' than an academic unit (*ibid.*).

Many academic criminologists have themselves been forced to bend to managerialist concerns as efficiency imperatives have been transposed from the world of business into the field of research. The impact of the Research Assessment Exercise, implemented in British universities since 1986, has stifled radical and critical criminology, encouraging researchers to produce uncritical research which has more chance of attracting public funding (Hillyard *et al.*, 2004, pp. 379–82). Researchers tend to censure their own work in an attempt to conform to the government's research agenda and to win lucrative research contracts (Morgan, 2008b). It would thus appear that, despite the official rhetoric on the need to promote evidence-based policy-making, policy is in reality determined by political considerations. 'Evidence' has itself become a political construct.

In terms of practical policy, managerialist concerns have led to increased punitiveness despite the fact that it might be thought that such concerns should militate against costly solutions to the crime problem, such as prison, and therefore mitigate punitive trends. Regardless of the technical and amoral appearance of managerialism, its logic is far from neutral. As Cavadino and Dignan have commented, it may be influenced by punitive strategies, resulting in what they have termed 'punitive managerialism' (2006, p. xiii). They suggest that concerns about efficiency and cost-effectiveness might undermine concerns for human rights (*ibid.*, p. 122), as is illustrated below in the case of private prisons. Furthermore, the logic of managerialism tends to represent victims as a consumers of criminal justice services (Rock, 2004, pp. 143–6), which may accord more legitimacy to their demands for ever-tougher sentences. Indeed, Loader suggests that it was this very tendency on the part of New Labour governments to respond to the demands of dissatisfied *consumers*, rather than to encourage a meaningful dialogue with *citizens* about the crime problem, that resulted in harsh penal policies (Loader, 2006b). Lacey also suggests that it was the same desire to satisfy 'clients' of the criminal justice system which led the Major governments to renege on implementing the progressive measures contained in the *Criminal Justice Act 1991* – after all, she writes, 'the customer is always right' (Lacey, 1994, p. 551). It is the same logic which presents the victim as a consumer of criminal justice services which leads to the dehumanisation of the offender: as Garland suggests, an amoral and technological approach to social order erodes the ideal of solidarity and can easily lead to policies of exclusion (Garland, 2001a, p. 183).

Managerialist concern with risk assessment as a quantifiable objective has also led to punitiveness in a number of ways. It has informed the decision to limit parole and eroded the principle of proportionality in sentencing as offenders are increasingly incarcerated for the risk they might pose as much as for the offence they have committed (Chapter 1). It has led to the blurring of the boundaries between the civil and the criminal law as merely risky behaviour has become redefined as criminal behaviour (Chapter 2). It has encouraged the proliferation of social and penal interventions with regard to children and young people in an attempt to nip risky behaviour in the bud (Chapter 3). It has made rehabilitation programmes, both inside and outside prison, principally utilitarian, concerned more with managing the risk posed by offenders than with bringing about qualitative behavioural changes (Chapter 3). At the same time, the role of the probation officer has been trans- formed from that of a social worker to a risk manager (Chapter 3). Finally, it has led to the extension of surveillance outside the prison walls and deeper than ever before into civil society, ensuring that 'risky' populations are constantly watched and monitored (Chapter 4).

The influence of managerialist concerns is also evident in the focus on quantifiable targets in the criminal justice system, such as the number of offences brought to justice. Rod Morgan has demonstrated that the increased use of summary justice, one of the indicators of increased puni- tiveness discussed above, has partly been driven by New Labour gov- ernments' drive to increase the number of offences brought to justice (Morgan, 2008a). Indeed, it is likely that police may use PNDs in inappro- priate circumstances in an attempt to meet government performance targets (*ibid.*, p. 19). The need to meet quantifiable targets has also led to a move towards 'situational crime prevention' which focuses on reducing the opportunities for crime rather than on tackling structural causes. It is obviously much easier to measure the effects of policies such as the increased installation of domestic security systems on burglary rates than the impact of reduced inequalities on specific kinds of crime rate. The penetration of such logic into crime policy has the potential to render policy more punitive on account of the fact that it promotes a view of criminals as rational actors who are wholly responsible for their actions. We shall now focus our attentions on the specific ways in which the privatisation of certain criminal justice services has led to increased punitiveness.

iii)   *Privatising the prison estate*

Prison privatisation is not entirely new. Indeed, up until the opening of the very first national prison in 1816 (HMP Millbank), the State did nothing more than provide prison buildings and structural main- tenance services – the system was largely managed by private individuals hoping to secure maximum profit (McConville, 1981, p. 8). Even after the prison service was nationalised in 1877, the private sector con- tinued to be involved in prison construction, in the provision of locks and bolts and other essential materials (Ryan, 1994, p. 14). As Roger

Matthews suggests, it would therefore be more appropriate to describe recent trends towards privatisation as 're-privatisation' (Matthews, 1989, p. 3). Yet, contrary to in the eighteenth century and before, the British State still retains overall control of the system and only 11 out of 138 penal establishments in England and Wales have been contracted-out to the private sector. Nonetheless, from the 1990s onwards, private interests have had an increasingly important influence over the British penal system. It is argued here that, along with the influence of managerialist concerns, this development has helped to exacerbate the 'pains of imprisonment' in UK prisons.

Although privatisation was accelerated under the New Labour governments, the groundwork had already been prepared by previous Conservative governments. In 1970, the Heath government signed a contract with Securicor (now G4S) to manage the first immigration detention centres constructed in Britain's four major airports (Jones and Newburn, 2005, p. 63). Then, in 1987, a Home Affairs Select Committee appointed to examine the penal system in England and Wales recommended that 'the Home Office should, as an experiment, enable private sector companies to tender for the construction and management of custodial institutions' (Home Office, 1987). A White Paper published the following year recommended that the Conservative government allow private companies to manage remand centres (Home Office, 1988). Finally, the *Criminal Justice Act 1991* permitted the government to contract any kind of penal establishment out to the private sector. The first private prison in Britain, HMP The Wolds, opened its doors in Yorkshire in 1992.

Since then, the UK has developed the most privatised justice system anywhere in Europe (Nathan and Solomon, 2004, p. 26). It was estimated in 2004 that England and Wales had more prisoners incarcerated in private prisons than the United States: 11 per cent compared to 7.2 per cent in America (Prison Reform Trust, 2010b). With the construction of a second private prison in Scotland, HMP Addiewell, it is estimated that 20 per cent of Scotland's prison population is now housed in private jails (SCCCJ, 2006). Northern Ireland has no private jails as yet. The private sector is not just involved in building and running prisons, it is also charged with prisoner escort services, the management of drug treatment centres, the provision of electronic monitoring technology and information technology systems as well as catering and laundry services. Following the enactment of the *Offender Management Act 2007*, private companies may now also compete alongside public bodies and voluntary organisations to run probation services. They also provide the technology necessary for the electronic monitoring of offenders. Given the growth of private security services in recent years, it is argued that there is not just a corrections or prisons industrial complex emerging in Britain but rather a 'security-industrial complex'. There are currently 75,500 private security officers employed in the UK (BSIA, 2010). This compares with a total of 140,000 police officers employed in England and Wales alone but it does not take into account the huge numbers of people employed in other related work, for example in the installation of alarms and CCTV and the surveillance of cameras. The 'security services company', G4S, has 40,000 people on its payroll in the UK, making it the biggest employer on the FTSE 100 (G4S, 2010).

Despite New Labour's opposition to prison privatisation whilst in opposition, it openly embraced the policy once in power. Whilst only two private prisons had been built under the Major governments – HMP The Wolds and HMP Doncaster – another nine prisons were built, financed and operated under the Private Finance Initiative between 1997 and 2010. Secure Training Centres for young people aged between 12 and 17 were also built and are managed by the private sector, as are seven out of the ten Immigration Removal Centres in Britain. The market is dominated by just four major companies – Serco, Kalyx, G4S and the GEO Group UK Ltd. – who together represent a multi-million pound industry.

The private security industry exercises considerable influence over government. Indeed, the initial decision by the Conservative Party to allow the private sector to run prisons was largely the result of lobbying by right-wing think tanks and private companies. It was the Adam Smith Institute who suggested that the British government contract the management of prisons out to the private sector in its 1984 report, *Justice Policy* (Ryan, 2003, p. 83). In 1986, several members of a Home Affairs Select Committee on the prison system visited a number of private prisons in the United States (Jones and Newburn, 2005, p. 64). Peter Young from the Adam Smith Institute commented that they were very impressed with what they saw and declared that 'privatisation is now being seen as a viable means of reducing the strain on Britain's grossly overcrowded jails' (Young, 1987, p. 5). In his report, *The Prison Cell*, he sang the praises of privatisation in America and recommended that it be adopted as a model in the UK (*ibid.*). A short time afterwards, UK Detention Services – a consortium made up of Corrections Corporation of America, one of the market leaders in the provision of carceral services in the States, and two British construction companies John Mowlem and Sir Robert McAlpine and Sons Ltd. – was formed with the express aim of lobbying government ministers in Britain in order to win contracts for the construction and management of prisons (Jones and Newburn, 2005, p. 64).

Since then, the private prisons lobby has only increased in importance and influence. Its interests were recently promoted by the Social Market Foundation (SMF), a free-market think tank chaired by Labour peer Lord Lipsey which counts key figures from the Liberal Democrats and the Conservative Party among the members of its policy advisory board (Vince Cable, the current Business Secretary, and George Osborne, the current Chancellor of the Exchequer). The SMF recently recommended that all offender management services for offenders serving less than 12 months should be contracted out to regional providers (Mulheirn *et al.*, 2010). Group 4 (now G4S) is reported to have donated £25,000 to the New Labour think tank, the Institute for Public Policy Research, in order to enable it to carry out research on private prisons (Mathiason, 2001). It therefore comes as no surprise that the IPPR's Commission into Public Private Partnerships gives a highly favourable account of the contracting out of public services to the private sector and privileges evidence from the private sector itself (IPPR, 2001).

Private security companies also manage to successfully promote their interests through their membership of certain powerful lobbies: G4S, for example, belongs to the British Security Industry Association, a professional body representing the industry which counts lobbying government as one of its main activities (BSIA, 2010). The industry has also set up its own research institutes. Gary Sturgess of the Serco Institute wrote a key report for the Confederation of British Industry in which prison privatisation was described as an 'overwhelmingly positive experience' (CBI, 2003, p. 47). A report by the Department for Trade and Industry, since renamed the Department for Business, Innovation and Skills, on the use of market-based approaches to public policy concluded that 'procurement of prison services has been successful' (DTI, 2005). Its claims about the superior cost efficiency of privately-run prisons relied exclusively on the CBI report written by Sturgess. The DTI failed to adopt a critical approach to this report, ignoring evidence to the contrary, such as that provided by the Centre for Public Services, an independent research group based at the University of London (Centre for Public Services, 2002). Even though it also claimed to draw on a National Audit Office report, the concerns raised by this report, notably that private prisons do less to reduce recidivism than those in the public sector, were overlooked (NAO, 2003, p. 19). Nevertheless, the Ministry of Justice cites the DTI Report as evidence of the benefits provided by the competitive tendering of prisons (Ministry of Justice, 2009h).

The CBI, as the largest lobby group for the private sector in the UK, enjoys a privileged position in the policy-making process, frequently contributing to government consultation exercises and networking within Parliament. The private security industry is particularly well-represented by the CBI: key members of the Public Services Strategy Board, set up specifically to campaign for an increased role for the private sector in the delivery of public services, include representatives from G4S (David Banks, Managing Director of the Group's Care and Justice Services), Serco (Clive Barton, Marketing Director for the Serco Group and Gary Sturgess from the Serco Institute) and the construction companies who were chosen by the New Labour government under the NOMS Strategic Alliance Framework Agreement to build penal facilities and to carry out minor refurbishment works on publicly-run prisons (John McDonough, Chief Executive of Carillion and Adrian Ringrose, Chief Executive of Interserve).

There is considerable cross-over of personnel between government and the private security industry. For example, John Reid, former Home Secretary, provided consultancy services to G4S whilst still a Labour MP (House of Commons, 2010, p. 200). Labour peer, Lord Filkin, is employed as a consultant for Serco (Serco, 2009). He voted in favour of the National Offender Management Bill which opened probation services up to contestability from the private and voluntary sectors (Hansard, 2007). Malcolm Stevens, manager of G4S Secure Training Centres (STCs) for 12- to 17-year-olds, used to be a senior government adviser on STC contracting, and the first director of Medway STC, Sue Clifton, was an adviser to the Youth Justice Board (Corporate Watch, 2000).

Both the New Labour government and the private sector had a common interest in presenting the contracting out of prisons as a cost-effective way of dealing with the overcrowding crisis in Britain's jails. Indeed, this is exactly how the case for prison privatisation was presented by Peter Young in his report for the Adam Smith Institute. He claimed private prisons would reduce costs for the public sector and also improve prison conditions (Young, 1987, p. 39). David Blunkett, when Home Secretary, echoed these arguments, stating, 'The Government are not interested in using the private sector for its own sake, whether in prisons or in the community. We want the most cost effective custodial and community sentences no matter who delivers them' (Home Office, 2004c, p. 14). He claimed that competition between the public and private sector had led to significant improvements in prison régimes, notably improved relationships between prison personnel and prisoners (*ibid.*).

Yet these arguments in favour of the contracting out of prisons are highly spurious. Firstly, the argument that the private sector is more efficient than the public sector when it comes to prison management has been described as a myth (Centre for Public Services, 2002). The comparisons between the two sectors ignore the cost differences between the new buildings held by the private sector and the old, often Victorian, buildings held by the public sector: for example, it is obviously less costly to install new security systems in new prisons than old (*ibid.*, p. 26). Comparisons also ignore the significant differences in salaries paid to public and private sector staff – the latter generally find themselves paid between 25 and 43 per cent less than the former (*ibid.*, p. 26; PPRI, 2004). These are false economies on account of the fact that working conditions in the private sector tend to be inferior and employees, of whom there are fewer per prisoner, are young and inexperienced (Prison Reform Trust, 2005). These disparities largely explain the higher rates of staff and prisoner assault in the private sector (*ibid.*). In addition, even if privately-run prisons represent cost savings in terms of cost per prisoner, they are actually more expensive in terms of costs per baseline and in-use Certified Normal Accommodation (the level at which prisons are considered not to be crowded) (Park, 2000, p. 26). In general, PFI projects, under which most private prisons in the UK are operated, are not more cost-effective than the public sector: there are extremely high consultation costs linked with such contacts (Centre for Public Services, 2002, p. 30); the Managerial State is still obliged to assume much of the risk whilst the private sector collects the profits (Harvey, 2007, p. 77); the government may be obliged to pay a premium to a private company to ensure that the contract is completed on time without exceeding its budget (Edwards *et al.*, 2004); and it may be left to pay for services long after they have ceased to be useful on account of the fact that it generally signs itself up for 25 to 30 year contracts with the private sector. A 2005 report on prison privatisation in Scotland described the Scottish government's claim that the expansion of PFI prison contracts would save it £700 million as 'highly questionable', especially on account of the fact that it ignored the difficulties in comparing the two sectors like for like and the costs that might be borne by other government agencies (Cooper and Taylor, 2005).

In addition, the argument that private prisons have offered overall improvements in régime quality does not stand up to scrutiny. The very first private prisons to open in the UK suffered from serious problems in this respect. For example, a 1995 report by the Prison Reform Trust exposed high assault and suicide rates, overcrowding and understaffing at newly-opened HMP Doncaster (Prison Reform Trust, 1995). These were more than just 'teething troubles' – 13 years after the first private prison was opened in the UK, similar problems were exposed at HMP Kilmarnock (opened in 1999) by an undercover journalist working for the BBC (BBC, 2005). After having spent 16 weeks working as a prison officer, the journalist noted severe staff shortages which meant that prisoners at risk of suicide were not adequately monitored and that prisoners were relatively free to use drugs (*ibid.*). The deputy governor of the prison from 1999 to 2003 attributed staff shortages to concerns about profitability, stating, 'The primary focus of running the prison was the financial outcomes. My view is that when I was there I never had enough officers to run it properly [...] my estimate would be, you would probably require another 30 per cent of resources' (*ibid.*). Rather than reporting problems to their superiors, prison officers were encouraged to say nothing so that Serco, the company responsible for managing the prison, would not incur financial penalties for breach of the terms of its contract with the government (*ibid.*). The existence of such penalties would therefore appear to have rather perverse effects, doing little to ensure that régime quality is upheld.

Despite the fact that all but two of the 11 private prisons in England and Wales scored highly according to the Ministry of Justice's most recent performance ratings, they did not score considerably better, or indeed worse, than prisons in the public sector (Ministry of Justice, 2010e). In some areas, notably safety, privately-managed prisons score less well – indeed public prisons are more than five times more likely to score well in this area (HM Inspectorate of Prisons, 2009, p. 14). Further problems are likely to result from the fact that private companies, out of concern for profitability, are more likely to want to accommodate the maximum number of prisoners possible in a single prison. Of the ten largest prisons in England and Wales, four are managed by the private sector (Hansard, 2008a). Current proposals to build five new 1500 place prisons under the Private Finance Initiative are likely to increase security problems, which have been found to be greater in larger prisons (HM Inspectorate of Prisons, 2009, p. 14). Prisoner rehabilitation will also be rendered more difficult as prisoners are more likely than ever to be accommodated far away from friends and family. The construction of large prisons runs totally counter to recommendations of the Woolf

Report which favoured the construction of small, local prisons in order to help maintain links between offenders and their communities.

Given these problems, it is likely that the involvement of the private sector in the management of the prison estate exacerbates the 'pains of imprisonment', thus helping to contribute to the more general move towards increased punitiveness in the treatment of offenders. There is also a risk that the involvement of the private sector in the delivery of probation services will further undermine the probation officer's social work role (see Chapter 3). Yet, the increasing role played by the private sector in the delivery of criminal justice services does not so far appear to have driven punitive sentencing policy in the UK, contrary to in the USA where two Pennsylvanian judges were jailed for taking bribes from private prison companies to send young people to prison for the most trivial of offences (*The Times*, 2009). Nonetheless, the idea that the private sector may be able to bear a significant proportion of the costs of criminal justice spending, particularly in times of economic recession necessitating swingeing public spending cuts, is likely to ensure that cost considerations will not act as a break on the use of costly penal interventions such as prison. Despite the fact that private prisons have not generally proved to be more cost effective, they do enable government to fulfil the cross-party ideological commitment to apply market solutions to the problems of public services. Hence, both government and the private sector share a 'correspondence of interests' in pushing for the further privatisation of criminal justice services.

iv)   *Privatising public space: Partners in (the fight against) crime*

Government and the private sector also share a correspondence of interests in the regeneration of city centres. Such policies enable government to repair the social and economic damage caused to the inner cities by phase one neoliberalism which dealt a hammer-blow to Britain's manufacturing industry, whilst enabling private capital to remodel these areas in such a way as to create maximum profit. Urban regeneration projects have been presented in a wholly positive light as a means of generating economic prosperity (notably through job creation) and of providing attractive, clean, crime-free public spaces. Private business has been given relatively free rein to control these spaces and has even been welcomed as an official government partner in the fight against crime. Consequently, it has played a significant role in shaping urban crime control policies, ensuring that any behaviour seen to potentially threaten economic prosperity may be targeted by the criminal law. This has resulted in a considerable ratcheting up of what kind of behaviour may be defined as criminal, thus also contributing to the intensification of punitiveness.

Despite the fact that private companies are often involved in criminal activities such as fraud or the failure to respect their duty of care towards their employees, particularly those employed in the construction industry (Coleman *et al.*, 2005, p. 2521), they are more commonly regarded as the victims than the perpetrators of crime (*ibid.*, p. 2518). Under New Labour, the Home Office website officially defined 'business crime' as 'all crime and disorder committed *by* or *against* businesses', yet only one of the many examples it cited of such crime may actually be committed by businesses themselves: 'fraud and forgery' (Home Office, 2010a, *my italics*). Similarly, the Chamber of Commerce affirms:

> Crime against business has many victims. Business owners are affected by the costs, both direct and indirect, that crime imposes on them. Employees are left frightened and demoralised by incidents of crime. The prosperity of local communities – that depend on thriving businesses to generate wealth – suffers, as crime against business serves to hamper business growth. In short, the economic, social and psychological impact of crime against business can be devastating (Hill, 2004).

Businesses are presented as victims but action against crime is justified not just in the interests of business but in the interests of society as a whole. Welcoming businesses as partners in the fight against crime is thus presented as being in the public interest. The creation of such partnerships was facilitated by the *Crime and Disorder Act 1998* (section 5) which places a duty on members of Crime and Disorder Reduction Partnerships (CDRPs) to develop crime-fighting strategies in consultation with local businesses.

Although the Chamber of Commerce considers that CDRPs are not sufficiently concerned about business crime (*ibid.*), the majority of the official strategies of the 371 CDRPs in England and Wales identify crimes committed against business as a major problem to be dealt with. Apart from CDPRs, other forms of partnership with business have been formed to tackle crime and to ensure that their interests are taken into account by government. For example, Business Improvement Districts (BIDs), created under *The Local Government Act 2003*, are partnerships between local authorities and businesses which aim to create conditions favourable to commerce. Businesses present in certain designated areas are given free rein to make any changes they think necessary to meet this aim. For example, they may decide to recruit private security guards to patrol the area and/or to forbid certain kinds of behaviour. Consequently, the notion of 'public' space is being redefined to fit with the concerns of local businesses.

Certain areas in Britain's cities are no longer freely accessible to any member of the public but rather to those who might contribute to the economic prosperity of the area: consumers, investors and tourists. As one city centre BID manager declared, 'High margins come with ABC1s, low margins with C2DEs. My job is to create an environment which will bring in more ABC1s' (cited by Minton, 2006, p. 20). The main priority of urban crime control policy has thus been to eliminate all those who may dissuade potential consumers from visiting city centres. This is not about tackling crime *per se* but rather about ensuring that people feel safe. As the London Bridge BID declares, 'We aim to make the London Bridge area as safe and secure as possible – and the perception of safety is just as important to us as crime statistics' (Team London Bridge, 2010). The notion of crime is thus extremely widely-defined to encompass all such behaviour which consumers may find off-putting. Thus, in Liverpool for example, where 34 streets in the city centre have effectively been privatised, rented out to a private company on a 250-year lease, activities such as skateboarding, rollerblading, begging, the consumption of food or alcohol outside designated areas, and protesting without police permission are banned (Minton, 2006, p. 14).

To the extent that the criminal law is invoked to protect commercial interests, it is appropriate to speak of the 'commodification of crime control', whereby private capital is given the power to define the legitimate targets of control (Coleman *et al.*, 2005, p. 2518). Parenti has noted similar trends in the United States and suspects that the aim of the criminal law in such situations is to create 'a new layer of regulation and exclusion, so as to protect the new hyper-aestheticized, playground quarters of the postmodern metropolis from their flipsides of misery' (Parenti, 2002, p. 70). It is hard to dispute the notion that such a strategy has helped to inform criminal justice policy in the UK. Rather than simply protecting the poor from anti-social behaviour, it might be suggested that ASBOs, dispersal orders and PNDs also aim to protect business interests. This may help to explain why the anti-social behaviour of the wealthy goes unchecked. Under the influence of corporate interests, the British government has been applying a form of 'revanchist urbanism' whereby the poor, rather than being incorporated within public spaces, are held responsible for crime and the decay of the inner cities and are thus deemed to have forfeited their right to inhabit 'public' space (Van Swaaningen, 2005). The punitive consequences of such trends are self-evident, not only for the individuals who find themselves excluded from 'public' spaces but also for entire communities who find themselves lumbered with problems displaced from other parts of the city without adequate means to deal with them.

The increasing influence of the private sector, and the managerialist logic which it promotes, over government policy-making can only be understood in the context of the neoliberal transformation of the State from provider of public services to facilitator of market solutions. This has not simply encouraged deregulation at the top of the social ladder and increased regulation at the bottom as crime control policies have become regarded as a means of protecting economic success. Indeed, there are many other crimes unrelated to business interests, such as sex offences, which are the focus of punitive penal interventions. Most importantly, it has become imperative for government to emphasise individual responsibility for social and crime problems as the Neoliberal State has become increasingly impotent to make the structural changes necessary to tackle them. Consequently, the penal consensus of social democracy has been replaced by a new managerialist logic which seeks to manage the risk presented by crime rather than to tackle its underlying causes. It is this obsession with risk management, together with the increasing role played by the private sector in the management of criminal justice services, which can be seen to underpin all of the punitive policies outlined in Part I. Yet, it would be a mistake to regard the private sector as the only significant influence on government policy-making. Government did of course have to pay regard to public opinion and to the media. The role played by the judiciary, without whom punitive policies would not have been translated into practice, is also relevant.

8
Constructing the Authoritarian Consensus

A punitive public?

New Labour certainly claimed that punitive penal policies were a direct response to public opinion. Tony Blair declared,

> [...] the culture of political and legal decision-making [...] has to change, to take account of the way the world has changed. It is not this or that judicial decision; this or that law. It is a complete change of mindset, an avowed, articulated determination to make protection of the law-abiding public the priority and to measure that not by the theory of the textbook but by the reality of the street and community in which real people live real lives (Blair, 2006b).

In this statement, the former Prime Minister expressed his desire to move towards a more democratic, open form of decision-making as opposed to the decision-making culture of the past, dominated by the 'platonic guardians' who felt that they had a duty to 'constrain the temptations of the rulers and keep on a tight leash the untutored passions of the ruled' (Loader, 2006a, p. 564). In the past, public opinion was in no way ignored (Morgan, 1979, p. 4) but the crime problem was not a major electoral issue to the extent that it is today. Up until 1959, no electoral manifesto mentioned the question of law and order (Downes and Morgan, 1997, p. 89). For the most part of the twentieth century, policy-makers did a very good job of steering public opinion: it has even been suggested that criminological expertise influenced popular culture (Garland and Sparks, 2000, p. 196). The most striking example of the power of the public élites to run against public opinion was the way in which they were able to abolish the death penalty with the *Murder [Abolition of the Death Penalty] Act 1965* in spite of widespread opposition – it was estimated that 76 per cent of British people remained in favour of it (Davies, 1975, p. 41). Policy-making was characterised by a culture of deference towards politicians which meant that the public generally left them alone to do their job (Ryan, 2003, p. 27). This culture did not change under the rule of Margaret Thatcher, despite the fact that she explicitly sought to dissociate herself with the post-war consensus and to show herself to be more in tune with the concerns of ordinary people by rejecting intellectual theories in favour of 'common sense'. It was only in the early 1990s that there was a radical change in the culture of decision-making from one of deference to one which sought to give expression to a wide variety of interests.

It became increasingly important for government to be seen to be responding to public opinion. Consequently, a number of 'popular' policies, such as the passing of a form of 'Sarah's Law', were implemented despite considerable opposition from professionals. The *Crime and Disorder Act 1998*, which introduced punitive crime-fighting measures such as ASBOs, was presented as 'a triumph of democratic politics', rooted in the lived experiences of local communities across the country (Ryan, 2004, p. 5). According to former Home Secretary David Blunkett, a number of policy initiatives were directly inspired by the public, namely curfews and dispersal orders, which he said emerged out of a public meeting held on the edge of his constituency at which people were shouting, 'Is there anybody on our side?' (Blunkett, 2010). Public opinion was valued over that of the professional élites who were described derisorily as 'the chattering classes', 'the sneer squad' or 'the intellectuals', curiously a term of insult for the New Labourites (Hall, 1998, pp. 13–14).

At first sight, the British public would indeed appear to be rather punitive. Indeed, as noted above, punitive sentiment is likely to run high in individualistic, unequal neoliberal societies. Yet Michael Tonry considers the British, along with the Americans, to be more punitive than other nationalities, writing, 'I believe a deeper strain of moralistic self-righteousness and punitiveness towards deviance and deviants characterizes British and American culture [...] than is the case in other countries' (Tonry, 2004a, p. 64). To support his case, he cites the International Crime Victimisation Survey (ICVS) from 2000 which showed the percentage of people in different countries preferring a prison sentence for a recidivist burglar: 56 per cent of North Americans, 54 per cent of Northern Irish people, 52 per cent of Scottish people and 51 per cent of English people, compared to between 12 and 16 per cent of people questioned in other European countries (*ibid.*). A more recent European survey shows similar results, with 50.4 per cent of British people preferring a prison sentence for such an offence, compared to just 12.7 per cent of respondents in France and 20.9 per cent in Germany (Kühnrich and Kania, 2007, p. 15). Surveys carried out in the UK also reflect punitive attitudes. A 2009 survey revealed that 70 per cent of British people think the UK should have the death penalty as the maximum possible penalty for at least one of 12 different types of crime surveyed ranging from armed robbery to child murder (IPSOS/MORI, 2009a). A 2003 survey asked a sample of the population which initiative from a list of six ('more police on the streets', 'harsher sentencing', 'better discipline at home/in school', 'more activities for young people to get involved in', 'eradicating poverty', 'community initiatives such as Neighbourhood Watch schemes') would be most effective at reducing crime rates. Thirty-three per cent chose 'harsher sentencing' and 35 per cent chose 'more police on the streets' (ICM/ *Observer*, 2003, p. 90). Only 11 per cent thought 'eradicating poverty' to be the best response (*ibid.*). The same survey found that 87 per cent of respondents thought that a person sentenced to life should never be released from prison (*ibid.*, p. 120) and 80 per cent favoured automatic 'three strikes' sentences for offenders convicted of any three crimes (*ibid.*, p. 120). Retribution seems to have been the principal motivation for such attitudes: in response to the question, 'Do you believe that prison should be used, primarily, as punishment, a deterrent or as rehabilitation?', the majority of people – 59 per cent – believed it should be used as punishment (*ibid.*, p. 125).

British people also tend to be very punitive with regard to young offenders. According to a study on public attitudes to the criminal justice system based on the results of the British Crime Survey 1998, 76 per cent of respondents considered the police and the courts to be too 'soft' on young offenders (Mattinson and Mirrlees-Black, 2000, p. 2). In 2003, despite a series of reforms rendering the system more punitive, this figure only fell by 5 per cent (Hough and Roberts, 2003, p. 2). Surveys have shown high levels of support for penalties such as ASBOs which tend to disproportionately affect young people: 82 per cent of respondents to a MORI poll said that they either 'strongly supported' or 'tended to support' ASBOs whilst only 4 per cent said they 'opposed' or 'strongly opposed' them (IPSOS/MORI, 2005, p. 32). A large majority of British people – 82 per cent – also believe that young people convicted of serious crimes such as murder should be prosecuted as adults (ICM/*Observer*, 2003, p. 137).

However, a number of studies have shown that these punitive sentiments are motivated by ignorance of how the criminal justice system actually works rather than by a genuine desire to get tough on crime. For example, a poll carried out for *The Guardian* in 2007 showed that 51 per cent of respondents would like the government to find means other than imprisonment for fighting crime and punishing offenders (Glover, 2007). In 2004, *Rethinking Crime and Punishment*, a research project sponsored by the grant-making foundation, the *Esmée Fairbairn Foundation*, asserts, 'Although public attitudes are complex, sometimes contradictory and often highly dependent on the wording of poll questions, they are in general much less punitive than is often thought to be the case' (RCP, 2004, p. 23). As evidence of less punitive attitudes, the report cites public support for measures aimed at crime prevention rather than punishment, scepticism concerning the value of prison as a solution to the crime problem, and support for community penalties and policies which seek to address the social causes of crime (*ibid.*, pp. 23–4). When British people are given more precise details about the criminal justice system or about individual offender case studies, they tend to be less punitive. For example, whilst they may criticise the juvenile justice system for being too lenient, when they are provided with personal information about offenders and their crimes, they tend to support community sentences or treatment programmes (Hough and Roberts, 2003). There would indeed appear to be a close correlation between ignorance about the criminal justice system and punitive sentiment. For example, British people tend to denounce living conditions in prison as being too comfortable without ever having had any direct experience of penal establishments (Roberts and Hough, 2005, pp. 288–9). Consequently, the punitive value of prison is undermined (*ibid.*, p. 292), which might explain why less than half the respondents to an earlier study considered that 'being put in prison punishes offenders' (Hough and Roberts, 1998).

Yet, public opinion is in no way homogeneous. It can be at once liberal and punitive and varies according to age, geographical regions and social background. Older people are, for example, more likely than younger people to support the death penalty, as are people living in the West Midlands (ICM/*Observer*, 2003, pp. 111–2). People from social classes A and B are less likely than people from social classes D and E to think that the main aim of prison should be punishment (*ibid.*, p. 125). Other surveys have demonstrated that those with a higher level of education tend to be more liberal-minded than those without qualifications (Park and Hough, 2002).

It is interesting to note that whilst the majority of the public may appear to support punitive crime policies, they lack faith in government's capacity to fight crime, despite the fact that it has implemented many of the tough policies demanded, namely sending more offenders to prison for longer periods of time. Whilst 41 per cent of British people who cited law and order/crime and anti-social behaviour as a significant problem considered the Labour Party to have the best policies on the issue in 1998, only 17 per cent thought so in 2008 (IPSOS/MORI, 2009b). Only 38 per cent of people in England and Wales believe the criminal justice system to be effective in terms of cutting crime (Thorpe and Hall, 2009, pp. 105–6). The British now consider crime to be the third most important issue facing Britain, after the economy and immigration (IPSOS/MORI, 2010). This might suggest that the British public's appetite for punitive policies is insatiable were it not for the existence of studies which show it to be less punitive when informed about how the criminal justice system actually works. It would appear that, rather than being *popular*, punitive crime policies are simply *populist* in the sense that they result from government responding blindly to what it perceives to be public demands without engaging in meaningful debate and discussion with the public about the crime problem. Despite attempts on the part of government to discuss policy issues in constituency surgeries and focus groups and to inform the public about how the penal system works (for example, via public information events organised during 'Inside Justice Week'), public opinion is not well understood or taken into account by policy-makers, and the public remains relatively ignorant (James and Raine, 1998, p. 65). Government tends to listen to the 'noise' of the public voice without really understanding what provokes these concerns (*ibid.*, p. 81). Consequently, it fails to adequately understand popular demands, thus condemning its policies to failure in the long term (*ibid.*). This would certainly appear to have been the case for New Labour.

Johnstone argues that populism in penal policy does not go far enough in the sense of democracy (Johnstone, 2001, p. 162). Yet, populism and democracy are, as Canovan has argued, but two sides of the same coin (Canovan, 1999). Just like democracy, populism presents itself as an anti-elitist project which speaks in the name of the silent majority whose interests have too long been ignored by the élites (*ibid.*). Indeed, a number of experts on the subject have noted that populist movements were originally popular movements in the sense that they aimed to overthrow the governing élites (Taggart, 2000; Collovald, 2004). The example which is most often cited is that of the 'People's Party', a popular movement elected in 1892 in Omaha to protect the interests of farmers against the big railroad companies and banking establishments (Taggart, *ibid.*, pp. 27–8).

Yet, the true meaning of populism has been distorted as it has become increasingly associated with the élites. Once populism is used by the élites in democratic government to legitimate the fact that they work within the confines of institutions which are in reality far removed from the people (Canovan, 1999, pp. 13–14), it ceases to be entirely 'popular'. Indeed, 'populist' policies may actually run counter to the best interests of the people. Punitive crime policy is, in many respects, not in the public interest. As noted above, it does little to prevent recidivism, it has not made the public feel safer, it has concentrated on street crime whilst ignoring extremely harmful white-collar crime, and it has meant that the structural causes of crime have been largely ignored. Despite New Labour's recognition that the poorest communities suffer disproportionately from crime, it would appear that it was unable to reverse this trend. According to social geographer Danny Dorling, whilst the poorest tenth of the population in England, Wales and Scotland were on average 143 per cent more likely to be murdered between 1981 and 1986, they were 182 per cent more likely to be murdered during the period 1996–2000 (Dorling, 2006, pp. 6–7). Those living in the poorest areas of England and Wales are more likely to feel that they are affected by anti-social behaviour (Thorpe and Hall, 2009, p. 101). It might also be argued that they are also more likely to suffer from unofficially-defined forms of anti-social behaviour perpetrated by companies which employ them in dangerous, low-paid jobs without respecting health and safety regulations. Although New Labour appeared to be inspired by 'left realism', the theory which argues that the Left needs to take crime seriously since it affects poorest communities most, it ignored the left realist argument that 'crime is endemic to capitalism because it produces both egalitarian ideals and material shortages' (Lea and Young, 1993, p. 96).

It is therefore misleading to describe New Labour's policies as populist since they ran counter to the popular interests that 'populism', in the original meaning of the word, is meant to protect. Despite involving victims and communities in the criminal justice process via Victim Personal Statements (see Chapter 4), Community Payback Schemes (see Chapter 1) and community policing schemes (see Chapter 4), the public has not been empowered in any meaningful way in the policy-making process or encouraged to really engage with the criminal justice system in a way which might encourage a less simplistic view of the issues at stake. Government instead encouraged the 'tyranny of simplicity' whereby the full complexity of problems is deliberately obfuscated and the people thus excluded from truly meaningful dialogue on these issues (Allen, 2005, p. 86). The complex issues involved in criminal justice were deliberately presented in simplistic terms in order to discredit expert opinion and better 'connect' with a narrowly-conceived notion of 'public opinion' or the popular 'common sense'. It is in the government's rather than the public's interests to do so. Indeed, fuelling simplistic punitive attitudes to both offenders and the poor focuses attention on the individual rather than the structural sources of social problems and thus absolves the State and its neoliberal policies from direct responsibility for the problem. As we noted above, a central aim of neoliberal policy is to responsibilise individuals so that market solutions may be made more readily acceptable to the public, framed as they are in a positive discourse of public choice and freedom from state control. In addition, being seen to respond to public concerns about crime helps to obfuscate the fact that government's chief priority has become the protection of market interests over the public interest. It might thus be suggested that the punitive form of populism encouraged by government is authoritarian since the government plays a role in the construction of public opinion, creating consensus around tough policies in fields such as law-and-order, immigration and social policies. Hence, the Blair government, as the Thatcher government before it, was in search of hegemony, attempting, as Stuart Hall (1988) wrote almost 20 years ago, 'to impose a new regime of social discipline and leadership "from above" which had to be rooted in popular fears and anxieties "below"' (*ibid.*). Yet, the construction of such a consensus could not be achieved alone. As Tonry has argued, 'it is not public opinion per se that leads to harsher policies, but politicians' proposals and posturing and sensational media crime coverage that lead to changes in public opinion' (Tonry, 2004c, p. 37).

The media: Hyping up the crime problem

The media has, in general, adopted a very punitive approach to law and order issues but it is unclear to what extent it has influenced or echoed government and public opinion. The media's punitive turn is not new – the number of crime stories published by newspapers increased significantly from the 1960s onwards when they began to represent crime as a growing problem, symptomatic of a widespread social crisis (Reiner *et al.*, 2003). Today, it is estimated that almost 20 per cent of newspaper articles are about crime, particularly murder, which represents one third of all crime stories (*ibid.*, pp. 17–18), despite the fact that murder only represented 0.01 per cent of all crimes recorded in England and Wales in 2008/09 (Home Office, 2010b). As mentioned above, some tabloids, such as *The Sun* and *The News of the World*, have explicitly campaigned for more punitive crime policies. In doing so, they claim to be representing public opinion. Yet, given that the majority of people have had no direct experience of crime, particularly the violent crime that is represented in the press, they are obliged to rely on the media as a source of information. Consequently, it is rather the press that informs public opinion. As the media expert Maxwell McCombs notes, although the general public are not mere robots programmed by the media, the media does hold a considerable influence over public opinion to the extent that it focuses attention on certain issues to the detriment of others (McCombs, 2005, pp. 1–8). Consequently, the public reacts more to perceived rather than lived reality. Indeed, the most recent research into fear of crime shows that fear of rarer crimes, such as knife crime, is particularly high, suggesting that perceptions are more likely to be influenced by media coverage than actual experience (Thorpe and Hall, 2009, p. 97). This is particularly worrying, given that the media as a whole tends to sensationalise and oversimplify events to add to their newsworthiness.

It goes without saying that all modern governments are acutely aware of the importance of building positive relationships with the media. Before becoming Prime Minister, Tony Blair personally sought the support of media giants such as Rupert Murdoch. Following several meetings between himself and Murdoch, New Labour promised to adopt a more relaxed approach to the regulation of media ownership, which undoubtedly encouraged Murdoch to put pressure on the chief editors of *The Sun* and *The News of the World* to back Labour in the 1997 election campaign (Seldon, 2005, pp. 250–3). Once in power, the Blair government sought to control the information the media could have access to by setting up a 'Strategic Communications Unit' under the direction of Alastair Campbell. It is alleged that journalists who opposed government policy were 'bullied in private, harangued in public and excluded from off-the-record briefings' (Franklin, 2004, p. 93).

Yet New Labour soon came to understand that the British media was a beast that was difficult to tame, as the very newspapers that had rallied behind it in 1997 became harsh critics of government policy, particularly accusing it of being too lenient on crime. The Brown government's eventual policy u-turn on the introduction of a 'Sarah's Law' in the UK might be understood as being as much a response to the pressures of the tabloid press as it was an attempt to respond to public opinion. It was, therefore, not only representatives from the world of business who had replaced the old civil service and academic professionals at the policy-making table but, it would appear, the media itself:

> As academics lost status and security with the retreat of public finance, so media people gained both prosperity and influence. No sector increased its power in Britain more rapidly than the media. [...] The hacks came in from the cold, not through the back door, but up the grand staircase. Tabloid editors, who forty years ago were despised and ignored, are now recognised as powers in the land, to be fêted, flattered and knighted [...] The masters of the media are the new aristocracy, demanding and receiving homage from politicians, big businessmen and the old aristocracy. Columnists and broadcasters are more famous than many of the politicians or public figures they interview (Sampson, 2005, p. 211).

That criticism of government policy on the part of high-ranking criminal justice professionals, such as Martin Narey or Rod Morgan, or from the judiciary itself, was often ignored, seems to confirm the validity of this statement. Far from controlling the press, the New Labour government instead became its hostage. It did, nonetheless, prove to be a rather accommodating hostage, easily ceding to the demands of the tabloids rather than resisting them.

This situation may be explained by the fact that government also shared a 'correspondence of interests' with the media. Both parties sought to simplify and emphasise the crime problem. For the media, this was a means of grabbing the attention of audiences in an increasingly competitive environment. In addition, on account of the fact that the majority of newspapers in Britain tend to lean to the right, it is unsurprising that they may be keen to focus on the individual responsibility of criminals and thus fuel punitive attitudes to crime. For successive New Labour governments, the simplification and mediatisation of the crime problem served to raise public awareness of an issue which it could use to appeal to the electorate across class lines. Although such 'wedge' issues are always important in electoral politics, they are arguably even more important at a time when the neoliberal transformation of the State has left political parties with relatively few issues on which they can campaign. Having abandoned commitments to full employment and social security, parties have had to find other issues on which to campaign. Campaigning on a plank of neoliberalism, which declares that the main aim of the State is now to facilitate the accumulation of capital and return economic power to the élites, is hardly likely to be popular. Campaigning on issues such as crime, however, which are seen to affect everyone, regardless of social class, is a means of achieving electoral success and thus securing the legitimacy of the neoliberal political project. This was particularly important for New Labour. Once it had distanced itself from the working class and the trade unions, the Party needed to find a new *raison d'être*. Crime was one issue amongst others which enabled it to appeal to both its core voters and the middle classes. It was also an issue which, presented in the most simplistic terms, gelled well with its new discourse on personal responsibility, thus enabling it to distance itself from the post-war consensus and its perceived emphasis on state responsibility. New Labour attempted to ensure that it would never again be seen as being 'soft on crime', as was the case in the 1970s and 1980s. The policy would appear to have backfired as the majority of British people came to consider that the Conservatives had the best policies on crime and anti-social behaviour (IPSOS/MORI, 2009b). Nonetheless, it is this correspondence of interests with the media which may help to explain why New Labour helped to fan the flames of punitive sentiment in the first place. The rising power of the media and public opinion is of course a key characteristic of contemporary society, and politicians from whatever political hue would ignore this fact at their peril. However, it was arguably the hegemony of neoliberalism which led New Labour to harness the power of the media and public opinion to advance such a narrow agenda. Had it not been in thrall to neoliberalism, the party may have been able to use these forces to advance a more progressive agenda and to develop a meaningful dialogue between government and the electorate. Yet, it remains to be explained why the judiciary participated in the construction of an authoritarian consensus on crime.

Judicial attitudes to sentencing

The British judiciary is in fact well-placed to resist punitive trends, unlike judges in countries such as the United States where they are often directly elected. Indeed, there is a strong tradition of judicial independence in the UK, despite attempts on the part of the executive to erode it by introducing mandatory minimum sentences. Judges still possess considerable latitude in determining sentences. For example, even though they are required by law to impose Indeterminate Sentences for Public Protection for any one of 153 offences, it is left up to them to set the minimum period which must be served before an offender's case may be examined by the Parole Board. Judges are guided by the independent Sentencing Guidelines Council and by the Sentencing Advisory Panel, both of which attempt to provide clear and consistent sentencing guidelines. However, the panel does not limit judicial discretion in any significant way on account of the fact that judges are under no obligation to follow the guidelines. This would suggest that penal policy could not have taken such a punitive direction in recent years were it not for judicial complicity. As the Halliday Report noted, 'Sentencing outcomes depend less on the content of the legal framework than on the way it is used. Judicial discretion, and its governance, are therefore crucial in determining sentences passed' (Halliday, 2001, p. 52).

There are even many examples from the past of judges being more punitive than the executive. A number of executive attempts to reduce the prison population were thwarted by the judiciary. For example, the Magistrates' Association successfully campaigned against the provision in the *Criminal Justice Act 1967* which obliged judges to impose suspended sentences on all offenders facing prison sentences of less than six months (Morris, 1989, pp. 115–16). With reference to judges' preference for incarceration, one commentator has remarked, 'Like the criminals they sentence, the Courts are incorrigible recidivists' (Elcock, 1984, p. 154). Opposition to punitive trends in government policy is generally confined to the highest rungs of the judiciary. Lord Chief Justices, notably Lord Bingham, Lord Woolf, Lord Phillips and the current Lord Chief Justice, Lord Judge, have often made outspoken criticism of these trends. Lord Woolf, for example, holder of the post from 2000–2005, frequently clashed with David Blunkett when he was Home Secretary from 2001–2004. And, in his capacity as a law lord in the House of Lords, Lord Bingham declared illegal the Blair government's policy of detaining terror suspects without trial (A [FC] and Others [FC] [Appellants] v. Secretary of State for the Home Department).

Yet, despite their independence, judges are not immune to public opinion (Ashworth, 1997, p. 1119). Lord Woolf has claimed that the increasingly punitive climate of opinion is responsible for the increase in the 'going rate' for sentence lengths in recent years (Woolf, 2003). Even though high-ranking judges condemn populist policy-making, they still believe that the judiciary should pay attention to public opinion:

[Judges] should take care not to be blown hither and thither by every wind of political or penal fashion. And in determining sentence in any given case the judge should close his or her ears to public and media clamour concerning that case [...] [But] [i]t is important to maintain public confidence in the justice and effectiveness of the sentencing process. If, for instance, informed public opinion perceives that the sentences which are imposed fail to match the gravity of the crimes committed, then the public will be tempted to take the law into their own hands and resort to private vengeance (Bingham, 1997).

The majority of judges, regarding themselves as public servants, consider that public opinion cannot be ignored. These concerns can, at times, lapse into populist sentencing. Even Lord Woolf succumbed to the public panic concerning mobile phone theft which erupted in 2002, raising 'excessively lenient' penalties handed down to two thieves. He recommended that the penalty for such offences should be at least 18 months, or even five years or more in cases involving violence (Dyer, 2002).

It would appear that, in practice, judges are also influenced by the executive with whom they share common interests. According to J. A. G. Griffith, judges form part of the Establishment and are therefore predisposed to follow the government, whatever their opposition might be to specific policies. He writes:

[Judges have a] unifying attitude of mind, a political position, which is primarily concerned to protect and conserve certain values and institutions. This does not mean that the judiciary invariably supports what governments do or even what Conservative governments do. Individually, judges may support the Conservative or Labour or the Liberal parties. Collectively, in their function and by their nature, they are neither Tories nor Socialists nor Liberals. They are protectors and conservators of what has been, of the relationships and interests on which, in their view, our society is founded. They do not regard their role as radical or even reformist, only (on occasion) corrective (Griffith, 1997, pp. 7–8).

Indeed, judges tend to share highly privileged backgrounds. Seventy per cent of British judges attended private school, whilst 78 per cent studied at Oxbridge (Slapper, 2007). The way in which they are elected also accounts for their partiality (Griffith, 1997, p. 337). Whilst the principle of judicial independence and the separation of powers between the three branches of government is well-established by the British constitution, judges were, until very recently, appointed by the Lord Chancellor who was also a member of the executive. Since April 2006, the independent Judicial Appointments Commission, set up under the *Constitutional Reform Act 2005*, is responsible for selecting judges. However, ultimate responsibility for judicial appointments rests with the Lord Chancellor who is free to accept or reject the recommendations of the Commission. Although the Lord Chancellor has lost his or her powers as head of the judiciary, he or she remains a member of the executive and sits as Minister of Justice.

In any case, since judges are recruited for life, it will take years before the composition of the judiciary changes in any significant way. According to Griffith, 'unorthodoxy in political opinion is a certain disqualification for appointment' (*ibid.*, p. 338). Whether or not this has changed is, as yet, irrelevant, since the majority of judges sitting today have been appointed under the old system. Given the similar social composition of the judiciary and the executive, it is perhaps not surprising if executive severity in penal policy-making is followed by judicial severity in sentencing, and *vice versa*. Once an authoritarian consensus has been constructed between government, the public and the media, it would be very difficult for the judiciary to follow a radically different direction without becoming involved in the political fray and stepping outside its constitutional boundaries. It is paradoxically the need to protect its independence that prevents the judiciary from taking an independent approach to sentencing.

Neoliberalism cannot be said to have directly influenced judicial sentencing decisions. However, it was arguably neoliberalism which helped to create the feelings of insecurity and egotism which fuelled the punitive sentiment which the judiciary could not ignore. It was also neoliberalism which rendered the Capitalist State relatively powerless to tackle the structural sources of that insecurity in the first place. Crime, just like immigration, has consequently become an issue around which all these fears may coalesce and which neoliberal governments can use as a wedge issue to garner electoral support. Rather than directly responding to public concern about crime, New Labour governments used that concern to serve their own electoral interests. It is in this sense that its populism is truly authoritarian. The public, along with the media and the judiciary, have themselves willingly formed part of an authoritarian consensus on law and order. The police, too, have willingly participated, motivated as they are by managerialist performance targets to apply government policy as intended. At the same time, opposition to this consensus has effectively been silenced as the post-war social-democratic criminological consensus has been discredited.

Conclusion: Towards Penal Dystopia?

The authoritarian consensus on law and order which has emerged in Britain over the past two decades is a cross-party consensus. It was shown in Chapter 5 that, despite superficial differences between the Conservatives and the Liberal Democrats, both parties largely follow New Labour thinking on crime and punishment in terms of their focus on individual responsibility for the crime problem and the need for the criminal justice system to be more responsive to what government perceives to be public demand. The new coalition government will continue to target not just crime but also anti-social behaviour and, in the context of swingeing spending cuts combined with a lack of political will, the root causes of crime are likely to remain unaddressed. Significantly, there is also cross-party consensus on the form of political economy to be applied to Britain. Despite the most recent crisis of capitalism which the UK, along with most other Western nations, is currently experiencing, there is no sign that the neoliberal consensus is breaking up. Whilst Gordon Brown declared in March 2009 that 'the 40-year-old prevalent orthodoxy known as the Washington consensus in favour of free markets has come to an end', he refused to countenance a return to considerable state intervention in the economic affairs of the nation or indeed any halt to the current direction of public service reform (Wintour and Watt, 2009). As Callinicos has noted, the state interventions of 2008 and 2009, involving the part-nationalisation of the banks in an attempt to save the British economy from collapse, were emergency measures only, designed to ensure the survival of the neoliberal order rather than to herald the beginning of a fundamental transformation of capitalism (Callinicos, 2010, pp. 128–9).

It is highly unlikely that the new Conservative-Liberal Democrat coalition will bring about such a transformation either. Although both parties have insisted on the need to responsibilise the financial sector, with Cameron promising to 'bring law and order to the financial markets' (Cameron, 2009), in practice the greatest efforts of the coalition are likely to be focused on reinforcing government's own fiscal responsibility. The emergency budget called in June 2010, just a month after the general election, has planned for public spending cuts to the tune of £6 billion. In order to honour its commitment to the provision of high-quality public services, the coalition has promised the continued privatisation of these services, thus facilitating capital accumulation and protecting the interests of the economic élites. The Neoliberal State is therefore set to retain its function as facilitator of market solutions rather than as provider of public services. Indeed, it would arguably be difficult for it to do otherwise: 'Three decades of neo-liberalism have left their mark, and in important respects there is no going back' (Gamble, 2009, p. 87). It will be hard for any new government to reverse the financialisation of the economy which has not just penetrated the public sector but also permeated everyday life and consciousness to the extent that it would be difficult for many people to contemplate changing their behaviour and rejecting their commitment to the credit culture (*ibid.*). Furthermore, even if the UK as a nation state had the will to turn its back on neoliberalism, 'disciplinary neoliberalism' would continue to be enforced by international agencies such as the IMF (*ibid.*). Finally, the extent of transnational economic integration has divested nation states of their capacity to enforce market regulation (Callinicos, 2010, p. 131).

It would be a serious mistake to suggest that the neoliberal order is crumbling simply because states are now becoming more interventionist and turning their back on pure *laissez-faire* politics (Dardot and Laval, 2009). Indeed, neoliberalism is about much more than *laissez-faire*: in practice, the neoliberal order has always required a strong state in order to create the conditions necessary to facilitate and stimulate market competition (Gamble, 1994). A strong state has also been required to legitimate such a system, as occurred during second phase 'roll out' neoliberalism when centre-left governments such as those of New Labour became highly interventionist in a failed attempt to manage the disastrous social consequences of phase one 'roll back' neoliberalism. Perhaps it could be said that we are today entering into a third phase of regulatory neoliberalism in which the practices of financial institutions and even of governments themselves are to be subjected to a series of new rules and standards. Far from threatening the neoliberal order, these regulatory reforms are intended to ensure its survival; they aim simply to render competition more effective and to help legitimate the system (Dardot and Laval, 2009).

Neoliberalism looks set to remain in place, not just as an economic policy, but also as a *system*, with all its legal, institutional, cultural and social dimensions, dominated by the rationality of free competition. In legal terms, there are no plans in the UK to alter the legal framework to divert power away from capital in favour of labour. Trade union legislation will remain draconian and the recent Conservative-Liberal Democrat agreement to limit the application to the UK of European legislation on labour issues such as the Working Time Regulations will ensure that labour flexibility is prioritised over workers' rights. In institutional terms, as the British State continues to regard its key function as facilitator of market solutions, it will find itself confronted with the same crisis of legitimacy that has beset all governments from Thatcher to Brown. As it divests itself of its key role of provider of social and economic security, it will need to find other sources of legitimation. As shown in Chapter 6, New Labour attempted to seek legitimation by repairing the social havoc reaped by destructive phase one neoliberalism. It promised to tackle social problems such as educational failure, crime and social exclusion by investing heavily in public services and, most importantly, by introducing policies designed to encourage individual responsibility. The party's embrace of neoliberalism severely circumscribed the extent to which it could address the structural causes of social problems, leading it to promote an egotistical culture of exclusive individualism. Such a culture is of course legitimated by the rationality of neoliberalism itself which aims to place citizens, as free-thinking, rational individuals, in competition with one another for access to employment and key public services.

Cameron's quest to ensure the legitimacy of his Conservative Party by differentiating it from its Thatcherite predecessors and thus casting off its 'nasty party' image, has led him to promote a form of 'caring conservatism', ostensibly concerned with repairing the problems of the 'broken society', characterised by high levels of crime, family breakdown, welfare dependency, debt, drugs, inadequate housing and failing schools (Cameron, 2008). Together with the Liberal Democrats, he aims to create the 'big society' whereby individuals and voluntary organisations are encouraged to get involved in their communities in a bid to resolve various social problems. Here, the coalition government once again demonstrates considerable continuity with its predecessors, promoting social policies which aim primarily to responsibilise and remoralise individuals rather than to address the structural causes of the social chaos which may be said to result from neoliberalism itself. Paradoxically, this has led to more rather than less state intervention as deregulation in the economic sphere is matched by increased regulation in the social sphere, exemplified by the development of an increasingly coercive welfare policy.

Neoliberalism as a system has led to increased punitiveness in criminal justice in a number of ways. Firstly, toughness in the face of the crime problem is another way in which government may attempt to secure legitimacy. This is what Garland has described as a 'sovereign state strategy' (Garland, 2001a) whereby the State attempts to show its capacity to protect citizens from the risk posed by crime whilst it remains relatively powerless to protect them from the various risks posed by 'late modernity', such as those created by the restructuring of the labour market. Yet, simultaneously, the State also adopts an 'adaptive strategy' whereby it effectively admits its weakness in face of the crime problem and attempts to offload its responsibility in that regard onto communities themselves. Both strategies were adopted by successive New Labour governments in Britain. On the one hand, the State's 'power to punish' was reasserted as a huge number of new offences were created and increasing numbers of people found themselves criminalised. On the other, communities were encouraged to join in the fight against crime by becoming members of Crime and Disorder Partnerships or by volunteering their services as Police Community Support Officers, for example. These two strategies are complementary rather than contradictory since they both facilitate the dispersal of state power throughout society. They also help to absolve the Neoliberal State of responsibility for the crime problem: the first strategy responsibilises the offender whilst the second responsibilises citizens and communities. Whilst Garland situates these strategies in the context of late modernity, it has been argued here that they can better be understood in the more specific context of neoliberalism in which the State has become relatively powerless to tackle the structural causes of crime. It is neoliberalism that has made the responsibilisation of individuals imperative.

Yet, New Labour failed to either to foster a culture of responsibility or to successfully legitimise its own power. It has instead fostered a culture of irresponsibility towards others by fostering a form of exclusive, egotistical individualism. This is one reason why the involvement of communities in the fight against crime exacerbated punitive trends. Moreover, no matter how tough New Labour governments got on crime, it was still perceived to be 'soft' in this respect. This would suggest that authoritarian crime policy failed to enable New Labour to secure legitimacy. Nonetheless, in the context of the neoliberal transformation of the State, crime, like immigration, represented one of the few 'popular' issues which it could regularly invoke in an attempt to appeal to the public at large. In the 2010 general election, these issues continued to be a hot topic for debate amongst all three major contenders for office. It is likely that both the Conservatives and Liberal Democrats will continue to use these issues to ensure political legitimacy, particularly in the context of massive public spending cuts which will inevitably exacerbate social and economic insecurities and undermine the already fragile popularity of the coalition government. If the Liberal Democrats initially offered the possibility of a less 'populist' approach to these issues before coming to power, they were rapidly forced to compromise, notably by dropping their commitment to an amnesty for immigrants already living in the UK and by abandoning their plans to halt the expansion of the penal estate. The coalition government is also likely to continue the trend towards 'punishment through welfare' in an attempt to manage the deleterious social effects of neoliberalism, particularly given the current economic crisis and the political desire on the part of both the Liberal Democrats and the Conservatives to present themselves as a force for 'progressive' politics. Indeed, there are plans to extend intervention programmes aimed at enforcing parental responsibility and the responsibility of welfare claimants. For those who fail to modify their behaviour, the sanctions will be severe.

Yet neoliberalism does not just help to explain why New Labour governments felt the need to adopt punitive crime policies in a quest for legitimation and electoral gain. It also explains the growing influence of managerialist logic which has undermined welfarist ideology in the penal system and placed risk management at the forefront of professional concerns. In welcoming the private sector as a new partner in criminal justice policy-making and the provision of criminal justice services, government has come to place private interests over those of offenders. It has been shown that offenders incarcerated in privately-run prisons may be more at risk of self-harm and violence than those held in publicly-run prisons, largely as a result of cost-cutting measures. The private sector has also been instrumental in extending punitiveness outside the four walls of the prison and into wider society as it has gained control over city centres and sought to exclude all those 'undesirables' who are seen to threaten commercial success. New Labour governments colluded, invoking a variety of new hybrid criminal/civil measures to address 'anti-social' behaviour such as begging and rowdy behaviour by young people. At the same time, they did little to pursue white-collar crime, particularly that caused by businesses themselves. These trends are also likely to continue under the new coalition government given that the privatisation of criminal justice services is to be extended. Indeed, the role of the private sector is likely to become ever-more important in the current economic crisis: whereas public spending cuts may have acted as a brake on punitiveness in the 1980s in Britain, it is likely that they will have the opposite effect today. The current government may pursue the expansion of the penal appara-tuses of the State, safe in the knowledge that the private sector will foot the bill, at least in the short term. Contracting out these services to the private sector may even be regarded as a means of boosting economic growth in the context of recession.

It might be argued that the intensification of punishment in Britain in recent years would have occurred irrespective of the shift from social democracy to neoliberalism. Indeed, it might be asked if punitive trends cannot simply be understood in the context of the development of a conservative authoritarian consensus. In many ways, it can. As has been shown, the British press and the judiciary have traditionally held conservative views. It might even be said that the British public has always held rather conservative views on social and legal reform (Marwick, 1996). Yet, the question remains unanswered as to why these attitudes were suddenly translated into particularly punitive penal pol-icies *circa* 1993. Certainly, 'the rise of the public voice' (Ryan, 2004) played some role as politicians were increasingly required to move away from a patrician style of governing and to become more responsive to public demands. Yet, it is arguably only with the neoliberal trans-formation of the State, which began to take shape in the 1990s, that it became imperative for governments to find new methods of legitimation and to succumb to pressure to submit the criminal justice system, as all other public services, to the processes of commodification.

Nonetheless, it cannot be said that penal punitiveness is intrinsic to neoliberalism. Indeed, it has been demonstrated that some key neoliberal thinkers such as Stigler would have been opposed to the recent trend towards disproportionality in punishment. Excessive state intervention into civil society in the name of the fight against crime may also be said to run counter to neoliberal orthodoxy which is traditionally mistrustful of the State. Yet, punitiveness has indeed resulted from neoliberalism as it is actually practiced in the UK. Actually existing neoliberalism created the conditions that made the development of the authoritarian consensus on law and order more likely. It helped to create a punitive culture, marked by rampant individualism rather than social solidarity. It exacerbated trends towards the deprofessionalisation of the welfare state and the creation of a new cadre of managerial élites. Most importantly, it made political triangulation necessary. As New Labour accepted the neo-liberal hegemony, it continued to pursue the welfarist policies which it hoped would enable it to repair the social damage wreaked by Thatcherite neoliberal policies. Yet because it could in reality do little to address the root causes of these problems, it ended up punishing through welfare. Nonetheless, none of these transformations could have occurred had the right social and political conjecture not already been in place. These changes need to be understood in the context of the need for New Labour to 'modernise or die', to drag itself out of the political wilderness where it had languished since its catastrophic electoral defeat of 1983. Reconciling itself to neoliberalism was a means of proving its competence in economic affairs and of regaining the trust of the business and finan-cial sectors. For the Conservative Party, the pursuit of welfarist policies today is a way for it to remodel itself as a more caring 'one nation' party. In addition, the particular culture of the media and the judiciary in the UK has meant that there has been little resistance to punitive trends.

Such an analysis allows us to explain why different neoliberal countries have experienced different levels of punitive intensity. The peculiar political culture of the United States, for example, where senior mem-bers of the judiciary are elected by the people, has made it particularly prone to penal populism. For experts such as Tonry, this is of particular significance given the peculiar punitive sensibilities of the American people (Tonry, 2009). The existence of such cultural sensibilities may go some way to explaining the fact that some American states are more punitive than others, even though all of them have embraced neo-liberalism. In the rest of Europe, neoliberalism has been gaining influ-ence in recent years, yet the extent to which it has led to increased penal punitiveness has been mediated to some extent by the particular cultural and political configuration of different countries. In France, for example, whilst punitive trends such as disproportional sentencing and the criminalisation of young people are evident, professionals have been more successful in resisting them (Genderot, 2006). The adoption of punitive penal policies in countries such as France may also be explained by factors which are not directly related to neoliberalism, such as the need to engage in political point-scoring with parties from the extreme right. Even within the UK, we have seen that there are variations in levels of punitiveness with, for example, some regions resorting to measures such as ASBOs more infrequently than others and imposing shorter aver-age sentence lengths. It is perhaps less surprising that such variations exist in the devolved regions which have had at least some degree of autonomy to diverge from national policy. Scotland, for example, whilst being far from 'a land of milk and honey' (Mooney and Poole, 2004), has succeeded in implementing some important social measures which have, in the opinion of some experts, allowed it to break from the neo-liberal consensus (Davidson, 2008). Others have argued that Scotland has a distinct civic culture characterised by a strong socialist culture which tends to favour more inclusive social and penal policies, whatever party finds itself in power (McAra, 1999, p. 378). This may go some way to explaining the fact that English punitive trends, whilst present in Scotland, have been diluted to some extent. Yet, it is more difficult to explain the dilution of these trends within England itself where neoliberalism is considerably harder to resist. This may serve as further proof that neoliberal punitive trends may be mediated by particular local factors.

Nonetheless, the general trend in the UK is likely, at least in the short term, to continue to be towards punitiveness in the social and penal spheres, the degree of economic and cultural integration ensuring that neoliberalism will remain as the dominant political model throughout the nation. The extent to which neoliberal punitive trends may be resisted suggests that we are not heading towards 'penal dystopia' (Zedner, 2002), but it will be nevertheless be increasingly difficult to resist punitiveness whilst the neoliberal hegemony remains in place. To turn a Hayekian metaphor on its head, neoliberal penality has produced a ratchet effect: once firmly anchored in society, it has become extremely difficult to reverse. To do so now would risk political suicide, given that crime has been clearly designated as a wedge issue capable of providing politicians with much-needed electoral legitimacy. There is currently no political will to propose alternative solutions to the crime problem which would tackle its structural causes and necessitate a degree of state expenditure which would be unthinkable in the present economic climate. Most significantly, regardless of the current crisis of capitalism, neoliberalism is not in its final death throes. Government intervention has paradoxically ensured that it is soon to be restored to its former glory, albeit in a newly mutated form.

Yet, alternative penal futures are not impossible. As the frailties of the neoliberal order become ever-more apparent and the promised austerity of the coalition government becomes increasingly hard to bear, there is a possibility that a political vacuum may emerge which could be filled by a truly progressive government willing to reassert the welfarist function of the State and to spurn managerialist imperatives. In such a context, it might be possible for welfarist measures to be promoted as genuine *alternatives* to punishment and thus for the State to be weaned off its current dependence on imprisonment. This is not to advocate a return to the heyday of the welfare state. As numerous experts have pointed out, the 'pains of imprisonment' were all too apparent throughout the post-war period, regardless of the optimistic and progressive rhetoric that might have been employed by those in power (Cohen, 2001; Sim, 2009). In addition, even the most ardent critics of the current politicisation of the crime problem would refrain from advocating a return to the profoundly undemocratic form of decision-making which characterised the post-war penal consensus. Rather, it is suggested here that a truly progressive government should engage with the public at large in meaningful debate about the crime problem, thus promoting greater understanding of the issues at stake and of offenders themselves. One way of involving victims and the public in the criminal justice process is via restorative justice programmes which encourage dialogue between all parties involved and seek to reintegrate offenders. Successive New Labour governments did attempt to place such initiatives at the heart of their youth justice programme and indeed to extend them to the criminal justice system as a whole. However, as noted above, restorative justice has in practice been hijacked by an authoritarian agenda and has consequently failed to operate as a progressive alternative to the current penal impasse. It is nonetheless to be hoped that a challenge to the neoliberal hegemony would depoliticise the crime problem and lead to the adoption of a genuinely inclusive form of penal politics, based perhaps on forms of restorative justice rather than the retributive justice that so dominates the penal agenda today. It would certainly allow the State to break free from managerialist logic, to focus its energies on redirecting power from private to public interests and to find new means of legitimation. It is to be hoped that a reassertion of the welfarist function of the State might encourage the kind of inclusionary politics which would allow penal dystopia to be avoided.

Bibliography

ACMD (2008) Advisory Council for the Misuse of Drugs, *Cannabis: Classification and Public Health* (London: Home Office).

Alcock, P. (1997) *Understanding Poverty* (Basingstoke and New York: Palgrave Macmillan).

Allen, Lord (1995) 'In Search of the Purpose of Prison' in Prison Reform Trust, *Gladstone at 100: Essays on the Past and Future of the Prison System* (London: Prison Reform Trust).

Allen, R. (2005) 'Rethinking Crime and Punishment' in Murray, C. *Simple Justice* (London: CIVITAS).

Amadi, J. (2008) *Piloting Penalty Notices for Disorder on 10- to 15-year-olds* (London: Ministry of Justice).

Anderson, P. and Mann, N. (1997) *Safety First: The Making of New Labour* (London: Granta).

Andrews, K. and Jacobs, J. (1990) *Punishing the Poor: Poverty under Thatcher* (Basingstoke and New York: Macmillan).

Archbishop of Canterbury (1985) 'Commission on Urban Priority Areas', *Faith in the City: A Call for Action by Church and Nation* (London: General Synod of the Church of England, Church House Publishing).

Ashworth, A. (2004) 'Social Control and "Anti-Social Behaviour": The Subversion of Human Rights?', *Law Quarterly Review*, 120, 263–91.

Ashworth, A. (1997) 'Sentencing' in Maguire, M., Morgan, R. and Reiner, R. (eds.), *The Oxford Handbook of Criminology*, 2nd edn (Oxford and New York: Oxford University Press).

Ashworth, A. and Hough, M. (1996) 'Sentencing and the Climate of Opinion', *Criminal Law Review*, 776–87.

Ashworth, A. and Gibson, B. (1994) 'Altering the Sentencing Framework', *Criminal Law Review*, 101–9.

Ashworth, A. (1989) *Custody Reconsidered: Clarity and Consistency in Sentencing*, Policy Study n°104 (London: Centre for Policy Studies).

Asquith, S. and Docherty, M. (1999) 'Preventing Offending by Children and Young People in Scotland' in Duff, P. and Hutton, N. (eds.), *Criminal Justice in Scotland* (Aldershot: Dartmouth Publishing).

Attorney General (2009) http://www.attorneygeneral.gov.uk/AboutUs/uls/Pages// ULSChart-2001to2008.aspx, date accessed 20 May 2010.

Audit Scotland (2008) *Managing Increasing Prisoner Numbers in Scotland*, http:// www.auditscotland.gov.uk/docs/central/2008/nr_080508_prisoner_numbers_ comparisons.pdf, date accessed 20 May 2010.

Baker, E. and Roberts, J. V. (2005) 'Globalization and the New Punitiveness' in Pratt *et al.* (eds.), *The New Punitiveness: Trends, Theories, Perspectives* (Cullompton: Willan Publishing).

Bailey, V. (1997) 'English Prisons, Penal Culture, and the Abatement of Imprisonment, 1895–1922', *Journal of British Studies*, 36(3), 285–324.

Bailey, V. (1993) 'The Fabrication of Deviance?: "Dangerous Classes" and "Criminal Classes" in Victorian England' in Rule, J. and Malcolmson, R. (eds.), *Protest and Survival: The Historical Experience* (London: Merlin Press).

Bailey, V. (1987) *Delinquency and Citizenship: Reclaiming the Young Offender* (Oxford: Clarendon Press).

Bale, T. (2010) *The Conservative Party: From Thatcher to Cameron* (Cambridge and Malden: Polity Press).

Ball, C. (2004) 'Youth Justice? Half a Century of Responses to Youth Offending', *Criminal Law Review*, 167–80.

Ball, C. (2000) 'The Youth Justice and Criminal Evidence Act 1999, Part I: A Significant Move Towards Restorative Justice, or a Recipe for Unintended Consequences?', *Criminal Law Review*, 211–22.

Barclay, G. and Tavares, C. (2003) *International Comparisons of Criminal Justice Statistics 2001*, http://rds.homeoffice.gov.uk/rds/pdfs2/hosb1203.pdf, date accessed 20 May 2010.

Barnardo's (2010) http://www.barnardos.org.uk/what_we_do/children_in_trouble_campaign.htm, date accessed 21 May 2010.

Barnardo's (2008) *Locking Up or Giving In – Is Custody for Children Always the Right Answer?* (London: Barnardo's).

Bauman, Z. (2000) 'Social Issues of Law and Order', *British Journal of Criminology*, 40(2), 205–21.

BBC (2009) 'Double Jeopardy "to be Abolished"', 10 December.

BBC (2006) 'Watchdog's Fears Over Megan's Law', 21 June.

BBC (2005) *Prison Undercover: The Real Story*, broadcast 9 March.

BBC (2001) 'Labour: "The Party of the Family"', 17 February.

Beccaria, C. (1996) 'On Crimes and Punishments' in Muncie, J., McLaughlin, E. and Langan, M. (eds.) (London and Thousand Oaks: Sage).

Beck, U. (1992) *Risk Society: Towards a New Modernity* (London and Thousand Oaks: Sage).

Becker, G. (1968) 'Crime and Punishment: An Economic Approach', *Journal of Political Economy*, 76(2), 169–217.

Becker, S. (1997) *Responding to Poverty: The Politics of Cash and Care* (London: Longman).

Beckett, K. and Sasson, T. (2004) *The Politics of Injustice: Crime and Punishment in America*, 2nd edn (London and Thousand Oaks: Sage).

Beckett, K. and Western, B. (2001) 'Governing Social Marginality: Welfare, Incarceration, and the Transformation of State Policy', *Punishment and Society*, 3(1), 43–59.

Beech, M. (2006) *The Political Philosophy of New Labour* (London: Tauris Academic Studies).

Bell, E. (2007) Interviews with male and female prisoners at HMP East Sutton Park and HMP Lewes (unpublished field research).

Berman, G. (2009) *Prison Population Statistics*, House of Commons Library, http://www.parliament.uk/commons/lib/research/briefings/snsg-04334.pdf, date accessed 15 March 2010.

BIBIC (2005) British Institute for Brain-Injured Children, *Ain't Misbehavin': Young People with Learning and Communication Difficulties and Anti-Social Behaviour* (London: BIBIC).

Bingham, Lord (1997) Speech made to the Police Federation, 10 July.

Birt, J. (2000) *A New Vision for the Criminal Justice System* (London: Cabinet Office).

Blakeborough, L. and Pierpoint, H. (2007) *Conditional Cautions: An Examination of the Early Implementation of the Scheme* (London: Ministry of Justice).

Blair, T. (2006a) with Porter, H., 'Britain's Liberties: The Great Debate', *The Observer*, 23 April.

Blair, T. (2006b) 'Our Nation's Future', speech made at the University of Bristol, 23 June.

Blair, T. (2004a) Speech on antisocial behaviour, 28 October 2004.

Blair, T. (2004b) Speech made on launching the government's new five-year crime strategy, 19 June.

Blair, T. (2001a) Speech to the Peel Institute, 26 January.

Blair, T. (2001b) Speech to the Christian Socialist Movement, 29 March.

Blair, T. (2000) Speech to the Labour Party Conference, 26 September.

Blair, T. (1997a) Speech made at the Aylesbury Estate, 2 June.

Blair, T. (1997b) Speech to the annual conference of the Confederation of British Industry, 11 November.

Blair, T. (1996) *New Britain: My Vision of a Young Country* (London: Fourth Estate).

Blair, T. (1988) 'Antisocial Behaviour', *The Times*, 12 April.

Blunkett, D. (2010) Interview with the author, 6 January.

Bottomley, K. and Coleman, C. (1984) 'Law and Order: Crime Problem, Moral Panic or Penal Crisis?' in Norton, P. (ed.), *Law and Order and British Politics* (Aldershot: Gower).

Bottoms, A. E. (1995) 'The Philosophy and Politics of Punishment and Sentencing' in Clarkson, C. and Morgan, R. (eds.), *The Politics of Sentencing Reform* (Oxford: Clarendon Press).

Bottoms, A. E., McClean, J. D. and Patchett, K. W. (1970) 'Children, Young Persons and the Courts – A Survey of the New Law', *Criminal Law Review*, 368–95.

Box, S. (1987) *Recession, Crime and Punishment* (London and New York: Macmillan).

Brake, M. and Hale, C. (1992) *Public Order and Private Lives: The Politics of Law and Order* (London and New York: Routledge).

Bratton, W. J. (1998) 'Crime is Down in New York City: Blame the Police' in Dennis, N. (ed.), *Zero Tolerance: Policing a Free Society*, Choice in Welfare No. 35 (London: CIVITAS).

Brenner, N. and Theodore, N. (2002) 'Cities and the Geographies of "Actually Existing Neoliberalism"', *Antipode*, 34(3), 349–79.

Broadhead, J. (2004) 'No More Uncertainty about Parole', *New Law Journal*, 1117.

Briggs, J., Harrison, C., McInnes, A. and Vincent, D. (1996) *Crime and Punishment in England: An Introductory History* (London: University College London Press).

Brody, S. (1978) 'Research into the Aims and Effectiveness of Sentencing', *Howard Journal*, 17(3), 133–45.

Brown, D. (2005) 'Continuity, Rupture, or Just More of the "Volatile and Contradictory"? Glimpses of New South Wales' Penal Practice Behind and Through the Discursive' in Pratt *et al.* (eds.), *The New Punitiveness: Trends, Theories, Perspectives* (Cullompton: Willan Publishing).

Bryans, S. (2000) 'The Managerialisation of Prisons – Efficiency Without a Purpose?', *Criminal Justice Matters*, 40(1), 7–8.

BSIA (2010) British Security Industry Association, http://www.bsia.co.uk/home, date accessed 26 May 2010.

Bullock, K. and Jones, B. (2004) *Acceptable Behaviour Contracts: Addressing Anti-Social Behaviour in the London Borough of Islington*, Home Office On-line Report 02/04, http://rds.homeoffice.gov.uk/rds/pdfs2/rdsolr0204.pdf, date accessed 21 May 2010.

Burney, E. (2008) 'The ASBO and the Shift to Punishment' in Squires, P. (ed.), *ASBO Nation: The Criminalisation of Nuisance* (Bristol: Policy Press).

Burney, E. (2005) *Making People Behave: Anti-Social Behaviour, Politics and Policy* (Cullompton: Willan Publishing).

Burrows, M. H. (2003) *Evaluation of the Youth Inclusion Programme* (London: Youth Justice Board).

Callinicos, A. (2010) *Bonfire of Illusions: The Twin Crises of the Liberal World* (Cambridge and Malden: Polity Press, 2010).

Cameron, D. (2009) 'Bringing Law and Order to the Financial Markets', speech made 24 March.

Cameron, D. (2008) 'Fixing Our Broken Society', speech delivered in Gallowgate, Glasgow, 7 July.

Cameron, D. (2006a) 'Thugs – Beyond Redemption?', speech to the Centre for Social Justice, 10 July.

Cameron, D. (2006b) Speech on young offenders made at the Annual Convention of the Youth Justice Board, Cardiff, 2 November.

Cameron, D. (2006c) Speech on police reform delivered in Dalston, East London, 16 January.

Cameron, D. (2006d) 'Balancing Freedom and Security – A Modern British Bill of Rights', speech to the Centre for Policy Studies, 26 June.

Canovan, M. (1999) 'Trust the People! Populism and the Two Faces of Democracy', *Political Studies*, 47(1), 2–16.

Carter, P. (2007) *Securing the Future: Proposals for the Efficient and Sustainable Use of Custody in England and Wales* (London: Ministry of Justice).

Carter, P. (2006) *Legal Aid: A Market-Based Approach to Reform* (London: Home Office).

Carter, P. (2003) *Managing Offenders, Reducing Crime: A New Approach*, Home Office Strategy Unit (London: Home Office).

Casey, L. (2006) Speech on socially-excluded families, 20 March.

Cavadino, M., Crow, I. and Dignan, J. (1999) *Criminal Justice 2000: Strategies for a New Century* (Winchester: Waterside Press).

Cavadino, M. and Dignan, J. (2006) *Penal Systems: A Comparative Approach* (London and Thousand Oaks: Sage).

Cavanagh, B. (2007) *A Review of Dispersal Powers* (Edinburgh: Scottish Government).

Cavanagh, B. (2009) *A Review of Police Fixed Penalty Notices (FPNs) for Antisocial Behaviour* (Edinburgh: Scottish Government).

CBI (2003) Confederation of British Industry, *Competition: A Catalyst for Change in the Prison Service* (London: CBI).

Centre for Public Services (2002) *Privatising Justice: The Impact of the Private Finance Initiative in the Criminal Justice System*, http://www.european-services-strategy.org.uk/news/2002/privatising-justice/privatising-justice-pdf.pdf, date accessed 26 May 2010.

Chatwin, R. (1981) 'Brixton and After', *Marxism Today*, September, 26–7.

Christie, N. (2000) *Crime Control as Industry: Towards Gulags, Western-Style* (London and New York: Routledge).

Christie, N. (1977) 'Conflicts as Property', *British Journal of Criminology*, 17(1), 1–15.

Christoph, G. (2010) 'Le néolibéralisme: un essai de définition' in Espiet-Kilty, R. (ed.) *Libéralisme(s)* (Clermont-Ferrand: Presses Universitaires Blaise-Pascal).

CIVITAS (2003) *Does Prison Work? Overseas Evidence*, http://www.civitas.org.uk/data/twoCountries.php, date accessed 20 May 2010.

CJINI (2008) Criminal Justice Inspection Northern Ireland, *Antisocial Behaviour Orders: An Inspection of the Operation and Effectiveness of ASBOs*, http://www.cjini.org/CJNI/files/90/9084a0a0-4404-4bd0-be20-fe9d021af1ad.pdf, date accessed 21 May 2010.

Clarke, J. and Newman, J. (2006) *The Managerial State*, 2nd edn (London and Thousand Oaks: Sage).

Clarke, K. (2010) 'The Government's vision for criminal justice reform', speech delivered to the Centre for Crime and Justice Studies on 30 June.

Coalition of Social and Criminal Justice (2006) *Neighbourhood by Neighbourhood: Local Action to Reduce Re-offending* (London: Local Government Association).

Cohen, N. (2003) *Pretty Straight Guys* (London: Faber and Faber).

Cohen, S. (2001) *Visions of Social Control: Crime, Punishment and Classification*, 2nd edn (Cambridge and Malden: Polity Press).

Coleman, R., Tombs, S. and Whyte, D. (2005) 'Capital, Crime Control and State-craft in the Entrepreneurial City', *Urban Studies*, 42(13), 2511–30.

Coleman, R. and Sim, J. (2005) 'Contemporary Statecraft and the "Punitive Obsession": A Critique of the New Penology Thesis' in Pratt, J. *et al.* (eds), *The New Punitiveness: Trends, Theories, Perspectives* (Cullompton: Willan Publishing).

Coleman, R. (2004) 'Reclaiming the Streets: Closed Circuit Television, Neo-liberalism and the Mystification of Social Divisions in Liverpool, UK', *Surveillance & Society* 2(2/3), http://www.surveillance-and-society.org/articles2(2)/liverpool.pdf, date accessed 22 May 2010.

Collovald, A. (2004) *Le 'populisme du FN': un dangereux contresens* (Broissieux: Éditions du Croquant).

Conservative Party (2010) Electoral manifesto, http://media.conservatives.s3.amazonaws.com/manifesto/cpmanifesto2010_lowres.pdf, date accessed 22 May 2010.

Conservative Party (2008) *Prisons with a Purpose: Our Sentencing and Rehabilitation Revolution to Break the Cycle of Crime*, Policy Green Paper, n°4 (London: Conservative Party).

Convery, U., Haydon, D., Moore, L. and Scraton, P. (2008) 'Children, Rights and Justice in Northern Ireland: Community and Custody', *Youth Justice*, 8(3), 245–63.

Cook, D. (1997) *Poverty, Crime and Punishment* (London: Child Poverty Action Group).

Cooke, G. and Lawton, K. (2008) *Working Out of Poverty: A Study of the Low-Paid and the 'Working Poor'* (London: IPPR).

Cooper, C., Anscombe, J., Avenell, J., McClean, F. and Morris, J. (2006) *A National Evaluation of Community Support Officers*, Home Office Research Development and Statistics Directorate, Research Study 297 (London: Home Office).

Cooper, C. and Taylor, P. (2005) 'Independently Verified Reductionism: Prison Privatisation in Scotland', *Human Relations*, 58(4), 467–522.

Corner, J. (2006) 'Just another service provider? The Voluntary Sector's Place in the National Offender Management Service' in Tarry, N. (ed.), *Returning to Its*

Roots? A New Role for the Third Sector in Probation (London: Social Market Foundation).

Corporate Watch (2000) 'Prison Privatisation', Issue 11, http://archive.corpora tewatch.org/magazine/issue11/cw11f6.html, date accessed 20 November 2009.

Cortellessa, A. (2008) Interview with Agamben, G., 'Le gouvernement de l'insécurité', *La revue internationale des livres et des idées*, March–April, 18–20.

Councell, R. (2003) *Prison Population in 2002: A Statistical Review*, Home Office Findings no. 228 (London: Home Office).

Crawford, A. and Lister, S. (2007) *The Use and Impact of Dispersal Orders: Sticking Plasters and Wake-Up Calls* (Bristol: The Policy Press).

Crawford, A. (1998) 'Community Safety and the Quest for Security: Holding Back the Dynamics of Social Exclusion', *Policy Studies*, 19(3/4), 237–53.

Crawford, R., Emmerson, C. and Tetlow, G. (2009) *A Survey of Public Spending in the UK* (London: Institute for Fiscal Studies).

Croall, H. (2006) 'Criminal Justice in Post-devolutionary Scotland', *Critical Social Policy*, 26(3), 587–607.

Cross, N., Evans, J. and Minkes, J. (2002) 'Still Children First? Developments in Youth Justice in Wales', *Youth Justice* 2(3), 151–62.

Crouch, C. (2008) 'What Will Follow the Demise of Privatised Keynesianism', *Political Quarterly*, 79(4), 476–87.

Crouch, C. (1997) 'The Terms of the Neo-Liberal Consensus', *Political Quarterly*, 68(4), 352–60.

Currie, E. (1998) 'The Politics of Crime: The American Experience' in Stenson, K. and Cowell, D. (eds.), *The Politics of Crime Control*, 2nd edn (London and Thousand Oaks: Sage).

Dardot, P. and Laval, C. (2009) *La nouvelle raison du monde: Essai sur la société néolibérale* (Paris: Éditions de la Découverte).

Davidson, N. (2008) 'Scotland's New Road to Reform?', *International Socialism*, 118, 31 March.

Davie, N. (2007) 'Le bras long de la justice? Biométrie, précrime et le corps criminel' in Prum, M. (ed.), *Changements d'aire: De la 'race' dans l'aire anglophone* (Paris: L'Harmattan).

Davie, N. (2005) *Tracing the Criminal: The Rise of Scientific Criminology in Britain, 1860–1918* (Oxford: The Bardwell Press).

Davies, C. (1975) *Permissive Britain: Social Change in the Sixties and Seventies* (London: Pitman).

Davis, J. (1980) 'The London Garrotting Panic of 1862: A Moral Panic and the Creation of a Criminal Class in mid-Victorian England' in Gatrell, V. A. C., Lenman, B. and Parker, G. (eds.), *Crime and the Law: The Social History of Crime in Western Europe since 1500* (London: Europa Publications Ltd.).

DCA (2006) Department of Constitutional Affairs, *Delivering Simple, Speedy, Summary Justice*, http://www.dca.gov.uk/publications/reports_reviews/deliverysimple-speedy.pdf, date accessed 21 May 2010.

Dean, H. and Taylor-Gooby, P. (1992) *Dependency Culture: The Explosion of a Myth* (Hemel Hempstead: Harvester Wheatsheaf).

De Giorgi, A. (2006) *Rethinking the Political Economy of Punishment: Perspectives on Post-Fordism and Penal Politics* (Aldershot: Ashgate).

Demker, M., Towns, A., Duus-Otterström, G. and Sebring, J. (2008) 'Fear and Punishment in Sweden: Exploring Penal Attitudes', *Punishment and Society*, 10(3), 319–32.

Demos (1997) *The Wealth and Poverty of Networks* (London: Demos).

Dennis, N. and Mallon, R. (1998) 'Confident Policing in Hartlepool' in Dennis, N. (ed.), *Zero Tolerance: Policing a Free Society*, Choice in Welfare No. 35 (London: CIVITAS).

Dixon, K. (1998) *Les évangélistes du marché* (Paris: Raisons d'agir).

Dobson, G. (2003) 'Custody Plus or Minus?', *Safer Society*, 16, 15–17.

Dorling, D. (2006) 'Prime Suspect: Murder in Britain', *Prison Service Journal*, 166, 3–10.

Downes, D. and Morgan, R. (2002a) 'The Skeletons in the Cupboard: The Politics of Law and Order at the Turn of the Millennium' in Maguire, M., Morgan, R. and Reiner, R. (ed.), *The Oxford Handbook of Criminology*, 3rd edn (Oxford and New York: Oxford University Press).

Downes, D. and Morgan, R. (2002b) 'The British General Election 2001: The Centre Right Consensus', *Punishment and Society*, 4(1), 81–96.

Downes, D. (2001) 'The *Macho* Penal Economy: Mass Incarceration in the United States – A European Perspective', *Punishment and Society*, 3(1), 61–80.

Downes, D. and Morgan, R. (1997) 'Dumping the "Hostages to Fortune"? The Politics of Law and Order in Post-War Britain' in Maguire, M., Morgan, R. and Reiner, R. (eds.), *The Oxford Handbook of Criminology*, 2nd edn (Oxford and New York: Oxford University Press).

Downes, D. (1993) *Contrasts in Tolerance: Post-War Penal Policy in the Netherlands and England and Wales* (Oxford and New York: Oxford University Press).

Driver, S. and Martell, L. (1997) 'New Labour's Communitarianisms', *Critical Social Policy*, 17(3), 27–46.

DTI (2005) Department of Trade and Industry, *Public Policy: Using Market-Based Approaches*, Economics Paper N° 14, http://www.berr.gov.uk/files/file14759.pdf, date accessed 26 May 2010.

Duménil, G. and Lévy, D. (2004) *Capital Resurgent: Roots of the Neoliberal Revolution* (Harvard: Harvard University Press).

Duncan Smith, I. (2010), 'Welfare for the 21st Century', speech delivered 27 May.

Durham, M. (1991) *Sex and Politics: The Family and Morality in the Thatcher Years* (Basingstoke and New York: Macmillan).

Dwyer, P. (1998) 'Conditional Citizens? Welfare Rights and Responsibilities in the Late 1990s', *Critical Social Policy*, 18(4), 493–515.

Dyer, C. (2002) 'Woolf: Jail All Mobile Phone Thieves', *The Guardian*, 30 January.

Eady, D. (2007) 'Prisoners' Rights since the Woolf Report: Progress or Procrastination?', *The Howard Journal*, 46(3), 264–75.

Edwards, P., Shaoul, J., Stafford, A. and Arblaster, L. (2004) *Evaluating the Operation of PFI in Roads and Hospitals* (London: Certified Accountants Educational Trust).

Elcock, H. (1984) 'Law, Order and the Labour Party' in Norton, P. (ed.), *Law and Order and British Politics* (Aldershot: Gower).

Elliott, F. and Hanning, J. (2009) *Cameron: The Rise of the New Conservative* (London and New York, Harper Perennial).

Emsley, C. (1996) *Crime and Society in England, 1750–1900*, 2nd edn (London: Longman).

EHRC (2010) Equality and Human Rights Commission, *Stop and Think: A Critical Review of the Use of Stop and Search Powers in England and Wales*, http://equalityhumanrights.com/uploaded_files/raceinbritain/ehrc_stop_and_search_report.pdf, date accessed 22 May 2010.

Etzioni, A. (1995) *The Spirit of Community: Rights, Responsibilities and the Communitarian Agenda* (London: Fontana Press).

Fairclough, N. (2000) *New Labour, New Language?* (London and New York: Routledge).

Farrall, S. and Hay, C. (2010) 'Not so Tough on Crime? Why Weren't the Thatcher Governments More Radical in Reforming the Criminal Justice System?', *British Journal of Criminology*, 50(3), 550–69.

Faulkner, D. (2001) *Crime, State and Citizen: A Field Full of Folk* (Winchester: Waterside Press).

Faulkner, D. (1996) *Darkness and Light: Justice, Crime and Management for Today* (London: Howard League).

Feeley, M. and Simon, J. (1994) 'Actuarial Justice: The Emerging New Criminal Law' in Nelken, D. (ed.), *The Futures of Criminology* (London: Sage).

Feeley, M. and Simon, J. (1992) 'The New Penology: Notes on the Emerging Strategy of Corrections and its Implications', *Criminology*, 30, 449–74.

Field, F. (1996) 'Stakeholder Welfare', *Choice in Welfare n° 32* (London: IEA).

Fionda, J. (1999) 'New Labour, Old Hat: Youth Justice and the Crime and Disorder Act 1998', *Criminal Law Review*, 36–47.

Fitzgibbon, D. (2007) 'Risk Analysis and the New Practitioner: Myth or Reality?', *Punishment and Society*, 9(1), 87–97.

Fletcher, H. (2006) 'Supervision in the Community – An Alternative Approach' in Tarry, N. (ed.), *Returning to Its Roots? A New Role for the Third Sector in Probation* (London: Social Market Foundation).

Fletcher, H. (2005) *Anti-Social Behaviour Orders: An Analysis of the First Six Years* (London: National Association of Probation Officers).

Forsythe, W. (1995) 'The Garland Thesis and the Origins of Modern English Prison Discipline: 1853 to 1939', *The Howard Journal*, 43(3), 259–73.

Forsythe, W. (1991) *Penal Discipline, Reformatory Projects and the English Prison Commission, 1895–1939* (Exeter: University of Exeter Press).

Foucault, M. (2004) *Naissance de la biopolitique: Cours au Collège de France, 1978–79* (Paris: Seuil/Gallimard).

Foucault, M. (1975) *Surveiller et Punir: Naissance de la prison* (Paris: Gallimard).

Fox, L. (1952) *The English Prison and Borstal Systems* (London: Routledge and Keegan Paul).

Franklin, B. (2004) 'A Damascene Conversion? New Labour and Media Relations' in Ludlam, S. and Smith, M. J. (eds.), *Governing as New Labour: Policy and Politics under Blair* (Basingstoke and New York: Palgrave Macmillan).

Freeden, M. (1999) 'The Ideology of New Labour', *Political Quarterly*, 70(1), 42–51.

G4S (2010) http://www.g4s.uk.com/en-GB/Who%20we%20are/, date accessed 26 May 2010.

Gamble, A. (2009) *The Spectre at the Feast: Capitalist Crisis and the Politics of Recession* (Basingstoke and New York: Palgrave Macmillan).

Gamble, A. (1994) *The Free Economy and the Strong State*, 2nd edn (Basingstoke and New York: Palgrave Macmillan).

Garland, D. (2005) 'Capital Punishment and American Culture', *Punishment and Society*, 7, 347–76.

Garland, D. (2001a) *The Culture of Control: Crime and Social Order in Contemporary Society* (Oxford and New York: Oxford University Press).

Garland, D. (2001b) 'The Meaning of Mass Imprisonment', *Punishment & Society*, 3, 5–7.

Garland, D. and Sparks, r. (2000) 'Criminology, Social Theory and the Challenge of Our Times', *British Journal of Criminology*, 40(2), 189–204.

Garland, D. (1996) 'The Limits of the Sovereign State: Strategies of Crime Control in Contemporary Society', *The British Journal of Criminology*, 36(4), 445–67.

Garland, D. (1985) *Punishment and Welfare* (Aldershot: Gower).

Garside, R. (2006) 'Right for the Wrong Reasons: Making Sense of Criminal Justice Failure' in Garside, R. and McMahon, W. (eds.) *Does Criminal Justice Work? The 'Right for the Wrong Reasons' Debate: Monograph n°3* (London: Centre for Crime and Justice Studies).

Gatrell, V. A. C. (1994) *The Hanging Tree: Execution and the English People, 1770–1868* (Oxford and New York: Oxford, University Press).

Genderot, S. (2006) 'France: The Politicisation of Youth Justice' in Muncie, J. and Goldson, B. (eds.), *Comparative Youth Justice: Critical Readings* (London and Thousand Oaks: Sage).

Ghate, D. and Ramella, M. (2002) *Positive Parenting: The National Evaluation of the Youth Justice Board's Parenting Programme* (London: Policy Research Bureau).

Giddens, A. (2000) *The Third Way and Its Critics* (Cambridge and Malden: Polity Press).

Giddens, A. (1998) 'Risk Society: The Context of British Politics' in Franklin, J. (ed.), *The Politics of Risk Society* (Cambridge and Malden: Polity Press/IPPR).

Gibb, F. (2005) 'Judges Set Against Plans for Victims' Advocates', *The Times*, 24 December.

Gil-Robles, A. (2005) *Report by the Commissioner for Human Rights on His Visit to the United Kingdom, 4th–12th November, 2004*, CommDH(2005)6 (Strasbourg: Council of Europe).

Girling, E. (2006) 'European Identity, Penal Sensibilities, and Communities of Sentiment' in Armstrong, S. and McAra, L. (eds.), *Perspectives on Punishment: The Contours of Control* (Oxford and New York: Oxford University Press).

Glover, J. (2007) 'More Prisons are not the Answer to Punishing Crime, says poll', *The Guardian*, 28 August.

Goldson, B. and Muncie, J. (2006) 'Rethinking Youth Justice: Comparative Analysis, International Human Rights and Research Evidence', *Youth Justice*, 6(2), 91–106.

Goldson, B. and Jamieson, J. (2002) 'Youth Crime, the "Parenting Deficit" and State Intervention: A Contextual Critique', *Youth Justice*, 2(2), 82–99.

Goldson, B. (2002) 'The New Punitiveness: The Politics of Child Incarceration' in Muncie, J., Hughes, G. and McLaughlin, E. (eds.), *Youth Justice: Critical Readings* (London: Sage).

Gottschalk, M. (2007) *The Prison and the Gallows: The Politics of Mass Incarceration in America*, 2nd edn (Cambridge and New York: Cambridge University Press).

Gray, E., Taylor, E., Roberts, C., Merrington, S., Fernandez, R. and Moore, R. (2005) *Intensive Supervision and Surveillance Programme: The Final Report* (London: Youth Justice Board).

Gray, J. (1996) *After Social Democracy: Politics, Capitalism and the Common Life* (London: Demos).

Green, D. A. (2009) 'Feeding Wolves: Punitiveness and Culture', *European Journal of Criminology*, 6(6), 517–36.

Green, D. (2003) 'Crime is Falling – Because Prison Works', *The Observer* 20 July 2003.

Grayling, C. (2009a) 'Tackling Antisocial Behaviour', speech delivered 9 April.

Grayling, C. (2009b) 'Our approach to law and order', speech delivered 17 November.

Griffith, J. A. G. (1997) *The Politics of the Judiciary*, 5th edn (London: Fontana Press).

Hale, S. (2002) 'Professor Macmurray and Mr Blair: The Strange Case of the Communitarian Guru that Never Was', *Political Quarterly*, 73(2), 191–7.

Halimi, S. (2004) *Le grand bond en arrière: Comment l'ordre libéral s'est imposé au monde* (Paris: Fayard).

Hall, S. (1998) 'The Great Moving Nowhere Show', *Marxism Today* (November/December), 9–14.

Hall, S. (1988) *The Hard Road to Renewal: Thatcherism and the Crisis of the Left* (London and New York: Verso).

Hall, S. and Scraton, P. (1981) 'Law, Class and Control' in Fitzgerald, M., McLennan, G. and Pawson, J. (eds.), *Crime and Society* (London and New York: Routledge).

Hall, S., Critcher, C., Jefferson, T., Clarke, J. and Roberts, B. (1978) *Policing the Crisis: Mugging, the State, and Law and Order* (Basingstoke and New York: Macmillan).

Halliday, J. (2001) *Making Punishment Work: Report of a Review of the Sentencing Framework for England and Wales* (London: Home Office).

Hallsworth, S. (2000) 'Rethinking the Punitive Turn: Economies of Excess and the Criminology of the Other', *Punishment and Society*, 2(2), 145–60.

Hammarberg, T. (2008) Memorandum by the Commissioner for Human Rights of the Council of Europe Following His Visits to the United Kingdom (5–8 February and 31 March–2 April 2008), CommDH(2008)27 (Strasbourg: Council of Europe).

Hansard (2010) Written answers, Hansard, 2010, 28 January, column 1042W, http://www.publications.parliament.uk/pa/cm200910/cmhansrd/cm100128/text/100128w0013.htm, date accessed 21 May 2010.

Hansard (2009a) Written answers, 16 June, column 257W, http://www.parliament.the-stationery-office.co.uk/pa/cm200809/cmhansrd/cm090616/text/90616w0025.htm, date accessed 20 May 2010.

Hansard (2009b) Lords Hansard, 12 January, column WA91, http://www.publications.parliament.uk/pa/ld200809/ldhansrd/text/90112w0002.htm, date accessed 20 May 2010.

Hansard (2008a) Written answers, 27 February, column 1719W, http://www.publications.parliament.uk/pa/cm200708/cmhansrd/cm080227/text/80227w0032.htm#08022816005384, date accessed 26 May 2010.

Hansard (2008b) Commons debates, 10 June, column 155, http://www.publications.parliament.uk/pa/cm200708/cmhansrd/cm080610/debtext/80610-0003.htm, date accessed 26 May 2010.

Hansard (2007) Lords Debate, 3 July, column 939, http://www.publications.parliament.uk/pa/ld200607/ldhansrd/text/70703-0006.htm, date accessed 26 May 2010.

Harding, C., Hines, B., Ireland, R. and Rawlings, P. (1985) *Imprisonment in England and Wales: A Concise History* (London: Crook Helm).

Harvey, D. (2007) *A Brief History of Neoliberalism*, 2nd edn (Oxford and New York: Oxford University Press).

Harris, R. (2001) in Institute of Economic Affairs (2001) *A Conversation with Harris and Seldon* (London: IEA).

Haydon, D. and Scraton, P. (2000) '"Condemn a Little More, Understand a Little Less": The Political Context and Rights Implications of the Domestic and European Rulings in the Venables-Thompson Case', *Journal of Law and Society*, 27(3), 416–48.

Hazel, N. *et al.* (2002) *Detention and Training: Assessment of the Detention and Training Order and Its Impact on the Secure Estate Across England and Wales* (London: Youth Justice Board).

HCJC (2010) House of Commons Justice Committee, *Cutting Crime: The Case for Justice Reinvestment*, http://www.publications.parliament.uk/pa/cm200910/cmselect/cmjust/94/94i.pdf, date accessed 22 May 2010.

Hewitt, M. (2002) 'New Labour and the Redefinition of Social Security' in Powell, M. (ed.) *Evaluating New Labour's Welfare Reforms* (Bristol: The Policy Press).

Hicks, J. and Allen, G. (1999) *A Century of Change: Trends in UK statistics since 1900*, House of Commons Research Paper 99/111, http://www.parliament.uk/documents/commons/lib/research/rp99/rp99-111.pdf, date accessed 22 May 2010.

Hill, S. (2004) *Setting Business Free from Crime* (London: The British Chambers of Commerce).

Hills, J. *et al.* (2010) *An Anatomy of Economic Inequality in the UK: Report of the National Equality Panel*, http://sticerd.lse.ac.uk/dps/case/cr/CASEreport60.pdf, date accessed 22 May 2010.

Hillyard, P. and Tombs, S. (2008) 'Beyond Criminology' in Dorling, D., Gordon, D., Hillyard, P., Pantazis, C., Pemberton, S. and Tombs, S. (2008) (eds.), *Criminal Obsessions: Why Harm Matters More than Crime*, 2nd edn (London: Centre for Crime and Justice Studies).

Hillyard, P., Sim, J., Tombs, S. and Whyte, D. (2004) 'Leaving a "Stain Upon the Silence": Contemporary Criminology and the Politics of Dissent', *The British Journal of Criminology*, 44(3), 369–90.

Hillyard, P. (1993) *Suspect Community: People's Experiences of the Prevention of Terrorism Acts in Britain* (London: Pluto Press).

Hillyard, P. and Percy-Smith, J. (1988) *The Coercive State* (London: Fontana).

HM Government (2010) http://programmeforgovernment.hmg.gov.uk/, date accessed 26 May 2010.

HM Government (2005) *Reducing Re-Offending Through Skills and Employment*, Cm 6702, http://www.official-documents.gov.uk/document/cm67/6702/6702.pdf, date accessed 22 May 2010.

HMICS (2010) Her Majesty's Inspectorate of Constabulary for Scotland, http://www.scotland.gov.uk/Resource/Doc/925/0078649.pdf, date accessed 22 May 2010.

HM Inspectorate of Prisons (2009) *The Prison Characteristics that Predict Prisons Being Assessed as Performing 'Well': A Thematic Review*, http://www.justice.gov.uk/inspectorates/hmi-prisons/docs/prison_performance_thematic-rps.pdf, date accessed 26 May 2010.

HM Inspectorate of Prisons (2008) http://www.justice.gov.uk/inspectorates/hmi-prisons/docs/ipp_pn-rps.pdf, date accessed 19 May 2010.

HM Inspectorate of Prisons (2005) *Annual Report of HM Chief Inspector of Prisons for England and Wales 2004–2005*, HC 883 (London: HMSO).

HM Inspectorate of Probation (2006) *An Independent Review of a Serious Further Offence Case: Anthony Rice* (London: HMSO).

HM Prison Service (2010a) Population figures, 30 April, http://www.hmprison-service.gov.uk/assets/documents/10004AA9population_bulletin_weekly_30_04_10.doc, date accessed 19 May 2010.

HM Prison Service (2010b) Offending behaviour programmes, http://www.hm-prisonservice.gov.uk/adviceandsupport/beforeafterrelease/offenderbehaviour-programmes/, date accessed 22 May 2010.

HM Treasury (2009) http://www.hm-treasury.gov.uk/d/pesa09_chapter4.pdf, date accessed 19 May 2010.

HM Treasury (2006) *PFI: Strengthening Long-term Partnerships*, http://webarchive.nationalarchives.gov.uk/+/http://www.hm-treasury.gov.uk/d/bud06_pfi_618.pdf, date accessed 22 May 2010.

HM Treasury (2003) *PFI: Meeting the investment challenge*, http://webarchive.national-archives.gov.uk/+/http://www.hm-treasury.gov.uk/media/F/7/PFI_604a.pdf, date accessed 22 May 2010.

Hobhouse S. and Brockway, F. (1984 [1922]) (eds.), *English Prisons Today* (New York: Garland).

Holdaway, S. and Desborough, S. (2004) *National Evaluation of the Youth Justice Board's Final Warning Projects* (London: Youth Justice Board).

Home Office (2010a) http://www.crimereduction.homeoffice.gov.uk/business/businesscrimeminisite01.htm, date accessed 15 April 2010.

Home Office (2010b) *A Summary of Recorded Crime Date from 2002/03 to 2008/09*, http://rds.homeoffice.gov.uk/rds/recordedcrime1.html, date accessed 26 May 2010.

Home Office (2007a) *Review of the Protection of Children from Sex Offenders* (London: Home Office).

Home Office (2007b) Victims' Advisory Panel, http://www.cjsonline.gov.uk/downloads/application/pdf/Victims'%20Advisory%20Panel%20Overview.pdf, date accessed 22 May 2010.

Home Office (2006a) *Penalty Notices for Disorder: A Guide*,http://www.asb.home-office.gov.uk/uploadedFiles/Members_site/Document_Library/step-by-step_guides/PENALTY%20NOTICES%20for%20disorder_step-by-step_May2006.pdf, date accessed 21 May 2010.

Home Office (2006b) *Criminal Statistics 2005: England and Wales* (London: Home Office).

Home Office (2006c) *Rebalancing the Criminal Justice System in Favour of the Law-Abiding Majority: Cutting Crime, Reducing Reoffending and Protecting the Public* (London: Home Office).

Home Office (2005a) *Use of Dispersal Powers* (London: Home Office).

Home Office (2005b) *Restructuring Probation to Reduce Re-offending: Consultation Paper* (London: Home Office).

Home Office (2004a) *Defining and Measuring Anti-Social Behaviour* (London: Home Office).

Home Office (2004b) *Building Communities, Beating Crime: A Better Police Service for the 21st Century*, Cm 6360 (London: Home Office).

Home Office (2004c) *Reducing Crime – Changing Lives: The Government's Plans for Transforming the Management of Offenders* (London: Home Office).

Home Office (2003a) *Respect and Responsibility: Taking a Stand Against Anti-Social Behaviour*, Cm5778 (London: HMSO).

Home Office (2003b) *Policing: Building Safer Communities Together* (London: Home Office Communication Directorate).

Home Office (2002) *Justice for All*, Cm5563 (London: Home Office).

Home Office (1997) *No More Excuses: A New Approach to Tackling Youth Crime in England and Wales*, Cm 3809 (London: Home Office).

Home Office (1990) *Crime, Justice and Protecting the Public*, Cm 965 (London: HMSO).

Home Office (1988) *Private Sector Involvement in the Remand System*, Cm 434 (London: HMSO).

Home Office (1987) Home Affairs Select Committee, *The Contract Provision of Prisons*, HC 291 (London: Home Office).

Home Office (1966) *Report of the Inquiry into Prison Escapes and Security* (London: HMSO).

Home Office (1960) *Prisons & Borstals: Statement of Policy and Practice in the Administration of Prisons and Borstal Institutions in England and Wales* (London: HMSO).

Hood, R., Shute, S., Feilzer, M. and Wilcox, A. (2002) *Reconviction Rates of Serious Sex Offenders and Assessments of their Risk*, Home Office Findings n° 164 (London: Home Office).

Hope, T. (2004) 'Pretend it Works: Evidence and Governance in the Evaluation of the Reducing Burglary Initiative', *Criminal Justice Matters*, 4(3), 287–308.

Hough, M., Clancy, A., McSweeney, T. and Turnbull, P. (2003) *The Impact of Drug Treatment and Testing Orders on Offending* (London: Home Office).

Hough, M. and Roberts, J. V. (2003) *Youth Crime and Youth Justice: Public Opinion in England and Wales* (London: Institute for Criminal Policy Research/The Nuffield Foundation).

Hough, M. and Roberts, J. V. (1998) *Attitudes to Punishment: Findings from the British Crime Survey*, Home Office Research Study 179 (London: Home Office).

House of Commons (2010) *The Register of Members' Financial Interests*, http://www.publications.parliament.uk/pa/cm/cmregmem/100412/100412.pdf, date accessed 26 May 2010.

House of Commons (2009) *Anti-social Behaviour Order Statistics*, http://www.parliament.uk/commons/lib/research/briefings/snsg-03112.pdf, date accessed 15 March 2010.

House of Commons (2008) *Meeting Needs? The Offenders' Learning and Skills Service*, http://www.publications.parliament.uk/pa/cm200708/cmselect/cmpubacc/584/584.pdf, date accessed 22 May 2010.

House of Commons Education and Skills Committee (2005) *Education and Skills: Seventh Report*, http://www.publications.parliament.uk/pa/cm200405/cmselect/cmeduski/114/11402.htm, date accessed 22 May 2010.

House of Commons Home Affairs Committee (2010) *Eighth Report: The DNA Database*, http://www.publications.parliament.uk/pa/cm200910/cmselect/cmhaff/222/22202.htm, date accessed 22 May 2010.

Howard, M. (1997) 'Cutting Social Security' in Walker, A. and Walker, C. (eds.), *Britain Divided: The Growth of Social Exclusion in the 1980s and 1990s* (London: Child Poverty Action Group).

Howard, M. (1993) Speech to the Conservative Party Conference, citation transcribed from a recording compiled by Peter Hill and BBC News, *Great Political Speeches* (audio cassette).

Howard League (2009) *Youth Justice in Wales: Thinking Beyond the Prison Bars*, http://www.howardleague.org/fileadmin/howard_league/user/online_publications/Wales_youth_justice.pdf, date accessed 21 May 2010.

Hoyle, C. and Rose, D. (2001), 'Labour, Law and Order', *The Political Quarterly*, 72(1), 76–85.

Hudson, B. (2010) 'Review Symposium: *Punishing the Poor – The Neoliberal Government of Insecurity* by Loïc Wacquant', *British Journal of Criminology*, 50(1), 589–608.

Hudson, B. (2003) *Understanding Justice: An Introduction to Ideas, Perspectives and Controversies in Modern Penal Theory*, 2nd edn (Buckingham: Open University Press).

Hudson, R. and Williams, A. M. (2000) *Divided Britain*, 2nd edn (Paris: Mallard Éditions).

Hutton, W. (1996) *The State We're In*, 2nd edn (London: Vintage).

ICM/*Observer* (2003) April, 'Crime Uncovered', http://www.icmresearch.co.uk/pdfs/2003_april_observer_crime_uncovered.pdf, date accessed 26 May 2010.

ICPS (2010) International Centre for Prison Studies, http://www.kcl.ac.uk/depsta/law/research/icps/worldbrief/, date accessed 20 May 2010.

Ignatieff, M. (1978) *A Just Measure of Pain: The Penitentiary in the Industrial Revolution, 1750–1850* (Basingstoke and New York: Macmillan).

IPPR (2001) *Building Better Partnerships: The Final Report of the Commission on Public Private Partnerships* (London: IPPR).

IPSOS/MORI (2010) 'April Issues Index: The Economy Remains the Top Issue as the Election Draws Near', 21 April, http://www.ipsos-mori.com/research-publications/researcharchive/poll.aspx?oItemId=2595, date accessed 26 May 2010.

IPSOS/MORI (2009a) 'Survey for Channel 4 on Attitudes Towards the Death Penalty', 28 October, http://www.ipsos-mori.com/researchpublications/researcharchive/poll.aspx?oItemId=2504, date accessed 26 May 2010.

IPSOS/MORI (2009b) 'Best Party on Key Issues: Crime/Law and Order', 29 September, http://www.ipsos-mori.com/researchpublications/researcharchive/poll.aspx?oItemID=29&view=wide, date accessed 26 May 2010.

ISPOS/MORI (2005) 'Public Concern about ASB and Support for ASBOs', 10 June, http://www.ipsos-mori.com/researchpublications/researcharchive/poll.aspx?oItemId=412, date accessed 26 May 2010.

Irwin, J., Austin, J. and Baird, C. (1998) 'Fanning the Flames of Fear', *Crime and Delinquency*, 44(1), 32–48.

Jacobson, J. and Gibbs, P. (2009) *Making Amends: Restorative Youth Justice in Northern Ireland* (London: Prison Reform Trust).

James, A. and Raine, J. (1998) *The New Politics of Criminal Justice* (London: Longman).

Jenkins, P. (1989) *Mrs Thatcher's Revolution* (London: Pan Books).

Jessop, B. (2007) 'New Labour or the Normalization of Neo-Liberalism?', *British Politics*, 2(2), 282–8.

Johnson, N. (1990) *Restructuring the Welfare State: A Decade of Change 1980–1990* (Hemel Hempsted: Harvester Wheatsheaf).

Johnstone, G. (2001) 'Penal Policy Making: Elitist, Populist or Participatory?', *Punishment and Society*, 2(2), 151–80.

Joint Committee on Human Rights (2004) *Third Report*, http://www.publications.parliament.uk/pa/jt200405/jtselect/jtrights/15/1507.htm, date accessed 22 May 2010.

Jones, C. and Novak, T. (1999) *Poverty, Welfare and the Disciplinary State* (London and New York: Routledge).

Jones, T. and Newburn, T. (2006) 'Three Strikes and You're Out: Exploring Symbol and Substance in American and British Crime Control Politics', *British Journal of Criminology*, 46(5), 781–802.

Jones, T. and Newburn, T. (2005) 'Comparative Criminal Justice Policy-Making in the United States and the United Kingdom: The Case of Private Prisons', *British Journal of Criminology*, 45(1), 58–80.

JRF (2001) Joseph Rowntree Foundation, *Recruiting and Employing Offenders: The impact of the Police Act* (London: JRF).

Karstedt, S. and Farrall, S. (2007) *Law-Abiding Majority? The Everyday Crimes of the Middle Classes* (London: Centre for Crime and Justice Studies).

Keegan, W. (1985) *Mrs Thatcher's Economic Experiment* (Harmondsworth: Penguin).

Kemshall, H. and Wood, J. (2010) *Child Sex Offender Review (CSOR) Public Disclosure Pilots, Research Report 32* (London: Home Office).

Kensey, A. and Tournier, P. (1999) 'Prison Population Inflation, Overcrowding and Recidivism: The Situation in France', *European Journal on Criminal Policy and Research*, 7(1), 97–119.

King, R. and McDermott, K. (1995) *The State of Our Prisons* (Oxford: Clarendon Press).

Kirkup, J. and Bunyan, N. (2008) 'Judge Blames Ministers for Yob Terror', *The Daily Telegraph*, 19 January.

Koffman, L. (2006) 'The Rise and Fall of Proportionality: The Failure of the Criminal Justice Act 1991', *Criminal Law Review*, 281–99.

Kühnrich, B. and Kania, H. (2007) *Attitudes Towards Punishment in the European Union: Results from the 2005 European Crime Survey*, http://www.europeansafetyobservatory.eu/, date accessed 29 April 2010.

Kury, H., Brandenstein, M. and Obergfell-Fuchs, J. (2009) 'Dimensions of Punitiveness in Germany', *European Journal on Criminal Policy and Research*, 15, 63–81.

Labour Party (1964) *Crime – A Challenge to Us All* (London: Labour Party).

Lacey, N. (2008) *The Prisoners' Dilemma: Political Economy and Punishment in Contemporary Democracies* (Cambridge and New York: Cambridge University Press).

Lacey, N. (1994) 'Government as Manager, Citizen as Consumer: The Case of the Criminal Justice Act 1991', *Modern Law Review*, 75(4), 534–54.

Lazergues, C. (2008) 'La mutation du modèle protectionniste de justice des mineurs', *Revue de science criminelle et de droit pénal comparé*, 1, 200–8.

Lea, J. and Young, J. (1993) *What is to be Done about Law and Order?*, 2nd edn (London, Pluto Press).

Leach, R. (2002) 'Christian Socialism: The Historical and Contemporary Significance of Christian Socialism within the Labour Party', Paper presented to the annual conference of the Political Studies Association, University of Aberdeen, 5–7 April, http://www.psa.ac.uk/journals/pdf/5/2002/leach.pdf, date accessed 22 May 2010.

Leapman, B. (2007) 'Penalty Notices for One Crime in Nine', *The Sunday Telegraph*, 8 January.

Leigh, A., Read, T. and Tilley, N. (1998) *Brit Pop II: Problem-Oriented Policing in Practice*, Police Research Series Paper 93, Home Office Research Development and Statistics Directorate (London: Home Office).

Letwin, O. (2002) *The Frontline Against Fear: Taking Neighbourhood Policing Seriously* (London: The Bow Group).

Levenson, J. (2002) *Prison Overcrowding: The Inside Story* (London: Prison Reform Trust).

Levi, M., Burrows, J., Fleming, M. and Hopkins, M. (2007) *The Nature, Extent and Economic Impact of Fraud in the UK: Report for the Association of Chief Police Officers' Economic Crime Portfolio* (London: ACPO).

Levitas, R. (2005) *The Inclusive Society?: Social Exclusion and New Labour*, 2nd edn (Basingstoke and New York: Palgrave Macmillan).

Leys, C. (2003) *Market-Driven Politics: Neoliberal Democracy and the Public Interest*, 2nd edn (London and New York: Verso).

Lianos, M. and Douglas, M. (2000) 'Dangerization and the End of Deviance: The Institutional Environment' in Garland, D. and Sparks, R. (eds.), *Criminology and Social Theory* (Oxford and New York: Oxford University Press).

Liberal Democrats (2010a) Electoral manifesto, http://network.libdems.org.uk/manifesto2010/libdem_manifesto_2010.pdf, date accessed 22 May 2010.

Liberal Democrats (2010b) Policy briefing: Crime and policing, http://www.nickclegg.com/siteFiles/resources/PDF/Policy%20Briefing%20-% 20 Crime%20Policing%20Oct%2009.pdf, date accessed 22 May 2010.

Liberty (2007) 'Terrorism Act 2006', http://www.liberty-human-rights.org.uk/issues/6-free-speech/terrorism-act-2006/index.shtml, date accessed 22 May 2010.

Liberty (2003) *Casualty of War: 8 Weeks of Counter-terrorism in Rural England*, http://www.liberty-human-rights.org.uk/publications/pdfs/casualty-of-war-final.pdf, date accessed 20 May 2010.

Lilly, R. and Knepper, P. (1993) 'The Corrections-Commercial Complex', *Crime and Delinquency*, 42(1), 150–66.

Lister, R. *et al.* (2003) 'Government Must Reconsider its Strategy for a More Equal Society' in Chadwick, A. and Heffernan, R. (eds.), *The New Labour Reader* (Cambridge and Malden: Policy Press).

Loader, I. (2006a) 'Fall of the "Platonic Guardians": Liberalism, Criminology and Political Responses to Crime in England and Wales', *British Journal of Criminology*, 46(4), 561–86.

Loader, I. (2006b) 'Rebalancing the Criminal Justice System?', letter sent to Tony Blair, 21 June.

Lobley, D. and Smith, D. (2000) *An Evaluation of Electronically Monitored Restriction of Liberty Orders: Crime and Criminal Justice Research Findings No. 47* (Edinburgh: Scottish Government).

Loveday, B. (2007) 'Community Policing under New Labour', *Criminal Justice Matters*, 67, 28–9.

Lund, B. (2002) *Understanding State Welfare: Social Justice or Social Exclusion?* (London and Thousand Oaks: Sage).

Lyon, D. (2003) *Surveillance as Social Sorting: Privacy, Risk and Digital Discrimination* (London and New York: Routledge).

Lyon, D. (1994) *The Electronic Eye: The Rise of the Surveillance Society* (Cambridge and Malden: Polity Press).

MacAskill, K. (2010) Scottish Parliament written answers, 22 February, http://www.theyworkforyou.com/spwrans/?id=2010-02-22.S3W-31340.h, date accessed 19 May 2010.

Macpherson, W. (1999) *The Stephen Lawrence Inquiry*, Cm 4262-I (London: Home Office).

Maguire, M. (2007) 'Crime Data and Statistics' in Maguire, M., Morgan, R. and Reiner, R. (eds.), *The Oxford Handbook of Criminology*, 4th edn (Oxford and New York: Oxford University Press).

Maguire, M. (2004) 'The Crime Reduction Programme in England and Wales: Reflections on the Vision and the Reality', *Criminal Justice Matters*, 4(3), 213–37.

Mair, G. and Mills, H. (2009) *The Community Order and the Suspended Sentence Order Three Years On: The Views and Experiences of Probation Officers and Offenders* (London: Centre for Crime and Justice Studies).

Mair, G., Cross, N. and Taylor, S. (2007) *The Use and Impact of the Community Order and the Suspended Sentence Order* (London: Centre for Crime and Justice Studies).

Mair, G. (1997) 'Community Penalties and the Probation Service' in Maguire, M., Morgan, R. and Reiner, R. (eds.), *The Oxford Handbook of Criminology*, 2nd edn (Oxford and New York: Oxford University Press).

Mandelson, P. and Liddle, R. (2002) *The Blair Revolution Revisited* (London: Politico's Publishing).

Mann, K. (1992) *The Making of an English 'Underclass'? The Social Divisions of Welfare and Labour* (Oxford and New York: Oxford University Press).

Margo, J. and Dixon, M. (2006) *Freedom's Orphans: Raising Youth in a Changing World* (London: Institute for Public Policy Research).

Marquand, D. (1988) *The Unprincipled Society: New Demands and Old Politics* (London: Jonathan Cape).

Martinson, R. (1974) 'What Works? Questions and Answers about Prison Reform', *The Public Interest*, 35, 22–54.

Marwick, A. (1996) *British Society Since 1945* (London: Penguin).

Marxism Today (1982) 'Policing in the Eighties: Interview with John Alderson', April, pp. 8–14.

Mathiason, N. (2001) 'Crime Pays Handsomely for Britain's Private Jails', *The Observer*, 11 March.

Matravers, A. and Hughes, G. (2003) 'Unprincipled Sentencing? The Policy Approach to Dangerous Sex Offenders' in Tonry, M. (ed.), *Confronting Crime: Crime Control Policy Under New Labour* (Cullompton: Willan Publishing).

Matthews, R., Easton, H., Briggs, D. and Pease, K. (2007) (eds.) *Assessing the Use and Impact of Anti-social Behaviour Orders* (Bristol: Policy Press).

Matthews, R. (2005) 'The Myth of Punitiveness', *Theoretical Criminology*, 9(2), 175–201.

Matthews, R. (2003) 'Rethinking Penal Policy: Towards a Systems Approach' in Matthews, R. and Young, J. (eds.), *The New Politics of Crime and Punishment* (Cullompton: Willan Publishing).

Matthews, R. (1989) (ed.) *Privatising Criminal Justice* (London: Sage).

Mattinson, J. and Mirrlees-Black, C. (2000) *Attitudes to Crime and Criminal Justice: Findings from the 1998 British Crime Survey*, Home Office Research, Development and Statistics Directorate, Research Findings n° 111 (London: Home Office).

Mayer, C. (2008) 'Britain's Mean Streets', *Time Magazine*, 26, March.

McAra, L. (2008) 'Crime, Criminology and Criminal Justice in Scotland', *European Journal of Criminology*, 5(4), 481–504.

McAra, L. (2006) 'Welfare in Crisis?: Key Developments in Scottish Youth Justice' in Muncie, J. and Goldson, B. (eds.), *Comparative Youth Justice: Critical Issues* (London and Thousand Oaks: Sage).

McAra, L. (1999) 'The Politics of Penality: An Overview of the Development of Penal Policy in Scotland' in Duff, P. and Hutton, N. (eds.), *Criminal Justice in Scotland* (Aldershot: Dartmouth Publishing Ltd.).

McCaughey, B. (2009) 'The Way Ahead' in Parkhill, T. (ed.), *Making the Difference: An Oral History of Probation in Northern Ireland* (Belfast: Probation Board for Northern Ireland).

McCombs, M. (2005) *Setting the Agenda: The Mass Media and Public Opinion* (Cambridge and Malden: Polity Press).

McConville, S. (1981) *A History of English Prison Administration, Volume I: 1750–1877* (London: Routledge and Keegan Paul).

McEvoy, K. and Mika, H. (2002) 'Restorative Justice and the Critique of Informalism in Northern Ireland', *The British Journal of Criminology*, 42(3), 534–62.

McGowen, R. (1995) 'The Well-Ordered Prison' in Morris, N. and Rothman, D. (eds.), *The Oxford History of the Prison: The Practice of Punishment in Western Society* (Oxford and New York: Oxford University Press).

McIvor, G. and Williams, B. (1999) 'Community-based Disposals' in Duff, P. and Hutton, N. (eds.), *Criminal Justice in Scotland* (Aldershot: Dartmouth Publishing Ltd.).

McNeill, F. (2005) 'Remembering Probation in Scotland', *Probation Journal*, 52(1), 23–38.

Melossi, D. (2004) 'Cultural Embeddedness of Social Control: Reflections on a Comparison of Italian and North American Cultures Concerning Punishment' in Newburn, T. and Sparks, R. (eds.), *Criminal Justice and Political Cultures: National and International Dimensions of Crime Control* (Collumpton: Willan Publishing).

Merton, R. (1938) 'Social Structure and Anomie', *American Sociological Review*, 3(5), 672–82.

Meyer, J. and O'Malley, P. (2005) 'Missing the Punitive Turn? Canadian Criminal Justice, "Balance" and Penal Modernism' in Pratt *et al.* (eds.), *The New Punitiveness: Trends, Theories, Perspectives* (Cullompton: Willan Publishing).

Midwinter, E.C. (1971) *Victorian Social Reform* (London: Longman).

Millie, A. (2008) *Anti-Social Behaviour* (Maidenhead: Open University Press).

Mills, H., Silvestri, A. and Grimshaw, R. (2010) *Police Expenditure 1999–2009*, (London: Centre for Crime and Justice Studies).

Ministry of Justice (2010a) *Sentencing Statistics England and Wales 2008*, http://www.justice.gov.uk/publications/docs/sentencing-stats-2008.pdf, date accessed 20 May 2010.

Ministry of Justice (2010b) *Criminal Statistics England and Wales 2008*, http://www.justice.gov.uk/publications/docs/criminal-stats-2008.pdf, date accessed 20 May 2010.

Ministry of Justice (2010c) *Restructuring the Delivery of Criminal Defence Services*, http://www.justice.gov.uk/publications/docs/restructuring-delivery-criminal-defence-services.pdf, date accessed 21 May 2010.

Ministry of Justice (2010d) 'Louise Casey to be First Victims' Commissioner', press release 30 March, http://www.justice.gov.uk/news/newsrelease300310b.htm, date accessed 22 May 2010.

Ministry of Justice (2010e) 'Prison Quarterly Ratings: Quarter 3 2009/10', http://www.justice.gov.uk/publications/docs/prison-ratings-q3-09-10.pdf, date accessed 26 May 2010.

Ministry of Justice (2009a) *Story of the Prison Population 1995–2009 England and Wales*, http://www.justice.gov.uk/publications/docs/story-prison-population.pdf, date accessed 20 May 2010.

Ministry of Justice (2009b) *Prison Population Projections 2009–2015 England and Wales*, http://www.justice.gov.uk/publications/docs/stats-prison-population-projections-2009-2015.pdf, date accessed 20 May 2010.

Ministry of Justice (2009c) *Population in Custody Monthly Tables March 2009: England and Wales*, http://www.justice.gov.uk/population-in-custody-march-09.pdf, date accessed 20 May 2010.

Ministry of Justice (2009d) 'First Birthday for Offender Community Payback Jackets', press release, 1 December, http://www.justice.gov.uk/news/newsrelease011209a.htm, date accessed 20 May 2010.

Ministry of Justice (2009e) *Offender Management Caseload Statistics 2008*, http://www.justice.gov.uk/publications/docs/offender-management-caseload-statistics-2008-2.pdf, date accessed 20 May 2010.

Ministry of Justice (2009f) 'Review of Cautions and On-the-Spot Fines', press release, 14 December, http://www.justice.gov.uk/news/newsrelease141209b.htm, date accessed 20 May 2010.

Ministry of Justice (2009g) *Capacity and Competition Policy for Prisons and* Probation, http://www.justice.gov.uk/about/docs/capacity-and-competition.pdf, date accessed 22 May 2010.

Ministry of Justice (2009h) 'Competition for Five Prisons Announced', press release, 16 November, http://www.justice.gov.uk/news/newsrelease161109a.htm, date accessed 26 May 2010.

Ministry of Justice (2008) *Prison Population Projections 2008–2015*, http://www.justice.gov.uk/publications/docs/stats-prison-pop-sep08.pdf, date accessed 20 May 2010.

Ministry of Justice (2007) *Criminal Statistics England and Wales 2007*, http://www.justice.gov.uk/docs/crim-stats-2007-tag.pdf, date accessed 20 May 2010.

Minton, A. (2006) *The Privatisation of Public Space* (London: The Royal Institution of Chartered Surveyors).

Moley, S. (2009) 'Property Crime' in Walker, A. *et al.* (eds.), *Crime in England and Wales 2008/09 Volume 1: Findings from the British Crime Survey and Police Recorded Crime* (London: Home Office).

Monbiot, G. (2006) 'The Business of Killing', *The Guardian*, 29 March.

Monbiot, G. (2005) 'Protest is Criminalised and the Huffers and Puffers say Nothing', *The Guardian*, 4 October.

Mooney, G. and Poole, L. (2004) '"A Land of Milk and Honey"? Social Policy in Scotland after Devolution', *Critical Social Policy*, 24(4), 458–83.

Moran, M. (2007) *The British Regulatory State: High Modernism and Hyper-Innovation*, 2nd edn (Oxford and New York: Oxford University Press).

Morgan, N. (1983) 'The Shaping of Parole in England and Wales', *Criminal Law Review*, 137–51.

Morgan, R. (2009) 'First-time Youth Offender Entrants: More Smoke and Mirrors', *Criminal Justice Matters*, 76(1), 10–12.

Morgan, R. (2008a) *Summary Justice: Fast – but Fair?* (London: Centre for Crime and Justice Studies).

Morgan, R. (2008b) Interview with the author, 22 May.

Morgan, R. (2006) 'Working with Volunteers and the Voluntary Sector – Some Lessons for Probation from Youth Justice' in Tarry, N. (ed.) *Returning to Its Roots? A New Role for the Third Sector in Probation* (London: Social Market Foundation).

Morgan, R. (1994) 'Just Prisons and Responsible Prisoners' in Duff, A., Marshall, S., Emerson Dobash, R. and Dobash, R., *Penal Theory and Practice: Tradition and Innovation in Criminal Justice* (Manchester: Manchester University Press).

Morgan, R. (1979) *Formulating Penal Policy: The Future of the Advisory Council on the Penal System* (London: NACRO).

Morris, N. (2006) 'Blair's "Frenzied Law-Making": A New Offence for Every Day Spent in Office', *The Independent*, 16 August.

Morris, T. (1989) *Crime and Criminal Justice Since 1945* (Oxford: Basil Blackwell).

MPS (2010) Metropolitan Police Service, *Investigation into the Death of Blair Peach*, http://www.met.police.uk/foi/units/blair_peach.htm, date accessed 22 May 2010.

Mulheirn, I., Gough, B. and Menne, V. (2010) *Prison Break: Tackling Recidivism, Reducing Costs* (London: Social Market Foundation).

Muncie, J. (2006) 'Governing Young People: Coherence and Contradiction in Contemporary Youth Justice', *Critical Social Policy*, 26, 770–93.

Murakami Wood, D. (2006) (ed.) *A Report on the Surveillance Society* (Wilmslow: Office of the Information Commissioner/Surveillance Studies Network).

Murray, C. (2005) *Simple Justice* (London: CIVITAS).

Murray, C. (1996) 'The Emerging British Underclass' in Lister, R. (ed.), *Charles Murray and the Underclass: The Developing Debate*, Choice in Welfare n° 33 (London: Institute of Economic Affairs).

Murray, C. (1990) *The Emerging British Underclass*, Choice in Welfare n° 2 (London: Institute of Economic Affairs).

NACRO (2009) *Youth Crime Briefing*, http://www.nacro.org.uk/data/files/nacro-2009070900-280.pdf, date accessed 21 May 2010.

NACRO (2003) *Youth Crime Briefing* (London: NACRO).

NAO (2006) National Audit Office, *The Home Office: Tackling Anti-Social Behaviour* (London: National Audit Office).

NAO (2004) National Audit Office, *The Drug Treatment and Testing Order: Early lessons*, HC366 (London: National Audit Office).

NAO (2003) National Audit Office, *The Operational Performance of PFI Prisons*, HC 700 (London: National Audit Office).

NAPO (2010) National Association of Probation Officers, *Performance of NOMS: The Case for Restructuring* (London: NAPO).

Nathan, S. and Solomon, E. (2004) 'The Perils of Private Prisons', *Safer Society*, 21, 26.

National Deviancy Conference (1980) (ed.) *Permissiveness and Control: The Fate of the Sixties Legislation* (Basingstoke: Macmillan).

Nelken, D. (2009) 'Comparative Criminal Justice: Beyond Ethnocentrism and Relativism', *European Journal of Criminology*, 6, 291–311.

Nellis, M. (2004) '"Into the Field of Corrections": The End of English Probation in the Early 21st Century', *Cambrian Law Review*, 35, 115–33.

Newburn, T. (2009) 'Contrasts in Intolerance: Cultures of Control in the United States and Britain' in Newburn, T. and Rock, P. (eds.), *The Politics of Crime Control: Essays in Honour of David Downes*, 2nd edn (Oxford and New York: Oxford University Press).

Newburn, T. (1998) 'Tackling Youth Crime and Reforming Youth Justice: The Origins and Nature of "New Labour" Policy', *Policy Studies*, 19(3/4), 199–212.

Nichol, D. (2006) Speech made by the President of the Parole Board to the Centre for Crime and Justice Studies, London, 14 December.

Nicholas, S., Kershaw, C. and Walker, A. (2007) (eds.), *Crime in England and Wales 2006–07* (London: Home Office).

NOMS (2009) National Offender Management Service, http://www.justice.gov.uk/noms-strategic-business-plans-0910-addendum.pdf, date accessed 22 May 2010.

NOMS (2007) National Offender Management Service, *A Century of Cutting Crime: 1907–2007* (London: Home Office).

Norris, C. and Cahill, M. A. (2006) 'CCTV: Beyond Penal Modernism', *British Journal of Criminology*, 46(1), 97–118.

Northern Ireland Office (2009) *Digest of Information on the Northern Ireland Criminal Justice System 9* (Belfast and London: Northern Ireland Office).

Northern Ireland Office (2008) *Together, Stronger, Safer: Community Safety in Northern Ireland* (Belfast and London: Northern Ireland Office).

Northern Ireland Office (2005) *Consultation on the Review of the Sentencing Framework* (Belfast and London: Northern Ireland Office).

Northern Ireland Prison Service (2008) *Foreign National Prisoner Strategy* (Belfast: NIPS).

Novak, T. (1984) *Poverty and Inequality* (London: Pluto Press).

Nuttall, J. (2003) 'The Labour Party and the Improvement of Minds: The Case of Tony Crosland', *The Historical Journal*, 46(1), 133–53.

O'Loan, C. and McKibbin, M. (2008) *The Northern Ireland Prison Population in 2007*, http://www.nio.gov.uk/2007_annual_prison_report.pdf, date accessed 20 May 2010.

O'Malley, P. (2004) 'Globalising Risk? Distinguishing Styles of "Neoliberal" Criminal Justice in Australia and the USA' in Newburn, T. and Sparks, R. (eds.), *Criminal Justice and Political Cultures: National and International Dimensions of Crime Control* (Collumpton: Willan Publishing).

OCJR (2006) Office for Criminal Justice Reform, *Penalty Notices for Disorder: Review of Practice across Selected Police Forces* (London: Ministry of Justice).

OECD (2008) Organisation for Economic Co-operation and Development, http://stats.oecd.org/Index.aspx?DatasetCode=SNA_TABLE1, date accessed 22 May 2010.

Oldfield, M. and Grimshaw, R. (2008) *Probation Resources, Staffing and Workloads 2001–2008* (London: Centre for Crime and Justice Studies).

Office for National Statistics (2004) http://www.statistics.gov.uk/cci/nugget.asp?id=455, date accessed 20 May 2010.

Office for National Statistics (2003a) *Prison Statistics England and Wales 2002*, Cm 5996 (London: HMSO).

Office for National Statistics (2003b) *Prison Population 1990–2002: Social Trends 33* (London: HMSO).

Ormerod, D. and Fortson, R. (2009) 'Serious Crime Act 2007: The Part 2 Offences', *Criminal Law Review*, 389–414.

Padfield, N. and Maruna, S. (2006) 'The Revolving Door at the Prison Gate: Exploring the Dramatic Increase in Recalls to Prison', *Criminology and Criminal Justice*, 6(3), 329–52.

Pantazis, C. and Pemberton, S. (2009) 'From the "Old" to the "New" Suspect Community: Examining the Impacts of Recent UK Counter-Terrorist Legislation', *British Journal of Criminology*, 49, 646–66.

Parenti, C. (2002) *Lockdown America: Police and Prisons in the Age of Crisis* (London and New York: Verso).

Park, A. and Hough, M. (2002) *Public Attitudes towards Crime and Punishment: Note for Rethinking Crime and Punishment* (London: Esmée Fairburn Foundation).

Park, I. (2000) *Review of Comparative Costs and Performance of Privately and Publicly Operated Prisons 1998–1999* (London: Home Office).

Pearson, G. (1983) *Hooligan: A History of Respectable Fears* (Basingstoke and New York: Macmillan).

Peck, J. and Tickell, A. (2002) 'Neoliberalizing Space', *Antipode*, 34(3), 380–404.

Phoenix, Jo (2008) 'ASBOs and Working Women: A New Revolving Door?' in Squires, P. (ed.), *ASBO Nation: The Criminalisation of Nuisance* (Bristol: Policy Press).

Piacentini, L. and Walters, R. (2006) 'The Politicization of Youth Crime in Scotland and the Rise of the "Burberry Court"', *Youth Justice*, 6(1), 43–59.

Pitts, J. (2001) *The New Politics of Youth Crime: Discipline or Solidarity?* (Basingstoke and New York: Palgrave Macmillan).

Piven, F. F. (2010) 'A Response to Wacquant', *Theoretical Criminology*, 14, 111–16.

Polanyi, K. (2001 [1944]) *The Great Transformation: The Political and Economic Origins of Our Time*, 2nd edn (Boston: Beacon Press).

Police Federation (2010) http://www.polfed.org/federationpolicy/52A6225A5CDC-4E7CB58E31B05C50835D.asp, date accessed 22 May 2010.

Pollard, C. (1998) 'Zero Tolerance: Short-term Fix, Long-term Liability?' in Dennis, N. (ed.), *Zero Tolerance: Policing a Free Society*, Choice in Welfare No. 35 (London: CIVITAS).

PPRI (2004) 'United Kingdom: Private sector: Lower Pay, Longer Hours, Higher Turnover', *Prison Privatisation Report International*, 65, http://www.psiru.org/justice/ppri65.htm, date accessed 26 May 2010.

Pratt J., (2008a) 'Scandinavian Exceptionalism in an Era of Penal Excess. Part 1: The Nature and Roots of Scandinavian Exceptionalism', *British Journal of Criminology*, 48(2), 119–37.

Pratt J., (2008b) 'Scandinavian Exceptionalism in an Era of Penal Excess. Part 2: Does Scandinavian Exceptionalism have a Future?', *British Journal of Criminology*, 48(3), 275–92.

Pratt, J., Brown, D., Brown, M., Hallsworth, S. J. and Morrison, W. (2005) (eds.), *The New Punitiveness: Trends, Theories, Perspectives* (Cullompton: Willan Publishing).

Pratt, J. (2005) 'Elias, Punishment, and Decivilization' in Pratt *et al.* (eds.), *The New Punitiveness: Trends, Theories, Perspectives* (Cullompton: Willan Publishing).

Prison Reform Trust (2010a) *Barred from Voting: The Right to Vote for Sentenced Prisoners* (London: Prison Reform Trust).

Prison Reform Trust (2010b) http://www.prisonreformtrust.org.uk/subsection.asp?id=268, date accessed 22 May 2010.

Prison Reform Trust (2009) *Bromley Briefings: Prison Factfile* (London: Prison Reform Trust).

Prison Reform Trust (2007) *Indefinitely Maybe? How the Indeterminate Sentence for Public Protection is Unjust and Unsustainable* (London: Prison Reform Trust).

Prison Reform Trust (2005) *Private Punishment: Who Profits?* (London: Prison Reform Trust).

Prison Reform Trust (1995) *HM Prison Doncaster: The Doncatraz File* (London: Prison Reform Trust).

Prison Reform Trust (1993) *Trends in Juvenile Crime and Punishment* (Juvenile Justice Paper 4) (London: Prison Reform Trust).

Prison Reform Trust (1991) *The Identikit Prisoner: Characteristics of the Prison Population* (London: Prison Reform Trust).

Prison Reform Trust (1989) *Comments on the Green Paper, 'Punishment, Custody and the Community'* (London: Prison Reform Trust).

Public Spending (2010) http://www.ukpublicspending.co.uk/uk_20th_century_chart.html, date accessed 22 May 2010.

Pugh, M. (1994) *State and Society: British Political and Social History 1870–1992* (London: Hodder Arnold).

Radzinowicz, L. and Hood, R. (1990) *The Emergence of Penal Policy in Victorian and Edwardian England* (Oxford: Clarendon Press).

Ramsay, P. (2004) 'What is Anti-Social Behaviour?', *Criminal Law Review*, 908–25.

Randall, N. (2004) 'Three Faces of New Labour: Principle, Pragmatism and Populism in New Labour's Home Office' in Ludlam, S. and Smith, M. J. (eds.), *Governing as New Labour: Policy and Politics under Blair* (Basingstoke and New York: Palgrave Macmillan).

RCP (2004) 'Rethinking Crime and Punishment', *The Report* (London: Esmée Fairbairn Foundation).

Reiner, R. (2009) 'Beyond Risk: A Lament for Social-Democratic Criminology' in Newburn, T. and Rock, P. (eds.), *The Politics of Crime Control: Essays in Honour of David Downes*, 2nd edn (Oxford and New York: Oxford University Press).

Reiner, R. (2007) *Law and Order: An Honest Citizen's Guide to Crime and Control* (Cambridge and Malden: Polity Press).

Reiner, R., Livingstone, S. and Allen, J. (2003) 'From Law and Order to Lynch Mobs: Crime News Since the Second World War' in Mason, P. (ed.), *Criminal Visions: Media Representations of Crime and Justice* (Cullompton: Willan Publishing).

Reiner, R. (2000) *The Politics of the Police*, 3rd edn (Oxford and New York: Oxford University Press).

Reiner, R. (1999) 'Order and Discipline' in Holliday, I., Gamble, A. and Parry, G. (eds.), *Fundamentals in British Politics* (Basingstoke and New York: Palgrave Macmillan).

Richards, S. (1998) 'The New Statesman Interview: Jack Straw', *New Statesman*, 3 April, 27–9.

Roberts, J. V. and Hough, M. (2005) 'The State of the Prisons: Exploring Public Knowledge and Opinion', *The Howard Journal*, 44(3), 286–306.

Roberts, J. V. (2003) 'Evaluating the Pluses and Minuses of Custody: Sentencing Reform in England and Wales', *The Howard Journal*, 42(3), 229–47.

Roberts, R. and Garside, R. (2005) *Punishment Before Justice? Understanding Penalty Notices for Disorder* (London: Centre for Crime and Justice Studies).

Robinson, G. (2008) 'Late-Modern Rehabilitation: The Evolution of a Penal Strategy', *Punishment and Society*, 10(4), 429–45.

Rock, P. (2004) *Constructing Victims' Rights: The Home Office, New Labour and Victims* (Oxford and New York: Oxford University Press).

Roe, S. and Ashe, J. (2008) *Young People and Crime: Findings from the 2006 Offending, Crime and Justice Survey* (London: Home Office).

Roe, S., Coleman, K. and Kaiza, P. (2009) 'Violent and Sexual Crime' in Walker, A. *et al.* (eds.), *Crime in England and Wales 2008/09 Volume 1: Findings from the British Crime Survey and Police Recorded Crime* (London: Home Office).

Rollock, N. (2009) *The Stephen Lawrence Inquiry Ten Years On: A Critical Review of the Literature* (London: The Runnymede Trust).

Rose, D. (2007) 'Locked Up to Make Us Feel Better', *New Statesman*, 19 March.

Rowlands, M. (2005) 'The State of ASBO in Britain – The Rise of Intolerance', *European Civil Liberties Network*, http://www.ecln.org/essays/essay-9.pdf, date accessed 20 June 2007.

Rusche, G. and Kirchheimer, O. (2003) *Punishment and Social Structure*, 3rd edn (New Jersey: Transaction Publishers).

Rutherford, A. (1999) 'Three Strikes for Domestic Burglars', *New Law Journal*, 82.

Rutherford, A. (1998) 'A Bill to be Tough on Crime', *New Law Journal*, 148, 13–14.

Ryan, M. (2005) 'Engaging with Punitive Attitudes Towards Crime and Punishment: Some Strategic Lessons for England and Wales' in Pratt *et al.* (eds.), *The New Punitiveness: Trends, Theories, Perspectives* (Cullompton: Willan Publishing).

Ryan, M. (2004) 'Red Tops, Populists and the Irresistible Rise of the Public Voice(s)', *Journal for Crime, Conflict and the Media*, 1(3), 1–14.

Ryan, M. (2003) *Penal Policy and Political Culture in England and Wales* (Winchester: Winchester Press).

Ryan, M. (1994) 'Privatisation, Corporate Interest and the Future Shape and Ethos of the Prison Service' in Prison Reform Trust, *Privatisation and Market Testing in the Prison Service* (London: Prison Reform Trust).

Ryan, M. (1978) *The Acceptable Pressure Group. Inequality in the Penal Lobby: A Case Study of the Howard League and RAP* (Farnborough: Saxon House).

Sabol, W., West, H. and Cooper, M. (2009) 'Prisoners in 2008', Bureau of Justice Statistics, http://bjs.ojp.usdoj.gov/content/pub/pdf/p08.pdf, date accessed 20 May 2010.

Salle, G. (2010) 'Petite histoire de la loi pénitentiaire allemande', *Le Monde Diplomatique*, March.

Sampson, A. (2005) *Who Runs This Place? The Anatomy of Britain in the 21st Century* (London: John Murray).

Samuels, A. (1968) 'The Criminal Justice Act 1967', *Modern Law Review*, 31(1), 16–39.

Scarman, Lord (1981) *Report of an Inquiry by the Right Honourable Lord Scarman presented to Parliament by the Secretary of State for the Home Department* (London: HMSO).

SCCCJ (2006) Scottish Consortium on Crime and Criminal Justice, *Prison Privatisation in Scotland*, http://www.scccj.org.uk/documents/Prison%20Privatisation %20in%20Scotland.pdf, date accessed 26 May 2010.

Schlosser, E. (1998) 'The Prison-Industrial Complex', *Atlantic Monthly*, December.

Scott, D. (2009) 'Arrested Development', *The Guardian*, 10 June.

Scott, D. (2008) *Penology* (London and Thousand Oaks: Sage).

Scottish Executive (2007) *Community Sentencing: Public Perceptions and Attitudes*, http://www.scotland.gov.uk/Resource/Doc/203436/0054193.pdf, date accessed 20 May 2010.

Scottish Government (2009a) *Prison Statistics Scotland 2008 and Beyond*, http://www.scotland.gov.uk/Resource/Doc/293705/0090774.pdf, date accessed 20 May 2010.

Scottish Government (2009b) *Statistical Bulletin: Criminal Proceedings in the Scottish Courts, 2007/08*, http://www.scotland.gov.uk/Resource/Doc/270433/0080553.pdf, date accessed 20 May 2010.

Scottish Government (2008a) *Prison Statistics Scotland 2007/08*, http://www.scotland.gov.uk/Publications/2008/08/14143909/57, date accessed 20 May 2010.

Scottish Government (2008b) *Protecting Scotland's Communities: Fair, Fast and Flexible Justice*, http://www.scotland.gov.uk/Resource/Doc/255089/0075587.pdf, date accessed 20 May 2010.

Scottish Government (2007a) *Reforming and Revitalising: Report of the Review of Community Penalties*, http://www.scotland.gov.uk/Resource/Doc/204067/0054359.pdf, date accessed 20 May 2010.

Scottish Government (2007b) *Use of Antisocial Behaviour Orders in Scotland*, http://www.scotland.gov.uk/Resource/Doc/198276/0053019.pdf, date accessed 21 May 2010.

Scottish Parliament (2009) Written answers: S3W-23933, Tuesday 26 May 2009, http://www.scottish.parliament.uk/business/pqa/wa-09/wa0526.htm#42, date accessed 20 May 2010.

Scottish Prisons Commission (2008) *Scotland's Choice*, http://openscotland.net/Resource/Doc/230180/0062359.pdf, date accessed 20 May 2010.

Scraton, P. (2003) 'Streets of Terror: Marginalisation, Criminalisation and Authoritarian Renewal', *Statewatch*, http://www.statewatch.org/news/2003/aug/philscraton.pdf, date accessed 22 May 2010.

Seldon, A. F. (2005) *Blair* (London: The Free Press).

Seldon, A. (2001) in Institute of Economic Affairs (2001) *A conversation with Harris and Seldon* (London: IEA).

Select Committee on Home Affairs (2002) *The Government's Drugs Policy: Is it Working?*, http://www.publications.parliament.uk/pa/cm200102/cmselect/cmhaff/318/31803.htm, date accessed 21 May 2010.

Serco (2009) http://www.serco.com/markets/homeaffairs/Copy_of_Copy_2_of_duncan.asp, date accessed 20 November 2009.

Sharpe, J. A. (1999) *Crime in Early Modern England 1550–1750*, 2nd edn (London and New York: Longman).

Shepherd, A. and Whiting, E. (2006) *Re-offending of Adults: Results from the 2003 cohort*, Home Office Statistical Bulletin 20/06 (London: HMSO).

Sim, J. (2010) 'Review Symposium: *Punishing the Poor – The Neoliberal Government of Insecurity* by Loïc Wacquant', *British Journal of Criminology*, 50(1), 589–608.

Sim, J. (2009) *Punishment and Prisons: Power and the Carceral State* (London and Thousand Oaks: Sage).

Simon, J. (2007) *Governing Through Crime: How the War on Crime Transformed American Democracy and Created a Culture of Fear* (Oxford and New York: Oxford University Press).

Sindall, R. (1990) *Street Violence in the Nineteenth Century: Media Panic or Real Danger?* (Leicester: Leicester University Press).

Slapper, G. (2007) 'The Law Explored: Ethnic Minorities and the Judiciary', *The Times*, 4 July.

Smith, D. (2003) 'New Labour and Youth Justice', *Children & Society*, 17(3), 226–35.

Soar, P. (2007) 'Legal Aid in Meltdown', *Criminal Justice Matters*, 34–5.

Social Exclusion Unit (2002) *Reducing Reoffending by Ex-Prisoners: Summary of the Social Exclusion Unit Report* (London: Cabinet Office).

Solomon, E. and Garside, R. (2008) *Ten Years of Labour's Youth Justice Reforms: An Independent Audit* (London: Centre for Crime and Justice Studies).

Squires, P. (2008) (ed.) *ASBO Nation: The Criminalisation of Nuisance* (Policy Press: Bristol).

Staley, K. (2005) *The Police National DNA Database: Balancing Crime Detection, Human Rights and Privacy*, http://www.genewatch.org/uploads/f03c6d66a9b354535738-483c1c3d49e4/NationalDNADatabase.pdf, date accessed 22 May 2010.

Statewatch (2010) http://www.statewatch.org/asbo/asbowatch-mentalhealth.htm, date accessed 21 May 2010.

Straw, J. (1998) *Making Prisons Work* (London: Prison Reform Trust).

Straw, J. and Michael, A. (1996) *Tackling Youth Crime: Reforming Youth Justice, A Consultation Paper on an Agenda for Change* (London: Labour Party).

Strickland, P. (2008) *Police Powers to Disperse Children and Groups under the Anti-Social Behaviour Act 2003*, http://www.parliament.uk/briefingpapers/commons/lib/research/briefings/snha-04048.pdf, date accessed 21 May 2010.

Stigler, G. (1970) 'The Optimum Enforcement of Laws', *Journal of Political Economy*, 78(3), 526–36.

STV (2010) 'Automatic Early Release Under Fire', 25 January, http://news.stv.tv/scotland/152822-automatic-early-release-under-fire/, date accessed 20 May 2010.

Sykes, G. M. (1958) *The Society of Captives* (Princeton: Princeton University Press).

Tawney, R. H. (1920) *The Acquisitive Society* (New York: Harcourt, Brace & Howe).

Taggart, P. (2000) *Populism* (Buckingham: Open University Press).

Team London Bridge (2010) http://www.teamlondonbridge.co.uk/default.aspx?m=3&mi=173, date accessed 26 May 2010.

Tham, H. (2001) 'Law and Order as a Leftist Project?: The Case of Sweden', *Punishment and Society*, 3(3), 409–26.

Thatcher, M. (1987a) Speech to Conservative Party Conference, 9 October. Available from The Margaret Thatcher Foundation, http://www.margaretthatcher.org/, date accessed 21 May 2010.

Thatcher, M. (1987b) Interview for *Woman's Own*, 23 September. Available from The Margaret Thatcher Foundation, http://www.margaretthatcher.org/, date accessed 21 May 2010.

Thatcher, M. (1987c) Televised interview for Channel Four, 'Face the People', 6 June. Available from The Margaret Thatcher Foundation, http://www.margaretthatcher.org/, date accessed 21 May 2010.

Thatcher, M. (1983) Speech to Conservative Party Conference, 14 October. Available from The Margaret Thatcher Foundation, http://www.margaretthatcher.org/, date accessed 21 May 2010.

Thatcher, M. (1981) Interview for *The Sunday Times*, 3 May. Available from The Margaret Thatcher Foundation, http://www.margaretthatcher.org/, date accessed 21 May 2010.

Thatcher, M. (1979) Speech to Conservative Rally, Cardiff, 16 April. Available from The Margaret Thatcher Foundation, http://www.margaretthatcher.org/, date accessed 21 May 2010.

The Herald (2008) 'Scotland Tops Euro Table for Sending Most People to Jail', 15 December.

The Independent (2007) 'Reid Unveils "Sarah's Law" proposals', 13 June.

The Sun (2006) 'We Demand Real Justice', 12 June.

The Times (2009) 'Judges Took Bribes to Jail Teenagers', 8 March.

Thomas, D. A. (1995) 'Sentencing Reform: England and Wales' in Clarkson, C. and Morgan, R. (eds.), *The Politics of Sentencing Reform* (Oxford: Clarendon Press).

Thorpe, K. and Hall, P. (2009) 'Public Perceptions' in Walker, A. *et al.* (eds.), *Crime in England and Wales 2008/09 Volume 1: Findings from the British Crime Survey and Police Recorded Crime* (London: Home Office).

Tilley, N. (2003) 'Community Policing, Problem-oriented Policing and Intelligence-led Policing' in Newburn, T. (ed.), *Handbook of Policing* (Cullompton: Willan Publishing).

Titmuss, R. M. (1976 [1958]) *Essays on 'The Welfare State'* (London: George Allen & Unwin Ltd.).

Tobias, J. J. (1967) *Crime and Industrial Society in the 19th Century* (London: Batsford).

Tombs, S. and Whyte, D. (2010) 'A Deadly Consensus: Worker Safety and Regulatory Degradation under New Labour', *British Journal of Criminology*, 50(1), 46–55.

Tombs, S. and Whyte, D. (2008) *A Crisis of Enforcement: The Decriminalisation of Death and Injury at Work* (London: Centre for Crime and Justice Studies).

Tombs, S. (2002) 'Focus on Crimes of Affluence': Beyond the Usual Suspects – Crime, Criminology and the Powerful', *Safer Society*, NACRO, 15, 18–20.

Tomlinson, J. (2002) 'The Limits of Tawney's Ethical Socialism: A Historical Perspective on the Labour Party and the Market', *Contemporary British History*, 16(4), 1–16.

Tonry, M. (2009) 'Explanations of American Punishment Policies: A National History', *Punishment Society*, 11, 377–94.

Tonry, M. (2004a) *Punishment and Politics: Evidence and Emulation in the Making of English Crime Control Policy* (Cullompton: Willan Publishing).

Tonry, M. (2004b) 'Why Aren't German Penal Policies Harsher and Imprisonment Rates Higher?', *German Law Journal*, 5(10), 1187–206.

Tonry, M. (2004c) *Thinking about Crime: Sense and sensibility in American Penal Culture* (Oxford and New York: Oxford University Press).

Tonry, M. (2003) (ed.) *Confronting Crime: Crime control policy under New Labour* (Cullompton: Willan Publishing).

Toynbee, P. and Walker, D. (2005) *Better or Worse? Has Labour Delivered?* (London: Bloomsbury).

Toynbee, P. (2003) *Hard Work: Life in Low-pay Britain* (London: Bloomsbury Publishing).

Travis, A. (2010) 'Prisoner Early Release Scheme to be Halted', *The Guardian*, 22 February.

Travis, A. (2007) 'Top Judge Attacks "Trapdoor to Prison"', *The Guardian*, 3 May.

TUC (2009) *Recession Report n°11*, http://www.tuc.org.uk/economy/tuc-17030-f0.cfm, date accessed 22 May 2010.

van Dijk, J., van Kesteren, J. and Smit, P. (2008) 'Criminal Victimisation in International Perspective: Key Findings from the 2004–2005 ICVS and EU ICS', http:// rechten.uvt.nl/icvs/pdffiles/ICVS2004_05.pdf, date accessed 19 May 2010.

van Swaaningen, R. (2005) 'Public Safety and the Management of Fear', *Theoretical Criminology*, 9(3), 289–305.

Varinard, A. (2008) *Commission de propositions de réforme de l'ordonnance du 2 février 1945 relative aux mineurs délinquants*, http://www.gouvernement.fr/ gouvernement/le-rapport-varinard-sur-la-reforme-de-la-justice-des-mineurs, date accessed 22 May 2010.

Von Hayek, F. (2001 [1944]) *The Road to Serfdom* (Abingdon and New York: Routledge).

Wacquant, L. (2009) *Punishing the Poor: The Neoliberal Government of Social Insecurity* (Durham and London: Duke University Press).

Wacquant, L. (2005) 'The Great Penal Leap Backwards' in Pratt *et al.* (eds.), *The New Punitiveness: Trends, Theories, Perspectives* (Cullompton: Willan Publishing).

Wacquant, L. (1999) 'Ce vent punitif qui vient de l'Amérique', *Le monde diplomatique*, April.

Waiton, S. (2006) 'Antisocial Behaviour: The Construction of a Crime', *Spiked Online*, 19 January, http://www.spiked-online.com/Articles/0000000CAF28.htm, date accessed 22 May 2010.

Walker, A. (1997) 'Introduction: The Strategy of Inequality' in Walker, A. and Walker, C. (eds.), *Britain Divided: The Growth of Social Exclusion in the 1980s and 1990s* (London: Child Poverty Action Group).

Walker, A., Flatley, J. and Kershaw, C. (2009) (eds.) *Crime in England and Wales 2008/09 Volume 1: Findings from the British Crime Survey and Police Recorded Crime* (London: Home Office).

Walklate, S. (2001) 'The Victims' Lobby' in Ryan, M., Savage, S. and Wall, D. (eds.), *Policy Networks in Criminal Justice* (Basingstoke and New York: Palgrave Macmillan).

Wallington, P. (1987) 'Some Implications for the Policing of Industrial Disputes [and the Public Order Act 1986]', *Criminal Law Review*, 179–91.

Walters, R. (2005) 'Boycott, Resistance and the Role of the Deviant Voice', *Criminal Justice Matters*, 62(1), 6–7.

Walters, R. (2003) 'New Modes of Governance and the Commodification of Criminological Knowledge', *Social Legal Studies*, 12(1), 5–26.

Walters, S. (2009) 'Mug a Hoodie: Tories Promise They Will put 100,000 in Jail to Clear Britain's Streets of Thugs', *The Daily Mail*, 4 October.

Ward, A. (1996) *Talking Dirty: Moral Panic and Political Rhetoric* (London: IPPR).

Webb, S. and Webb, B. (1922) *English Prisons Under Local Government* (London: Longmans, Green & Co.).

Welsh, B. C. and Farrington, D. P. (2002) *Crime Prevention Effects of Closet Circuit Television: A Systematic Review*, Home Office Research Study n° 252 (London: Home Office).

Welshman, J. (2006) *Underclass: A History of the Excluded 1880–2000* (London: Hambledon Continuum).

Whitman, J. Q. (2003) *Harsh Justice: Criminal Punishment and the Widening Divide between America and Europe* (Oxford and New York: Oxford University Press).

Whyte, B. (2009) 'Counterblast: Youth "In Justice" in the UK – Which Way for Scotland?', *The Howard Journal*, 48(2), 200–4.

Whyte, D. (2004) 'Punishing Anti-social Business', *New Law Journal*, 1293.

Wiener, M. (1994) *Reconstructing the Criminal: Culture, Law, and Policy in England, 1830–1914* (Cambridge and New York: Cambridge University Press).

Wilkinson, R. R. (2005) *The Impact of Inequality* (London and New York: Routledge).

Wilson, C. (2001) 'Networking and the Lobby for Penal Reform: Conflict and Consensus' in Ryan, M., Savage, S. and Wall, D. (eds.), *Policy Networks in Criminal Justice* (Basingstoke and New York: Palgrave Macmillan).

Wilson, J. Q. and Herrnstein, R. J. (1996) *Crime and Human Nature*, 2nd edn (Touchstone, New York).

Wilson, J. Q. and Kelling, G. L. (1982) 'The Police and Neighbourhood Safety: Broken Windows', *Atlantic Monthly*, 249(3), 29–36.

Wilson, J. Q. (1975) *Thinking About Crime* (New York: Random House).

Wilson, W. J. (1987) *The Truly Disadvantaged: The Inner City, the Underclass, and Public Policy* (Chicago: Chicago University Press).

Windlesham, Lord (1993) *Responses to Crime Vol. 2: Penal Policy in the Making* (Oxford: Clarendon Press).

Wintour, P. and Watt, N. (2009) 'Brown: I Should Have Done More to Prevent Bank Crisis', *The Guardian*, 17 March.

Woollacot, M. (1998) 'The Politics of Prevention' in Franklin, J. (ed.), *The Politics of Risk Society* (Cambridge and Malden: Polity Press/IPPR).

Woolf, H. Lord (2003) Speech delivered to the Anglo-Australian Lawyers' Society, 9 April.

Woolf, H. Lord (2001) 'The Woolf Report: A Decade of Change?', address to the Prison Reform Trust, 31 January.

Woolf, H. (1991) *Prison Disturbances April 1990: Report of an Inquiry by the Rt. Hon. Lord Justice Woolf*, Cm 1456 (London: HMSO).

Wootton, B. (1978) *Crime and Penal Policy: Reflections on Fifty Years' Experience* (London: George Allen and Unwin).

Wootton, B. (1968) 'The White Paper on Children in Trouble', *Criminal Law Review*, 465–73.

Wright, M. (1996) *Justice for Victims and Offenders: A Restorative Response to Crime* (Winchester: Waterside Press).

YJB (2010a) Youth Justice Board, *Custody Figures*, http://www.yjb.gov.uk/en-gb/yjs/Custody/CustodyFigures/, date accessed 19 May 2010.

YJB (2010b) Youth Justice Board, http://www.yjb.gov.uk/en-gb/yjs/Sentences-OrdersandAgreements/LocalChildCurfew/, date accessed 21 May 2010.

YJB (2010c) Youth Justice Board, http://www.yjb.gov.uk/en-gb/practitioners/Workingwithvictims/Restorativejustice/, date accessed 21 May 2010.

YJB (2010d) Youth Justice Board, http://www.yjb.gov.uk/en-gb/yjs/Custody/Custodyfigures/, date accessed 21 May 2010.

YJB (2009) Youth Justice Board, *Youth Justice Annual Workload Data 2007/08*, http://www.yjb.gov.uk/publications/scripts/prodView.asp?idproduct=441&eP=, date accessed 21 May 2010.

YJB (2006) Youth Justice Board, *A Summary of Research into Anti-Social Behaviour Orders Given to Young People between January 2004 and January 2005*, http://www.yjb.gov.uk/Publications/Resources/Downloads/ASBO%20Summary.pdf, date accessed 21 May 2010.

YJB and WAG (2004) Youth Justice Board and Welsh Assembly Government, *All Wales Youth Offending Strategy*, http://wales.gov.uk/dsjlg/publications/

communitysafety/youthoffendingstrategy/strategye?lang=en, date accessed 21 May 2010.

Young, J. (2002) 'Crime and Social Exclusion' in Maguire, M., Morgan, R. and Reiner, R. (eds.), *The Oxford Handbook of Criminology*, 3rd edn (Oxford and New York: Oxford University Press).

Young, J. (1999) *The Exclusive Society* (London and Thousand Oaks: Sage).

Young, J. (1988) 'Radical Criminology in Britain: The Emergence of a Competing Paradigm', *British Journal of Criminology*, 28(2), 159–83.

Young, P. (1987) *The Prison Cell: The Start of a Better Approach to Prison Management* (London: Adam Smith Institute).

Zander, M. (2003) 'Lord Woolf's Criticisms of Mr Blunkett's Criminal Justice Bill – Pt II', *New Law Journal*, 1266.

Zedner, L. (2009) 'Opportunity Makes the Thief-Taker: The Influence of Economic Analysis on Crime Control' in Newburn, T. and Rock, P. (eds.). *The Politics of Crime Control: Essays in Honour of David Downes*, 2nd edn (Oxford and New York: Oxford University Press).

Zedner, L. (2002) 'Dangers of Dystopia', *Oxford Journal of Legal Studies*, 22(2), 341–66.

Index